THE PEER-EFFECT: NON-TRADITIONAL MODELS OF INSTRUCTION IN SPANISH AS A HERITAGE LANGUAGE

The Peer-Effect: Non-Traditional Models of Instruction in Spanish as a Heritage Language guides an important pedagogical conversation on the relevance of heritage language and literacy practices as resources for instruction, framing heritage teaching and learning as a social justice issue.

Presenting ethnographic and discourse analyses of a heritage peer tutoring program at a university in California, this book focuses on the ways in which the dynamic translanguaging practices that Spanish heritage language (SHL) peer tutors mobilize in a non–classroom, student-led, collaborative academic space directly respond to the literacy demands of academic language development. Based on the in-depth analysis of peer tutors' translingual practices, the book advances scholarship in SHL pedagogy, providing concrete classroom-based examples, techniques, and activities that nurture equitable pedagogies for heritage student belonging, while challenging the deficit discourse that has traditionally governed the dialogue around literacy instruction for multilingual students.

This versatile volume is designed for educators, researchers, practitioners, and students in the fields of heritage language pedagogy, bilingual education, educational linguistics, and literacy studies for multilingual students.

Lina M. Reznicek-Parrado is Teaching Assistant Professor of Spanish and Founding Director of the Spanish Program for Heritage and Bilingual Speakers at the University of Denver, USA.

ROUTLEDGE INNOVATIONS IN SPANISH LANGUAGE TEACHING

The *Routledge Innovations in Spanish Language Teaching* series showcases cutting-edge research in the field of Hispanic Applied Linguistics. It publishes titles in English or Spanish that strike a balance between theoretical, methodological, and empirical discussions in Spanish Language Teaching. Books in the series are intended for postgraduate students, language teachers, university lecturers, and researchers who would like to keep abreast of the latest developments in the field, both from a theoretical and practical point of view.

Series editors: Javier Muñoz-Basols, *University of Oxford,* and Elisa Gironzetti, *University of Maryland.*

Traducción, competencia plurilingüe y español como lengua de herencia (ELH)
Laura Gasca Jiménez

The Peer-Effect: Non-Traditional Models of Instruction in Spanish as a Heritage Language
Lina M. Reznicek-Parrado

For more information about this series please visit: https://routledge.com/Routledge-Innovations-in-Spanish-Language-Teaching/book-series/RISLT

THE PEER-EFFECT: NON-TRADITIONAL MODELS OF INSTRUCTION IN SPANISH AS A HERITAGE LANGUAGE

Lina M. Reznicek-Parrado

Series Editors: Javier Muñoz-Basols and Elisa Gironzetti
Spanish List Advisor: Javier Muñoz-Basols

LONDON AND NEW YORK

First published 2024
by Routledge
4 Park Square, Milton Park, Abingdon, Oxon OX14 4RN

and by Routledge
605 Third Avenue, New York, NY 10158

Routledge is an imprint of the Taylor & Francis Group, an informa business

© 2024 Lina M. Reznicek-Parrado

The right of Lina M. Reznicek-Parrado to be identified as author of
this work has been asserted in accordance with sections 77 and 78 of the
Copyright, Designs and Patents Act 1988.

All rights reserved. No part of this book may be reprinted or reproduced
or utilised in any form or by any electronic, mechanical, or other
means, now known or hereafter invented, including photocopying and
recording, or in any information storage or retrieval system, without
permission in writing from the publishers.

Trademark notice: Product or corporate names may be trademarks
or registered trademarks, and are used only for identification and
explanation without intent to infringe.

British Library Cataloguing-in-Publication Data
A catalogue record for this book is available from the British Library

Library of Congress Cataloging-in-Publication Data
Names: Reznicek-Parrado, Lina M., author.
Title: The peer-effect: non-traditional models of instruction in Spanish
as a heritage language/Lina M. Reznicek-Parrado.
Description: Abingdon, Oxon; New York, NY: Routledge, 2023. |
Series: Routledge innovations in Spanish language teaching |
Includes bibliographical references and index. Identifiers:
LCCN 2023006397 (print) | LCCN 2023006398 (ebook) |
ISBN 9781032042602 (hardback) | ISBN 9781032042640 (paperback) |
ISBN 9781003191179 (ebook) Subjects: LCSH: Spanish language—Study
and teaching (Higher)—Social aspects. | Heritage language speakers—
Education. | Translanguaging (Linguistics) Classification:
LCC PC4065 .R45 2023 (print) | LCC PC4065 (ebook) |
DDC 468.0071—dc23/eng/20230512
LC record available at https://lccn.loc.gov/2023006397
LC ebook record available at https://lccn.loc.gov/2023006398

ISBN: 978-1-032-04260-2 (hbk)
ISBN: 978-1-032-04264-0 (pbk)
ISBN: 978-1-003-19117-9 (ebk)

DOI: 10.4324/9781003191179

Typeset in Bembo
by Deanta Global Publishing Services, Chennai, India

Para Francisco X. Alarcón, su misión y su memoria.

CONTENTS

Foreword   xi

Introduction: Teaching Spanish as a Heritage Language: A
Social Justice Issue   1

Belonging in Heritage Language Learning 1
Heritage Language Learners: Histories and Profiles 3
Bilingual Education: The Emergence of Spanish Heritage
    Education in the US 5
The Field of Spanish as a Heritage Language: Looking Ahead
    Toward Non-Traditional Models of Instruction 8
"The Peer-Effect": Belonging in Heritage Language Learning 13
Notes 15
References 15

1 Peer-to-Peer Tutors in a California Heritage Language Program   20

Toward a Pedagogy of Language and Literacy as a Social Act:
    Implications for Heritage Academic Writing 20
    Academic Literacy as Social: Heritage Language Writing 24
"The Peer-Effect": Illustrating Heritage Language Practices for Pedagogy 29
Demographic Growth of Latinxs in and out of the Academy 31
The Spanish for Native Speakers Program 32
Peer-to-Peer Tutoring by and for Heritage Students of Spanish 33
Participant Selection and Background 34
    Concepción 35

viii Contents

Maité 37
Vanessa 37
Joaquín 37
Cristal 38
Esmeralda 38
Data Collection 39
   Video Recordings of Tutoring Sessions and Field Notes 39
   Tutor Interviews 41
On Belonging in Language Learning: Positionality 42
Notes 45
References 45

2 Hybrid Literacy Practices in a Translingual Academic Space   48

Methods of Inquiry 48
Sociolinguistic Ethnography 49
Tutors' Language and Literacy Practices: Translanguaging in Context 51
Literacy Practices 53
   Talking About Social Media 54
   Consulting an Expert: Asking Metalinguistic Questions 57
   Peer-to-Peer Academic Advising: Searching the Internet for
      Academic Information 61
   Personal Storytelling: Esmeralda 63
   Defining Norms of Academic Writing: Guiding Student Responses 67
Tutors' Literacy Practices: Summary 72
Notes 72
References 72

3 Translanguaging for Academic Literacy Development and
  Community Building   74

Hybridity in Heritage Language Development: Going Beyond
   "Academic Language" 74
Tutors' Linguistic Hybridity 76
   Tutors' Translanguaging 77
Tutors' Literacy Practices for Academic Development and
   Community Building 83
   Academic Literacy Development 84
     Academic Support 84
     Tutor as Expert 88
   Community Building 92
     Academic Empathy 92
     Belonging to a Community 94

Contents **ix**

Considerations for Student Impact 96
Note 97
References 97

4 The Peer as the Expert: Tutors Mobilizing Academic Personas   99

The Relevance of Casual Talk in Heritage Academic Spaces 99
  Beyond the Classroom: The Tutoring Room as Locus of Study 100
The Peer-to-Peer Collaborative Academic Learning Space 101
Constructing an Academic Persona: Analysis of Tutor Lexico-
  Grammatical Resources 107
  Providing Academic Support 109
  Metalinguistic Knowledge 120
Casual Talk Matters for Academic Literacy Development in
  Heritage Language Learning 127
Note 128
References 128

5 The Peer as Ally: Tutors Creating Community in an
   Academic Space   130

Creating an Academic Community: Mediating Collaborative Learning 130
  Through the Use of Evaluative Language 130
Academic Empathy: Leveraging Tutees' Experiences for Learning 132
Building Community for and with Tutees 137
  Concepción 137
Translating Peer Community Engagement and Heritage Literacy
  Practices into the Classroom 144
References 145

6 Students' Hybrid Language Practices at the Core of SHL
   Pedagogy: How to Foster Equitable Pedagogies in SHL   146

Heritage Language Learning for Institutional Belonging 146
The Spanish Program for Heritage/Bilingual Speakers at the
  University of Denver 149
  Key Theoretical Notions Guiding the Pedagogical Work 150
The Four Motions for Equitable Pedagogies in Spanish Heritage
  Learning 151
  Collaboration 151
  Exploration 157
  Production 162
  Self-Reflection 165

x Contents

The Peer-Effect: Heritage Student Tutors Mirroring Equitable Pedagogies in Spanish Heritage Language Instruction 167
Peer-to-Peer Tutoring for Spanish Heritage Language Instruction: Considerations 168
Academic Literacy in Spanish as a Heritage Language 170
Belonging in Both Heritage and Academic Literacies 172
References 172

Appendix A	*175*
Appendix B	*176*
Appendix C	*178*
Appendix D	*179*
Acknowledgments	*182*
Index	*184*

FOREWORD

Damián Wilson Vergara

I am honored and thrilled to give introductory comments on a book that is a rich contribution to the growing field of research on Spanish as a heritage language. From the opening pages of this manuscript, the reader will be introduced to the very important and inclusive notion of *belonging*, which is an organizing concept that weaves the diverse strands of this work together and serves as a goal for creating educational spaces for our students. We need a sense of belonging. As a heritage speaker of Spanish myself who has had the pleasure of taking SHL classes during the 1990s, I can firmly attest to the importance of belonging. Many readers who are also heritage speakers, and others familiar with our positionality, will know that we do not always feel as though we belong in educational spaces. Because the language is so dear to us, whether we are receptive bilinguals or confident speakers, it is especially alienating to find ourselves in Spanish classes that contribute to this *enajenamiento* through aggressive approaches that eradicate our ways of speaking or passive ones that merely erase us. The sense of belonging that I felt in those SHL classes reinforced an emerging interest in my own culture and inspired me to pursue the goal of regaining my heritage language. That experience set me on a path that puts me before you today writing these words and I know that the SHL experience has been the key for many others to open doors previously locked to them.

In *The Peer-Effect: Non-Traditional Models of Instruction in Spanish as a Heritage Language*, Dr. Lina Reznicek-Parrado describes an innovative and original ethnographic study and discourse analysis of data collected primarily from tutors involved in a peer-study program. To my knowledge, there is no other work looking at a peer tutoring program and the interactions contained within that context, especially not on this scale. While many studies on SHL focus on student perceptions of their learning experience, either through interviews or questionnaires, this looks at the learning experience itself, which adds to its originality. In

xii Foreword

doing so this book shows how many emerging movements in heritage language teaching can have practical implications in working with our students. Many of us return from conferences with visions of CLA, translanguaging, multiliteracies, and raciolinguistics dancing in our heads and then struggle with how to implement these alluring but elusive concepts in our own classes. Whether applying the concepts to a peer tutoring program itself or to a classroom setting, this book shows how to apply the most innovative and fruitful ideas in SHL education to our own circumstances. Ideally, this work will inspire the reader to move forward with confidence that they have a solid resource upon which they can rely.

One of the other terms that Dr. Reznicek-Parrado immediately highlights at the forefront of this work is *social justice*. This book serves as a cogent reminder that in enacting heritage language research and teaching, we are (or should be) contributing to social justice for groups who have been deprived of an opportunity to value their own ways of speaking and being. In other words, creating a sense of belonging is social justice itself.

INTRODUCTION

Teaching Spanish as a Heritage Language: A Social Justice Issue

Belonging in Heritage Language Learning

In advocating for the inclusion of students' spoken varieties of Spanish within the pedagogical frameworks of Spanish Heritage Language Pedagogy, Mexican-American author and linguist Eduardo Hernández-Chávez writes the following:

> The goals for Spanish revitalization cannot be separated from those for cultural pluralism ... The important goal is the development of the community—educationally, economically, socially, politically—through Spanish, through English, or bilingually [...] The *native language* is a critical ingredient in all of this precisely because it can contribute to these goals, and *without it, individuals are uprooted*, and the community tends to fragment.
>
> *(1993, p. 67, my emphasis)*

When referring to the "native language", Hernández-Sánchez invokes the intimate and personal relationship that heritage students—and all human beings—experience with their language, crucial in defining how individuals navigate relationships with others and with the world. Hernández-Chávez also refers to the relevance of both "cultural pluralism" and "the community" as inseparable from language, thus further implying that literacy—the ways in which we read and write with language—and our social existence are intrinsically connected. Importantly, Hernández-Chávez frames language and literacy as having educational, social, and political implications, essentially asserting that language and literacy are crucial for social participation and ultimately, social survival. Language and literacy, in this sense, represent

DOI: 10.4324/9781003191179-1

2 Introduction

the conglomeration of experiences, values, routines, habits, ideologies, and practices through which we, as human beings, consistently and continuously engage as we are socialized into our communities. Our "language" and our "literacy", therefore, represent *us*. In other words, they represent the multiple ways through which we *belong*.

Social justice advocates and literacy education specialists Kalantzis et al. (2016) refer to "belonging" in literacy learning as the ability to connect at a deep personal level within a classroom context where students' practices with literacy and their educational experiences and trajectories are clearly and explicitly reflected. This book examines how heritage language educators can intentionally design, develop, and maintain a sense of belonging for their students as a way to prioritize social justice in their classrooms, or as a way to intentionally create quality pedagogical experiences that do not dismiss students' unique trajectories as heritage language speakers. It accomplishes this by exploring how the everyday language and literacy practices of Spanish speakers as a heritage language play out—and are integral—in academic contexts. I illustrate how a clear sense of students' belonging can be created and maintained, specifically within a peer-to-peer tutoring space. I show that the variable ways heritage peer tutors use their own language and literacy repertoires to leverage their tutees' academic literacy development is productive—and even necessary—for heritage language learning, highlighting the fact that prioritizing social justice in the SHL classroom is accessible for educators and researchers alike. Additionally, by exploring how heritage students mediate their participation in contexts of learning through unique language and literacy practices, this empirical goal draws from and seeks to inform the notion of "equitable pedagogies"—pedagogies that create spaces of belonging through the inclusion of students' full literacy repertoires in service of their learning (Martínez, Morales, & Aldana, 2017). Equitable pedagogies intentionally embrace students' linguistic variability as a key process in encountering new academic genres and ways of making meaning, framing the process of literacy development as one that is intentionally designed for students who mobilize literacy practices beyond the standard. Thus, this book encourages educators and researchers to consider the range of possibilities when frameworks of social justice are prioritized, that is, when heritage speakers can engage in academic trajectories that facilitate learning through the mobilization of a wide range of language and literacy practices that go beyond those traditionally framed as academic, rather than at the expense of them. In other words, this book answers the question: what happens when students truly belong in their heritage language learning journey?

Before exploring such questions in the subsequent chapters, I present a brief overview of the heritage language student profile, considering the relevance that this student population has had in the trajectory of bilingual education in the US as well as for the pedagogical models of heritage language education proposed up until today. For a discussion of heritage language writing and academic literacy specifically, see Chapter 1.

Introduction **3**

Heritage Language Learners: Histories and Profiles

Marco Antonio,[1] now 15 years old, arrived in the United States from El Salvador eight years ago. His parents immigrated north when he was three years old. After waiting in his country for four years after his parents left, Marco Antonio was able to reunite with his family and is now completing tenth grade in a North Carolina high school. As he writes in his composition notebook for his Spanish class, he loves to play basketball, and even if he misses celebrating Christmas in the way he did back in El Salvador, he is sure that learning English will help him get into a good university.

Lucio is 22 years old and a transfer student at a large public university in the Midwest. He proudly identifies as a non-traditional student and tells of the years he has been in and out of college, juggling several full-time jobs and the responsibility of taking care of his three siblings. Lucio was born in the United States to a Mexican father and a Guatemalan mother, and Spanish was mostly spoken at home. He became fully responsible for his family when his father decided to return to Mexico and his mother struggled with addiction. As a young adult, Lucio speaks of his strong desire to reencounter his identity as a Spanish speaker and is determined to face the insecurities that surface when reading and writing in Spanish, having had no previous schooling in Spanish until his arrival at college. Lucio is a Spanish major with plans to study abroad in Latin America.

Luisa María arrived in San Antonio, Texas, when she was five years old. Her father, who was a high-achieving businessman in Lima, Peru, found work in Texas and immigrated with his wife and three daughters. Several years later, the family moved to Nebraska, where Luisa María is finishing high school. She is studious and writes in Spanish with nostalgia about being back in Peru, where she would play with her cousins until late and night. Luisa María has many aspirations for the future and says that even though everything is different now, she is happy to have the privilege of being bilingual and receiving a good education.

Marco Antonio, Lucio, and Luisa María are all students I have encountered in Spanish courses for *heritage speakers*. Their stories point to the relevance of not just their linguistic profile as bilingual people, but also the personal and sociopolitical factors of their stories that directly affect their academic trajectories. Thus, the definition of the heritage language student profile must consider and critically frame the linguistic features of heritage language repertoires with the sociopolitical implications of the stories that belong to those students we encounter in our classrooms.

In general, a heritage language is defined as a language spoken in minority communities within familiar contexts (for example, the home, church, neighborhoods, local schools, etc.) and in situations where there is a majority language more widely used, such as the case of Catalán, Gallego, or Euskera in Spain, Creole in Haiti, or Spanish in the United States. However, historically, we do not have well-established systems of understanding heritage language processes of acquisition, though linguists continue to be hard at work figuring better and

4 Introduction

more exact ways of describing how a heritage language is acquired and develops in the internal linguistic systems of bilingual people. While the tendency would be to explain the acquisition of a heritage language as a similar or identical process to the successive acquisition of a second language, Montrul (2012) advocates, naturally, that the only way to understand the acquisition process, as well as the linguistic profile of heritage speakers, is considering not just the order of acquisition of the first vis-à-vis the second language, but the functional dimensions of the languages spoken by the individual (primary language vs. secondary language) as well as the sociopolitical factors (minority language vs. majority language) that play out in the acquisition process. Additionally, Montrul states that the acquisition process of a heritage language must be highlighted as just that— a process—because when the first language becomes a minority language (for example, when a Spanish-speaking individual begins to exist in an English-only context) there is a functional dimension transformation of the languages spoken; the first language, or the primary language, becomes, soon enough, the language of secondary use. Thus, this functional change, which can happen several times and in different ways throughout an individual's life, affects the linguistic as well as the communicative features of the first language. In other words, the acquisition process of the heritage language could be conceived as a hybrid process between systems of first language *and* second language acquisition.

According to Cummins (2005), the term "heritage languages" has been used in Canada since 1977 with the beginning of the Heritage Language Programs of Ontario. Van Deusen-Scholl reminds us, however, that it is imperative to consider such a term has differing connotations according to the context used and the cultural framework of the country where the term is being used (2003). For example, in Europe and South Africa, both the terms *home language* and *origin language* are used, while in the Netherlands the term *immigrant minority language* is preferred as a more neutral term (2003, p. 218). Likewise, in Canada, academics differentiate between *immigrant languages* and *First Nations languages*, while in Australia the term *community languages* is preferred. In the United States, however, the most widely used term in the academic literature to refer to a minority language used by students such as Marco Antonio, Lucio, and Luisa María is *heritage language*. In the context of this country, demographic shifts and the use of such a term by academic communities have contributed to two phenomena: first, minority language communities have gained greater presence and relevance in the public eye, and second, those immigrants of the second or third generation who have likely had minimal contact with the country of their ancestors have begun to desire to reconnect with their cultural heritage. As Van Deusen-Scholl (2003) and Wiley (2001) explain, this has contributed to the definition of *heritage language* as one that is variable and dynamic, given that, among other things, what constitutes a "heritage" changes and develops according to immigration patterns of the host country. Thus, the elasticity of the term implies a variety of additional considerations, such as, for example, *who* is considered a "legitimate" heritage speaker. Are individuals who are not currently a part of the minority community and who do not speak the community language on a daily basis, but carry the cultural heritage of their ancestors, considered "heritage" speakers? What is most important, the use of the heritage language or the cultural identity of a speaker? On the other hand, there are those who reject the term "heritage language", framing it as a term that depicts a long-lost image of the past. Academics that dismiss the term assert the need to reimagine a term that can highlight not just tradition but a contemporary reality that can gain relevance for the future (Baker & Jones, 1998). Regardless of the debate, it is crucial to consider the sociopolitical factors that define, under the umbrella of a unique cultural history, what makes a language a *heritage language*.

In terms of the pedagogical context of teaching and learning a heritage language in the United States, educators often adopt the term "heritage language learner" when referring to students who are "raised in a home where a non-English language is spoken, who speaks or at least understands the language, and who is to some degree bilingual in that language and in English" (Valdés, 2001). Considering such a definition, Guadalupe Valdés, one of the most renowned heritage language educators in the US, reiterates the importance of recognizing that the term "bilingual" rejects the mythical assumption that a speaker uses both (or more) languages to superior levels, such as that they can complete all communicative tasks in one language as well as the other or that they can go unnoticed by a native speaker of the same language(s). Instead, Valdés recognizes that bilingual people generally do not have the opportunity to mobilize both (or all) of their languages in the same contexts and with the same group of people throughout their lives. She concludes, thus, that one must conceptualize a variety of "bilinguals" and that their profiles vary across a range of linguistic and pragmatic skills. As such, heritage speakers present a highly variable and dynamic linguistic profile.

Bilingual Education: The Emergence of Spanish Heritage Education in the US

To appropriately illustrate the context of study explored in this book, it is imperative to consider the complex trajectories that both bilingual education and Spanish heritage education have launched in California and the broader United States and the relationship that these trajectories have with efforts to both include and exclude the language and literacy practices of multilingual students. While this book explores a Spanish heritage program within the higher educational system, the historical context of K–12 bilingual education has direct consequences for the type of language learning experiences that heritage speakers and other linguistically diverse students in the United States receive before entering the university.

Both the incorporation and eradication of bilingual programs in public education have been deeply tied to the demographic changes and immigration waves observed in recent history. In the early 19th century, for example, dual-language

6 Introduction

instruction was available to both immigrant and native populations in more than 12 American states. Bilingual programs in German, Swedish, Norwegian, Danish, Italian, Czech, French, and Spanish were common (Ovando, Collier, & Combs, 2005). Further, in the late 1700s, the evident pro-German sentiment that remained after the American Revolution contributed to Americans' desire to learn German in school, illustrated by the fact that, for example, out of 57 K–12 public schools in St. Louis, Missouri, 52 were German-English bilingual schools (Escamilla, 1980). But after the arrival of the Irish in the late 19th century and the popular rise of consequent xenophobic sentiments against immigrants—especially from Germany (a sentiment which was exacerbated by WWI)—dual-language education was eradicated throughout the country. While just 14 of the 45 states had English-only legislation toward the end of the 19th century, by 1923 a total of 34 out of the 48 states prohibited dual-language education (Lessow-Hurley, 2015).

Later, the Cuban Revolution and the arrival of Cuban political refugees in 1959 prompted small pockets of Spanish bilingual programs in both east and southwestern states. The first fully bilingual program was founded in 1963 in Dade County, Miami, where both L1 students (those who spoke Spanish as a first language) and L2 students (those who spoke it as a second language) were fully immersed in Spanish beginning in first grade and gradually received English instruction; this ultimately served as the first model for modern-day two-way bilingual education programs across the nation (Keller & Van Hooft, 1982). During the same time period, however, the Civil Rights movement was brewing, and Mexicans, Mexican-Americans, and Chicanxs[2] (mostly from the Southwest) joined African Americans in demanding equal rights. From a people whose distinctive trait was that they spoke Spanish, Latinxs quickly became a people who did not speak English, becoming first LES (Limited English Speakers) and then LEP (Limited English Proficient). As García posits, native Spanish-speaking proficiency was no longer an asset but a problem that needed to be remediated (1993, p. 78).

As more attention was placed on the "lack" of English-speaking abilities among multilingual students, in 1974 a group of Chinese American families sued the San Francisco Public School District in the well-known case of *Lau v. Nichols*. Families argued that because they did not understand English, and instruction didn't account for their limited English proficiency, more than 1,800 Chinese students in English-only schools were being denied their right to a meaningful education. The United States Supreme Court unanimously ruled that the use of the exact same resources, materials, curricula, and teachers for all children, both English and non-English speaking, was unconstitutional. They mandated that those students who spoke English as a second language be provided some type of differentiating instruction. While *Lau v. Nichols* made it illegal for students whose primary language is not English to receive English-only instruction exclusively without assessing appropriate accommodations to understand instruction, it did not legislate the specific type of instruction that should be used to teach them. This omission of detail made way for the creation of many (and some detrimental) types of "bilingual" programs, such as those that seek to assimilate students into English as soon as possible while discouraging the in-school use of home language and literacy practices.

In the late 1980s, xenophobic attitudes around bilingual education continued, and the English-Only movement was born, exacerbated by the growth in the immigrant population across the US. Later, in 1994, the short-lived approval of Proposition 187 in California denied public school assistance to children of undocumented immigrants, though it was deemed unconstitutional and revoked shortly thereafter. Since then, however, in support of the English-Only movement, millionaire Ron Unz dismantled local and national efforts for bilingual education through funding propositions that eliminated the establishment of dual language programs. In California, for example, home to almost a third of the nation's English language learners by 2004 (National Center for Education Statistics, 2014), Ron Unz helped pass Proposition 227 in 1998.[3] Later, in 2000 and 2002, Arizona and then Massachusetts, a state where 71% of voters approved the "English for the Children" movement, eradicated all remaining bilingual programs in the state.

It was against this anti-bilingual education backdrop that the field of Spanish as a Heritage Language emerged. Simultaneous with the dismantling of bilingual education and to counter the negative linguistic image of Spanish in the US, US Latinx Spanish language professionals began to advocate for a positive view of the Spanish language, establishing that Spanish was not a "problem" but a resource of the community while highlighting its essential role in public life (García, 1993). By 1972, when bilingual education was gaining renewed interest among educators and began to be re-established, the American Association of Teachers of Spanish and Portuguese (AATSP) issued, for the very first time, a recommendation of courses designed for "Native Speakers of Spanish". By 1975, renowned education specialist Guadalupe Valdés had published the first newsletter on the "Teaching of Spanish to Native Speakers (SNS)". In 1976 she edited, along with García-Moya, the first collection of academic articles about the teaching of Spanish to native speakers in the US. In 1977, Valdés and Teschner wrote the first commercial textbook for a Spanish Native Speaker course (*Español escrito: curso para hispanohablantes bilingües*), ultimately opening the doors to an emerging field within Spanish education in the US.

The most recent national presidential tenure must also be addressed in relation to how it has affected the possibilities and limitations of bilingual and heritage education in the United States. Unsurprisingly, the xenophobic and racist ideologies that propelled Donald Trump's campaign fueled detrimental policies attacking immigration, immigrants, and multilingualism—both within the American public education system and beyond. For example, shortly after Trump's election, the White House discontinued the use of the Spanish-language social media handle @LaCasaBlanca, which had been consistently managed by former presidents Barack Obama and George W. Bush. Both used the handle to grant

8 Introduction

the nationwide Spanish-speaking public access to critical information. Trump's dismissive move made Spanish, and the people who speak it, symbolically irrelevant to his presidency. Despite the overturn of the late 1990s-era Proposition 227 in 2016, when Donald Trump was elected president amid the slow re-implementation of bilingual programs across the nation, the exclusive and toxic rhetoric surrounding bilingualism and multilingualism in the US continued to present important obstacles to the creation, implementation, and retention of academic spaces that intentionally and responsibly consider linguistic diversity as an asset and societal advantage in spaces of teaching and learning.

Despite societal linguistic hostility against Spanish documented throughout history, linguists, educators, and academics continue their efforts to demonstrate the importance of bilingualism and motivate collective support for the field of Spanish as a Heritage Language in the United States. This collective effort dates back a couple of decades, involving several milestones. In 1999, for example, the University of California, Los Angeles, sponsored the first conference for the study of heritage languages (including Spanish as a heritage language). Titled First Heritage Languages in America, the initiative was organized by the Center for Applied Linguistics (CAL) and the National Foreign Language Center (NFLC). At the beginning of the 1990s, the Spanish in the US and Spanish in Contact with Other Languages Conference was founded, and the field of Spanish as a Heritage Language—defined as "an area of study that draws from political, psychological, linguistic, pedagogical, and other disciplines and has as one of its main objectives Spanish language maintenance"— was in full force (Beaudrie & Fairclough, 2012, p. 5). Most recently, the National Symposium on Spanish as a Heritage Language (NSSHL), which was founded by Spanish linguist Diego Pascual y Cabo, held its tenth reiteration in 2023, consistently growing its members, participants, and overall interest in many complex issues surrounding Spanish as a Heritage Language in the US context.

The Field of Spanish as a Heritage Language: Looking Ahead Toward Non-Traditional Models of Instruction

As Latinxs continue to represent one of the fastest growing segments of the US population, and as they continue to gather more presence in educational, public, and political institutions and the media, therefore gaining economic power and political influence,[4] research in the teaching and learning of Spanish across educational contexts has also grown. According to Beaudrie (2012), many language departments across the country, especially at the postsecondary level, have initiated or increased the number of course offerings specifically designed for speakers of Spanish as a heritage language since the turn of the century.

Thanks to the growing interest in the unique linguistic and socio-educational profile of the Spanish heritage student population, researchers today have moved forward by incorporating several established tenets that operationalize Spanish heritage language pedagogy as separate from Spanish foreign language pedagogy.

Thus, heritage language educators have access to information regarding innovative pedagogical approaches envisioned exclusively for Spanish heritage speakers (for example, Potowski, 2010; Roca & Colombi, 2003; Webb & Miller, 2000). These emerging pedagogical frameworks highlight the heterogeneity and diversity of the Spanish heritage student population, prompting instructors to understand that developing or utilizing a single set of learning objectives or curricular generalizations is impossible. Thus, they should attain objectives that address the contextual and unique linguistic, social, and educational needs of Spanish heritage learners. While this heterogeneity makes it challenging for the field to grow and, instead, gives way to highly localized models of instruction (according to the needs of the context), many researchers in the field have begun to elaborate research and pedagogical goals that could be conceived for all educational contexts of Spanish heritage language. The first six goals of Spanish heritage language research and teaching were proposed by Valdés (1995) and the final two were added subsequently by Aparicio (as cited in Beaudrie, Ducar, & Potowski, 2014). As summarized by Martínez (2016), the seven goals of Spanish heritage teaching are:

1. Maintenance of the heritage language
2. Acquisition of a prestige language variety
3. Expansion of the bilingual range
4. Transfer of literacy skills
5. Acquisition of academic skills in the heritage language
6. Cultivation of positive attitudes toward the heritage language
7. Acquisition or development of cultural awareness

While a collection of personalized pedagogical goals is a step in the right direction (that is, toward unifying the field), these seven goals tend to overemphasize formal registers and so-called "prestige varieties", which come at the expense of leveraging speakers' heritage language practices for instruction. Researchers have long cautioned that such a "limited normative" approach, where the explicit instruction of unmarked "standard" or "academic" language is regarded as a priority, erases the complicated racialized reality of the Spanish spoken in the US (Faltis, 1990; Mena & García, 2021). As such, researchers continue to advance work that advocates for the importance of Spanish/English bilingualism, biculturalism, and biliteracy in the US, raising questions regarding the social, linguistic, and educational implications of this work (Pascual y Cabo, 2016) in order to advance more equitable pedagogical frameworks where educators can leverage the linguistic, literacy, and cultural practices of students as crucial tools for academic literacy development and in light of social justice tenets (Martínez, Morales, & Aldana, 2017).

Regardless, some of the most researched issues in Spanish heritage language pedagogy include linguistic attitudes and ideologies (see Rivera-Mills, 2012; Potowski, 2002, for example), linguistic identity (Leeman, 2012, 2015), and

10 Introduction

language policy and planning (Martínez, 2012; Potowski & Carreira, 2004). Other topics remain less researched, such as heritage language assessment (except for Beaudrie, 2016), teaching strategies for mixed classrooms (except for Bowles et al., 2014; Carreira, 2016), online teaching in the heritage classroom (except for Henshaw, 2016a, 2016b), and pedagogical strategies for receptive heritage speakers (except for Beaudrie, 2009a, 2009b). Importantly and most recently, researchers have risen Critical Language Awareness (CLA) frameworks to the surface to further reframe heritage language pedagogy from a critical perspective (Beaudrie & Vergara Wilson, 2021). As Beaudrie and Vergara Wilson posit, for example, CLA frameworks are essential to guiding students as they become aware of the complex ways in which language and power are interconnected, and the social privilege that some language varieties have over others. Earlier on, well-known American linguist Jennifer Leeman posited that developing critical perspectives on language has great value for heritage students, in part because many of them have personal experience with multilingualism, both in their own families and in their local communities. For her, many of the experiences of heritage speaker students remain unexamined, as well as the ideologies that affect them directly, such as the historical erasure of non-English languages in the US, the monolingual ideologies that denigrate hybrid language practices, the assignation of greater moral and intellectual value to "standard" and "national language varieties", and the role of educational institutions in enforcing language hierarchies (2005). In fact, Beaudrie and Loza (2021) make reference to a "critical turn" in heritage language pedagogy, whereby critical paradigms based on educational equity are paramount in informing research and practice, given that "a CLA framework in HL classrooms fosters social justice, educational equity, and the elimination of language disparities in educational contexts" (Beaudrie & Vergara Wilson, 2021, p. 63).

Of most relevance to the present study is the closely related and growing attention that the field has recently placed on exploring pedagogical frameworks that promote leverage of students' involvement in hybrid and translingual literacies to expand their linguistic repertoires (see, for example, Zapata & Lacorte, 2018). Following tenets of CLA, these pedagogical frameworks pay close attention to the way heritage students use language to navigate academic language learning, including—but not limited to—the ways students draw from a variety of repertoires (formal/informal registers of English, informal/formal registers of Spanish, colloquialisms, dialectal uses of a variety of Spanish, so-called academic language, etc.) while they collectively participate in a space of teaching and learning Spanish as their heritage language. Spanish heritage specialists Torres, Pascual y Cabo, and Beusterein (2017), for example, posit that a crucial area of concern in Spanish heritage pedagogy is the development of pedagogical materials that address the promotion of "multiliteracies" in the heritage classroom, urging for pedagogies that are intentionally inclusive of the multilingual, multimodal, and globally connected reality of the world today. As such, the authors emphasize the relevance of not only classroom-based literacies but also those "pertaining to heritage learners' experiences in their homes" (2017, p. 273). Similarly, Zapata (2018), who studies Spanish heritage pedagogies from a multiliteracies perspective, states that the point of departure toward re-envisioning Spanish heritage pedagogies is the need to develop curricula that are "based on relevant materials that connect closely to who the learners are—to their personal world, including the community to which they belong—by taking into account their diverse social and cultural backgrounds" (p. 3). Through this approach, the field is beginning to finally challenge theoretical narratives that stigmatize students' literacy practices as deficient and instead intentionally normalize the multilingual and multidialectal repertoires of heritage speakers (Martínez, Morales, & Aldana, 2017).

Non-traditional models of instruction such as the one described by Zapata and Lacorte connect deeply to other theoretical frameworks that seek to validate and intentionally highlight heritage language and literacy practices for teaching and learning. One such framework is that of translanguaging (García, 2009; Prada, 2021) in which the alternative uses of language that bilinguals deploy take center stage, both as we understand how social interaction happens and importantly as we explore how teaching and learning take place in linguistically diverse academic spaces. When envisioning language pedagogy, both CLA and translanguaging frameworks posit that heritage speakers draw from translingual practices and repertoires to successfully participate in socially situated contexts and across linguistic boundaries since their repertoires are not represented as single languages. Indeed, for translanguaging scholars, "single languages" like "English" or "Spanish" merely represent ideological inventions tied to nation-states traditionally meant to support nationalist and expansionist ideas in earlier centuries (Otheguy, García, & Reid, 2015). These restrictive linguistic ideologies are thus not useful for reimagining equitable spaces of learning for multilingual students. In all, the intentional incorporation of translanguaging frameworks as well a CLA in heritage language pedagogy "puts forth an idea that is still today received with reticence by many bilingual educators: that of making the bilingual practices of racialized minoritized students legitimate in academic contexts" (Prada, 2021, p. 103). Ultimately, both translanguaging frameworks and CLA tenets emphasize the potential of non-traditional models and spaces for teaching and learning in Spanish heritage language pedagogy.

A clear example of the intentional incorporation of the socially situated implications within Spanish heritage language teaching and learning rooted in translanguaging and CLA frameworks for pedagogy in heritage language education is the relevance of non-traditional models of pedagogy and the incorporation of students' hybrid literacies in Leeman et al.'s critically engaged service-learning initiative, which encourages activism and the critical exploration of identity through an out-of-classroom experience (2011). In their action research model, the authors emphasize that students' mobilizing agency in their language trajectory outside of the classroom is of inherent importance to critical pedagogy. The experiences that students gain as they teach Spanish literacy to elementary school

12 Introduction

learners are designed, according to the authors, so that students develop their expert identities as Spanish speakers:

> If students could deploy their linguistic knowledge and skills as teachers in the program, they might be able to challenge dominant ideologies that construct bilingual and heritage speakers as "limited" or "deficient", and to enact identities in which their knowledge of Spanish was seen as wholly legitimate, and indeed experts in this scope.
>
> *(Leeman et al., 2011, p. 487)*

The authors show that heritage speakers who complete out-of-school critically engaged service-learning experiences consistently express that heritage language learning is not just about formal language study. They assert that the teaching of culture—and the integration of heritage language practices—is integral to the role of heritage language curricula. Other examples of these same non-traditional models of pedagogy that respond to the pressing need to critically integrate heritage language practices as part of teaching and learning trajectories are Trujillo's learning community course model for heritage learners (2009), Parra's integration of community art and community poetry in Spanish heritage language learning (2013), and Lowther-Pereira's integration of service-learning for heritage language critical pedagogies (2015, 2018), among others.

Less common is the implementation of peer-to-peer tutor programming in heritage language curricula. At the time of writing this book, I did not find any published work referencing tutoring models in heritage-to-heritage dyads, or as a non-traditional, out-of-classroom academic experience to Spanish heritage programs beyond the one described here. However, perhaps one of the most closely aligned pedagogical frameworks which describes the relevance of combining critical language awareness with peer social interaction is Faltis' description of a pedagogical framework that integrates Freirean critical pedagogy with Vygotskian social learning (1990), where a more advanced peer guides learners for language development. According to Faltis, the theory of learning presented by Vygotsky in the early 1960s is relevant for heritage langue development, since it necessarily involves a process that requires social interaction with significant others or peers that relate to the same personal and social experiences unique to the heritage language trajectory. Additionally, Faltis' integration of Freire's problem-posing approach, or ways to guide students to perceive critically the way they exist in the world, allows for a consistent questioning of the power dynamics involved in language, and especially in academic language vis-à-vis language that is deemed "non-academic". As such, Faltis' model posits that in tandem, Freirean and Vygotskian perspectives offer a viable and much-needed alternative to heritage language pedagogy approaches that posit the learning of the "standard" as the primary goal (Faltis, 1990).

While there are no current models of heritage language education that integrate an out-of-classroom peer-to-peer model such as the one described in this book, in general, tutoring as a complement to the academic trajectories of students is not new. In fact, models for peer education and support are widely prevalent in education as illustrated by the College Reading and Learning Association's historical overview of the various interpretations and applications of peer education spanning many years (Keller & Porter, 2020). Peer education is widely accepted as a high-impact educational practice, and scholars commonly agree that "peer education has the potential for both breadth and depth as an influential force in a community … [a]nd the very act of connecting to others in that kind of relationship builds the sort of community our institutions aspire to be" (Williams, 2011b, p. 98, as cited in Reznicek-Parrado & Gonzalez, 2022). Importantly, heritage language programs are uniquely positioned to implement academic spaces for peer support in the eyes of CLA and translanguaging frameworks, especially as a model that supports re-framing pedagogy as a site for social justice. Unfortunately, there is a lack of research and interest around the impact of student communities of practice for instruction, or what Martínez calls "the embeddedness of the community" (2016). Because programs and terminologies differ, "we are only now beginning to approach this work with the sort of rigor and attention to learning outcomes that have become the expected norm of program evaluation in the more formal curriculum" (Williams, 2011a, p. 5). As such, the establishment of programs like the one described in this book contributes valuable information regarding the impact of peer education on heritage language learners, leveraging CLA and translanguaging frameworks, bringing heritage language and literacy practices to the forefront, and helping inform future models that support heritage language student retention and success through equitable spaces for teaching, learning, and belonging.

"The Peer-Effect": Belonging in Heritage Language Learning

By drawing on more recent trends to build on the linguistic profile that students already possess through critical linguistic and pedagogical frameworks based on equity and inclusion, the peer-to-peer Spanish heritage program discussed in this book aims to intentionally leverage students' full linguistic repertoires within and across academic spaces, completely eliminating the "language of lacking" (Ladson-Billings, 1995, p. 479) in favor of acceptance and acknowledgment of students' language practices and identities as part of the program experience. By giving students the responsibility of taking center stage in navigating academic spaces outside of the classroom in support of their writing trajectories, students learn *from and about* their linguistic, cultural, and ethnic diversity (Vergara Wilson & Pascual y Cabo, 2019, p. 179). I describe a model for student-led academic support centered on equitable pedagogies that can enrich the heritage language student experience and engage learning not only from and about, but also *through* students' linguistic, cultural, and ethnic diversity (Reznicek-Parrado & Gonzalez, 2022). Later, in Chapter 6, I discuss the program's implication for in-classroom pedagogies.

14 Introduction

As such, this book centers on the language and literacy practices that speakers of Spanish as a heritage language mobilize as they engage with peers in an autonomous, non-classroom academic context of Spanish literacy learning. I seek to demonstrate that an intentional curiosity for how heritage speakers navigate academic language holds deep implications for the development of new pedagogical frameworks in Spanish Heritage Language pedagogy. Such purposeful curiosity requires that educators and researchers consider the embeddedness of the community (Martínez, 2016) and the extent to which heritage student literacy practices already respond to the cultural and linguistic context surrounding their own learning and development (Martínez, 2010). After exploring the empirical data, I illustrate pedagogical examples that can help educators envision a pedagogy inclusive of all linguistic repertoires, which relies on heritage language pedagogies as a tool to recreate a class space representative of all lived experiences of belonging—not just those of the mainstream. The remainder of this book adheres to the following outline.

In Chapter 1, I situate the peer-to-peer program from which the data is based as an illustration of the equitable pedagogies described in this introduction and after a discussion on current frameworks of heritage writing and academic literacy for belonging. The second part of this first chapter frames the sociodemographic relevance of Latinxs and Spanish in California to contextualize the founding of the University of California, Davis' Spanish heritage program. Here, I will introduce the six focal participants while narrating the experience of being and becoming a peer tutor as I observed it while I worked with this group of students—highlighting the emotional, academic, and social advantages that it brought for those students involved. Before finishing the chapter, I offer a brief discussion of my own positionality in regard to the analysis presented in subsequent chapters.

In Chapter 2, I begin describing the ethnographic data analysis by exploring the literacy practices mobilized by the focal participants in the peer-to-peer tutoring session to show what tutors are doing with language as they work collaboratively with their tutees. I describe tutors' linguistically hybrid literacy practices before detailing the thematic analysis of the socially situated goals with which tutors mobilized such practices.

In Chapter 3, I illustrate specific translanguaging moments in the data, where tutors intentionally mobilize linguistic hybridity to engage with their tutees as they frame a unique linguistic and pedagogical experience for their peers. I then highlight tutors' practices with language but primarily focus on the specific socially situated goals they mobilize by way of the translanguaging literacy practices described in Chapter 2. This chapter demonstrates how tutors continually position themselves as experts, allies, friends, and peers as they mobilize hybrid language practices to frame a welcoming, like-minded community of practice, illustrating the impact of their literacy repertoires on this student-led community.

In Chapter 4, I initiate a dialogue between the theoretical framework and the second part of the methodology grounded in discourse analysis of tutor–tutee

Introduction **15**

interactions. I explore how tutors intentionally and functionally position themselves as experts in the content matter, as well as in navigating the academic contexts of the college experience, all while mobilizing heritage language practices.

In Chapter 5, I advance the dialogue between the theoretical framework and discourse analysis of tutor–tutee interactions to continue framing the tutoring room as a context where equitable pedagogies benefit students' learning experiences. Specifically and following Appraisal Analysis (Martin & White, 2005), I include analysis of the evaluative language in the peer interactions to illustrate the varied ways in which tutors actively and intentionally create community as they work with their students. The chapter ends by highlighting tutors' efficacy in mobilizing equitable pedagogies as peers.

In Chapter 6, I summarize the data findings to illuminate the implications of pedagogical frameworks in Spanish heritage learning that can re-conceptualize students' translingual literacy practice as relevant for pedagogy in the same way that tutors intentionally re-frame academic literacy development and as illustrated in the analysis. I discuss and offer concrete classroom-based examples to illustrate how educators can begin to nurture equitable pedagogies by reflecting the range of everyday translingual literacy practices that Spanish heritage speakers already mobilize in service of their learning. I include a variety of student voices to reflect on my last four years as Director of the Spanish for Bilingual/Heritage Speakers Program at my current institution and consider how I have drawn on this research for the conception, development, and assessment of Spanish heritage courses.

Notes

1 All names and places are fictionalized to assure anonymity.
2 While the use of the non-binary morpheme "-x" has been harshly criticized due to its limited use among non-academic Spanish-speaking communities, I choose to use it solely for the purposes of using gender-inclusive forms that, while not all-encompassing, allow me to use gender-inclusive language. Throughout the book, I make all efforts to use other gender-inclusive language forms, such as the use of gender-neutral possessives ("their" for "hers" or "his") and pronouns ("they" for "she" or "he"). Spanish-specific gender-inclusive language, like the insertion of the non-binary gender morpheme "-e" (such as in "chicanes", "latines", etc.), is not used here since the original language of this book is English, and such gender-neutral markers are used most commonly in texts originally written in Spanish.
3 Proposition 227 was repealed in 2016 by Proposition 58, dismantling restrictions for bilingual programs in California.
4 In 2014, for example, Latinxs became the "majority-minority" in California, surpassing the population of non-Hispanic whites (Pew Hispanic Center, 2014).

References

Baker, C., & Jones S. P. (1998). *Encyclopedia of Bilingual Education and Bilingualism.* Clevedon, UK: Multilingual Matters.

16 Introduction

Beaudrie, S. M. (2009a). Spanish receptive bilinguals: Understanding the cultural and linguistic profile of learners from three different generations. *Spanish in Context, 6*(1), 85–104.

Beaudrie, S. M. (2009b). Receptive bilinguals' language development in the classroom: The differential effects of heritage versus foreign language curriculum. In M. Lacorte & J. Leeman (Eds.), *Spanish in the United States and Other Contact Environments: Sociolinguistics, Ideology and Pedagogy* (pp. 325–345). Madrid: Iberoamericana.

Beaudrie, S. M. (2012). Research on university-based Spanish heritage language programs in the United States: The current state of affairs. In S. Beaudrie & M. Fairclough (Eds.), *Spanish as a Heritage Language in the United States: The State of the Field* (pp. 203–222). Washington, DC: Georgetown University Press.

Beaudrie, S. M. (2016). Advances in Spanish language heritage assessment. Research and instructional considerations. In D. Pascual y Cabo (Ed.), *Advances in Spanish as a Heritage Language*. Amsterdam: John Benjamins Publishing Company.

Beaudrie, S. M., & Fairclough, M. A. (2012). *Spanish as a Heritage Language in the United States: The State of the Field* (p. 203). Washington, DC: Georgetown University Press.

Beaudrie, S. M., & Vergara Wilson, D. (2021). Reimagining the goals of HL pedagogy through critical language awareness. In S. Loza & S. M. Beaudrie (Eds.), *Heritage Language Teaching: Critical Language Awareness Perspectives for Research and Pedagogy* (pp. 63–79). London: Routledge.

Beaudrie, S. M., Ducar, C., & Potowski, K. (2014). *Heritage Language Teaching: Research and Practice*. New York: McGraw-Hill.

Bowles, M. A., Adams, R. J., & Toth, P. D. (2014). A comparison of L2–L2 and L2–heritage learner interactions in Spanish language classrooms. *The Modern Language Journal, 98*(2), 497–517.

Carreira, M. (2016). A general framework and supporting strategies for teaching mixed classes. In D. Pascual y Cabo (Ed.), *Advances in Spanish as a Heritage Language* (pp. 159–176). Amsterdam: John Benjamins Publishing Company.

Cummins, J. (2005). A proposal for action: Strategies for recognizing heritage language competence as a learning resource within the mainstream classroom. *The Modern Language Journal, 89*(4), 585–592.

Escamilla, K. (1980). German-English bilingual schools 1870–1917: Cultural and linguistic survival in St. Louis. *Bilingual Journal, 5*(2), 16–20.

Faltis, Christian. (1990). Spanish for native speakers: Freirian and Vygotskian perspectives. *Foreign Language Annals, 23*, 117–126.

García, O. (1993). From Goya portraits to Goya beans: Elite traditions and popular streams in U.S. Spanish language policy. *Southwest Journal of Linguistics, 12*, 69–86.

García, O. (2009). *Bilingual Education in the 21st Century: A Global Perspective*. Malden and Oxford: Wiley/Blackwell.

Henshaw, F. G. (2016a). Technology-enhanced heritage language instruction. Best tools and best practices. In M. Fairclough & S. Beaudrie (Eds.), *Innovative Strategies for Heritage Language Teaching* (pp. 237–254). Washington, DC: Georgetown University Press.

Henshaw, F. G. (2016b). Online courses for heritage learners. Best practices and lessons learned. In D. Pascual y Cabo (Ed.), *Advances in Spanish as a Heritage Language* (pp. 281–298). Amsterdam: John Benjamins Publishing Company.

Hernández-Chávez, E. (1993). Native language loss and its implications for revitalization of Spanish Chicano communities. In B. J. Merino, H. T. Trueba, & F. A. Samaniego (Eds.), *Language and Culture in Learning: Teaching Spanish to Native Speakers*. London: The Falmer Press.

Kalantzis, M., Cope, B., Chan, E., & Dalley-Trim, L. (2016). *Literacies*. Cambridge, UK: Cambridge University Press.

Keller, G. D., & Van Hooft, K. S. (1982). A chronology of bilingualism and bilingual education in the United States. In J. A. FIshman & G. D. Keller (Eds.), *Bilingual Education for Hispanic Students in the United States*. New York: Teachers College Press.

Keller, P., & Porter, H. D. (2020). A terminological study of peer education in higher education [White paper]. College Reading and Learning Association. https://crla.net /images/whitepaper/CRLA_2020_WhitePaper_Peer_Ed_FA.pdf

Ladson-Billings, G. (1995). Toward a theory of culturally relevant pedagogy. *American Educational Research Journal*, *32*(3), 465–491.

Leeman, J. (2005). Engaging critical pedagogy: Spanish for native speakers. *Foreign Language Annals*, *38*, 35–45.

Leeman, J. (2012). Investigating language ideologies in Spanish as a heritage language. In S. Beaudrie & M. Fairclough (Eds.), *Spanish as a Heritage Language: The State of the Field* (pp. 43–59). Washington, DC: Georgetown University Press.

Leeman, J. (2015). Identify and heritage language education in the United States. *Annual Review of Applied Linguistics*, *35*, 100–119.

Leeman, J., Rabin, L., & Román-Mendoza, E. (2011). Identity and activism in heritage language education. *The Modern Language Journal*, *95*(4), 481–495.

Lessow-Hurley, J. (2015). *The Foundations of Dual Language Instructions* (4th ed.). Boston: Pearson Education.

Lowther-Pereira, L. (2015). Developing critical language awareness via service-learning for Spanish heritage speakers. *Heritage Language Journal*, *12*(2), 159–185.

Lowther-Pereira, L. (2018). *Community Service-learning for Spanish Heritage Learners: Making Connections and Building Identities* (Vol. 18). Amsterdam: John Benjamins Publishing Company.

Loza, S., & Beaudrie, S. M. (Eds.). (2021). *Heritage Language Teaching: Critical Language Awareness Perspectives for Research and Pedagogy*. London: Routledge.

Martin, J. R., & White, P. R. R. (2005). *The Language of Evaluation: Appraisal in English*. New York: Palgrave.

Martínez, D., Morales, P. Z., & Aldana, U. S. (2017). Leveraging students' communicative repertoires as a tool for equitable learning. *Review of Research in Education*, *41*, 477–499.

Martínez, G. (2012). Policy and planning research for Spanish as a heritage language: From language rights to linguistic resource. In S. Beaudrie & M. Fairclough (Eds.), *Spanish as a Heritage Language: The State of the Field* (pp. 61–78). Washington, DC: Georgetown University Press.

Martínez, G. (2016). Goals and beyond in heritage language education. In M. Fairclough & S. Beaudrie (Eds.), *Innovative Strategies for Heritage Language Teaching: A Practical Guide for the Classroom* (pp. 39–55). Washington, DC: Georgetown University Press.

Martínez, R. A. (2010). Spanglish as literacy tool: Toward an understanding of the potential role of Spanish-English code-switching in the development of academic literacy. *Research in the Teaching of English*, *45*(2), 124–149.

Mena, M., & García, O. (2021). 'Converse racialization' and 'un/marking' language: The making of a bilingual university in a neoliberal world. *Language in Society*, *50*, 343–364.

Montrul, S. (2012). Is the heritage language like a second language? *EUROSLA Yearbook*, *12*, 1–29.

National Center for Education Statistics (NCES) (2014). Number and percentage of public School students participating in English language learner (ELL) programs, by

18 Introduction

state: Selected years, fall 2004 through fall 2014. https://nces.ed.gov/programs/digest/d16/tables/dt16_204.20.asp

Otheguy, R., García, O., & Reid, W. (2015). Clarifying translanguaging and deconstructing named languages: A perspective from linguistics. *Applied Linguistics Review, 6*(3), 281–307.

Ovando, C. J., Collier, V. P., & Combs, M. C. (2005). *Bilingual and ESL Classrooms: Teaching in Multicultural Contexts* (4th ed.). Boston: McGraw Hill.

Parra, M. L. (2013). Expanding language and cultural competence in advanced heritage- and foreign-language learners through community engagement and work with the arts. *Heritage Language Journal, 10*(2), 253–280.

Pascual y Cabo, D. (2016). Charting the past, present, and future of Spanish heritage language research. In D. Pascual y Cabo (Ed.), *Advances in Spanish as a Heritage Language* (pp. 1–8). Amsterdam: John Benjamins Publishing Company.

Pew Hispanic Center. (2014). Latinos will surpass whites as largest racial/ethnic group in California. http://www.pewresearch.org/fact-tank/2014/01/24/in-2014-latinos-will-surpass-whites-as-largest-racialethnic-group-in-california/

Potowski, K. (2002). Experiences of Spanish heritage speakers in university foreign language courses and implications for teacher training. *ADFL Bulletin, 33*(3), 35–42.

Potowski, K. (2010). *Conversaciones escritas: Lectura y redacción en contexto.* Hoboken: Wiley & Sons.

Potowski, K., & Carreira, M. (2004). Teacher development and national standards for Spanish as a heritage language. *Foreign Language Annals, 37*(3), 427–437.

Prada, J. (2021). Translanguaging awareness in heritage language education. In S. Loza & S. M. Beaudrie (Eds.), *Heritage Language Teaching: Critical Language Awareness Perspectives for Research and Pedagogy* (pp. 101–118). London: Routledge.

Rivera-Mills, S. V. (2012). Spanish heritage language maintenance. In S. Beaudrie & M. Fairclough (Eds.), *Spanish as a Heritage Language in the United States: The State of the Field.* Washington, DC: Georgetown University Press.

Reznicek-Parrado, L.M, Gonzales, A. (2022). Curricular integration of academic support services: Supporting heritage writing. *Spanish Heritage Language Journal, 2*(2), 250–267.

Roca, A., & Colombi, M. C. (Eds.) (2003). *Mi lengua: Spanish as A Heritage Language in the United States. Research as Practice.* Washington, DC: Georgetown University Press.

Torres, J., Pascual y Cabo, D., & Beusterien, J. (2017). What's next? Heritage language learners shape new paths in Spanish teaching. *Hispania, 100*(5), 271–278.

Trujillo, J. A. (2009). Con todos: Using learning communities to promote intellectual and social engagement in the Spanish curriculum. In M. Lacorte & J. Leeman (Eds.), *Spanish in the United States and Other Contact Environments: Sociolinguistics, Ideology and Pedagogy* (pp. 369–395). Madrid, Spain: Iberoamericana.

Valdés, G. (1995). The teaching of minority languages as academic subjects: Pedagogical and theoretical challenges. *Modern Language Journal, 79*(3), 299–328.

Valdés, G. (2001). Heritage language students: Profiles and possibilities. In J. K. Peyton, Ranard D. A., & McGinnis S. (Eds.), *Heritage Languages in America: Preserving a National Resource* (pp. 37–77). DC/McHenry: Center for Applied Linguistics/Delta Systems.

Van Deusen-Scholl, N. (2003). Toward a definition of heritage language: Sociopolitical and pedagogical considerations. *Journal of Language, Identity, and Education, 2*(3), 211–230.

Vergara Wilson, D., & Pascual y Cabo, D. (2019). Linguistic diversity and student voice: The case of Spanish as a heritage language. *Journal of Spanish Language Teaching, 6*(2), 170–181.

Webb, J. B., & Miller, B. L. (Eds.) (2000). *Teaching Heritage Language Learners: Voices from the Classroom*. Yonkers: American Council on the Teaching of Foreign Languages (ACTFL).

Wiley, T. (2001). On defining heritage languages and their speakers. In J. K. Peyton, D. A. Ranard, & S. McGinnis (Ed.), *Heritage Languages in America: Blueprint for the Future* (pp. 29–36). Washington, DC: Center for Applied Linguistics and Delta Systems.

Williams, L. B. (2011). The ongoing, and emerging, place of peer education. *New Directions for Student Services, 2011*(133), 1–7.

Zapata, G. C., & Lacorte, M. (2018). *Multiliteracies Pedagogy and Language Learning: Teaching Spanish to Heritage Speakers*. Cham, Switzerland: Palgrave Macmillan.

1

PEER-TO-PEER TUTORS IN A CALIFORNIA HERITAGE LANGUAGE PROGRAM

Toward a Pedagogy of Language and Literacy as a Social Act: Implications for Heritage Academic Writing

For many heritage speakers, a high school or university Spanish language course often represents their very first encounter with academic literacy in the language of their heritage. Because traditional language classrooms are often limited to the incorporation of standard academic language, students risk the conclusion that their heritage literacy repertoires are incompatible with those of a formal academic context encountered at the university or in any formal educational context and ultimately choose not to study their heritage language. Unfortunately, many secondary and higher education Spanish courses continue to emphasize formal academic literacies with minimal room for students to explore how their heritage literacies, often deemed "non-academic" or "non-standard", can in fact complement the curriculum or be leveraged within it. In all, courses for Spanish as a heritage language largely fail to successfully address the incongruence between how students have been socialized to communicate in their home communities and the differing literacy expectations of school (Martínez, Morales, & Aldana, 2017). Importantly, this disconnect has profound implications for students' understanding of their selves—their identity, their community networks, and how they conceive their potential linguistic capital for their own professional futures. In other words, if we do not center a commitment to redesigning our curricula so that it is deeply committed to framing belonging at its core, where students see themselves reflected and find themselves as legitimate language users, we are doing entire student communities of heritage speakers a disservice.

It is also pertinent to ask the question of how to redesign curricula that potentially diverges from the goal of academic literacy (or the acquisition of the

DOI: 10.4324/9781003191179-2

"standard") which we can agree is relevant for students who have had little to no formal schooling in the language of their heritage. Let me clarify from the outset of this book: I am not advocating divergence from the standard goal of expanding students' linguistic spectrum. I too believe that students who can mobilize academic language will be positioned to participate in social spaces where the standard varieties—namely socially prestigious ways of talking—are needed. However, I also do not ascribe to an "appropriateness model" (Leeman, 2018) which equates formal or standard language as exclusively "appropriate" and informal or non-standard language as always "inappropriate" for use in academic contexts. Importantly, for me, it is also crucial that students build the critical knowledge to see that informal language such as heritage language practices is not "inappropriate" for academic spaces, but rather that it is stigmatized and given less social prestige by specific social groups, necessarily implying issues of power. In addition, I do not believe heritage language practices should simply act as a temporary scaffold for bilingual speakers to adopt dominant literacy. Rather, much like critical language awareness models and as a way to push back against the ways that appropriateness-based models of literacy development further the linguistic ideologies that frame heritage language practices as "deficient" or "unacceptable", I frame heritage language practices as *needed* for academic literacy development. What I illustrate in this book is how we can do away with the notion of appropriateness altogether and, instead, leverage heritage language practices as an inherent tool for academic literacy. As such, students develop critical awareness surrounding language use while they develop academic literacy and, most importantly, as they increase their ability for belonging, connecting with a classroom context where their practices with language and literacy are explicitly and consistently reflected.

With this goal in mind, it is useful to understand how the field of Literacy Studies has conceived the idea that because language reflects the social world, there is no real or inherent difference between language that is academic and language that is not, but that language is simply a reflection of our experiences. If we want to convey the message to our heritage students that they belong in our classroom, does that not mean that we should also frame the language that we use in that space to send that very message? With the goal of theoretically exploring the notion of belonging in language and literacy pedagogy to which I refer earlier, this book adopts views that frame language as a system that cannot be separated from its social context and function—that is, views that position language as a meaning-making resource (Scribner & Cole, 1981; Gee, 1992; Heath, 1982; Street, 1993). In this way, *The Peer-Effect: Non-Traditional Models of Instruction in Spanish as a Heritage Language* follows tenets put forth by the research collective of New Literacy Studies (NLS), an interdisciplinary movement that began in the mid-1980s and challenged the traditional notion of literacy that presumes centrality of the text in its definition. As such, social literacy theory conceives literacy not as a "skill" that is learned, but rather as a "practice" that is developed in a social context over time, using the notion of "literacy practice"

22 Heritage Tutors in CA

to distinguish it from dominant conceptions of literacy that establish the sole standard of what counts as "true literacy". In this way, this book draws attention to how literacy practices—recurrent, goal-oriented, socially situated uses of language in meaningful human activities (Scriber & Cole, 1981)—of dominant communities are not inherently "more sophisticated" but remain privileged simply because they are the ones mobilized by those in power (that is, they reflect the social experiences of the privileged).

Understanding language and literacy through a social lens is useful in framing heritage language and literacy practices as relevant for heritage pedagogies in several ways. First, literacy conceived through the lens of social participation never remains neutral, apolitical, or ahistorical. Rather, a "literacy as social" lens focuses on the everyday meanings and uses of literacy in specific, complex, and socially situated cultural contexts. Thus, social approaches to literacy extend far beyond the traditional notion of literacy as a cognitive-based and socially devoid skill to simply "read and write". Rather, it emphasizes that literacy is not just a cognitive ability but instead a cover-term for a variety of different socio-cultural practices. As posited by Gee, social approaches to literacy position it as "tied up with socialization, enculturation and development in social and cultural groups" (1996, p. 52). Additionally, the lens of linguistic hybridity has been central in capturing the consequences of intercultural exchange and "boundary crossing" experienced by students from non-dominant communities. As posited by Gutiérrez, Morales, and Martínez, "the resulting 'linguistic bricolage' [of students' repertoires] reflects the ways that the local and the global are always implicated in the everyday linguistic practices of non-dominant students, thus challenging narrow and essentialized notions of [heritage and/or multilingual] students' linguistic repertoires" (2009, p. 80).

Street (2005) conceptualizes the importance of social approaches to literacy as having implications for the framing of literacy as well as how we understand the process of literacy acquisition with intentional consequences for the inclusion and exclusion of people. In his view, when conceptualizing "literacy as social", it is useful to make a distinction between an "autonomous" model and an "ideological" model of literacy (Street, 1984), where an "autonomous model" refers to the assumption that the acquisition of literacy will "in itself—autonomously—have effects on other social and cognitive practices" and that literacy as an isolated skill "will lead to higher cognitive skills, improved economic performance, greater equality, and so on" (Street, 2005, p. 417). The problem with this model, according to Street, is that it disguises the cultural and ideological assumptions that underpin it, imposing Western conceptions of literacy onto other cultures. Conversely, an "ideological" model of literacy posits that literacy is a social practice that is always embedded in socially constructed epistemological principles:

It is about knowledge: The ways in which people address reading and writing are themselves rooted in conceptions of knowledge, identity, being. Literacy, in this sense, is always contested, both its meanings and its practices, hence particular versions of it are always "ideological"; that is, they are always rooted in a particular worldview and a desire for that view of literacy to dominate and to marginalize others.

(Street, 2005, p. 418)

Importantly and especially relevant to this book are the implications that social approaches to literacy provide for the contexts of teaching and learning literacy in diverse academic spaces. Traditionally, literacy instruction focused on passing along the "autonomous model" to emergent writers, where literacy was seen as a universal, generic skill devoid of context. However, with the conception of literacy as an "ideological" process, social approaches to literacy have allowed educators to not only emphasize cultural meanings but also expose the power dimension of reading and writing processes (Street, 2005). Additionally, social approaches to literacy have allowed both researchers and educators to step away from the traditionally decontextualized, abstract, rule-governed, and fragmented conception of literacy to one not based on the notion of "correctness" (or monolingualism) but that includes a representation of meanings in a broader, richer, and more complex social experience. Such an experience includes non-traditional conventions and complex relationships between the visual, the spatial, and the written word(s) (Kalantzis et al., 2016). A literacy pedagogy based on social approaches reframes the antiquated, basic understandings of literacy to modern-day basic understandings, as illustrated in the new types of foundations that this framework poses in relation to literacy instruction (Table 1.1).

These "new basics" for literacy teaching and learning have pivotal implications for the reconceptualization of what "academic literacy" means, with a

TABLE 1.1 Old and New Basics in Literacy Instruction

Old Basics for Literacy Education	New Basics for Literacy Education
• Reading and writing are two of the three "Rs" (the third being "arithmetic")	• Literacy and numeracy as fundamental life skills
• Phonics rules	• Multiple "literacies" for a world of multimodal communications
• Correct spelling and grammar	• Many social languages and variations applied in communication appropriate to settings
• Standard, educated speakers	• "Kinds of people" who can innovate, take risks, negotiate diversity, and navigate uncertainty
• Appreciating "literary" value of "prestige texts"	• A wide and diverse range of texts valued, with growing access to different media and text types
• Well-disciplined "kinds of people"	• People who can negotiate different human contexts and styles of communication

Source: Adapted from Kalantzis et al., 2016, p. 5.

particular understanding that for literacy to reflect social reality, "researchers instead of privileging the particular literacy practices familiar in their own cultures, now [must] suspend judgement as to what constitutes literacy among the people they are working with until they can understand what it means to the people themselves" (Kalantzis et al., 2016, p. 419). As such, in recent years, scholars not just in heritage language education but in literacy education overall have mobilized new conceptualizations of academic literacy more consistent with the tenets of the new basics for literacy education described earlier.

Academic Literacy as Social: Heritage Language Writing

If we are to reconceptualize language and literacy as social acts, we must also consider how the language and literacy practices utilized in school settings, as well as the literacy demands of academic contexts, should be framed around the complex socially situated context in which they exist. This book also incorporates frameworks that consider *academic* literacy development through social approaches to literacy, highlighting that academic literacy learning must "reflect the kind of reality and learning that students experience in their everyday life" (Zapata & Lacorte, 2018, p. 3) and that it must be "more responsive to the diversity of cultures, including subcultures, such as communities and affiliations, and the variety of languages within societies" that students bring (Mills, 2011, p. xiii). To access more holistic realities of all students engaging with academic tasks and to consider the complete repertoire of literacy practices that students are already mobilizing in academic contexts as part of their academic literacy development, it is also useful to explore frameworks which see academic language as situated practice (see Cummins, 1979, 1981; Lave & Wagner, 1991; Antilla-Garza & Cook-Gumperz, 2015). In line with a literacy framework that incorporates the hybrid, translingual literacy practices of multilingual students, my research explores how bi/multilingual students use and combine language and literacy practices, including "academic" and "non-academic" uses of language that are fluidly and strategically aligned with the academic context in which students participate.

In academic settings, social approaches to literacy problematize the fact that academic literacy continues to reflect the literacy practices of the mainstream— namely, the privileged. How do we decide and therefore communicate which are "the language practices used to construct knowledge or negotiate membership in an academic or professional community" (Colombi, 2015, p. 6) if traditional academic literacy practices are shaped by those literacies that exclude heritage speakers' day-to-day literacies, for example? The answers to that question continue to be contested, as I will show. We must first consider and reframe what scholars have understood as "academic literacy" and how particular frameworks have shaped the conversation with implications for heritage language teaching and learning.

Our current understanding or definition of "academic literacy" or "academic language", that is, the type of requisites written and spoken language students acquire to perform well in school, has been deeply influenced by Cummins' 1981 seminal model of second language acquisition. In this model, Cummins makes a fundamental distinction between conversational and academic aspects of language proficiency (the distinction between Basic Interpersonal Communicative Skills [BICS] and Cognitive Academic Language Proficiency [CALP]). The distinction operationalizes an assumption that "everyday" uses of language are highly contextualized, whereas academic uses of language are relatively less context-embedded, more complex, and more abstract. Cummins posits that "as a student progresses through the grades, they are increasingly required to manipulate language in cognitively demanding and context-reduced situations that differ significantly from everyday conversational interactions" (2000, p. 67). Context-embedded communication, such as day-to-day interactions, is distinguished from context-reduced communication in that speakers can actively negotiate meaning while supported by a variety of situational and interpersonal cues (such as asking for feedback, gesturing, etc.). Context-reduced communication, on the other hand, relies primarily on linguistic cues, meaning that successful interpretation of the message depends heavily on knowledge of the language itself (Cummins, 2000). As such, according to this model, context-embedded communication is more typical to the everyday realities experienced outside of the classroom, whereas many of the linguistic demands of the classroom reflect communicative activities that represent context-reduced tasks (Cummins, 2000).

The BICS-CALP dichotomy has been, as noted, particularly influential among researchers and practitioners, informing current popular conceptualizations of the notion of "academic language". However, in examining this notion, Valdés, Poza, and Brooks (2015) recall that the conceptualizations of the language needed by students to succeed in school have been presented in the field of education as a series of oppositions, including "standard versus non-standard", "academic versus conversational", and "effective versus noneffective reading/writing", including the "BICS/CALP" dichotomy. These oppositions, they argue, are based on assumptions that there is only one type of academic literacy with specific aspects of language (i.e., vocabulary, syntax, non-stigmatized pronunciation, etc.) that students must acquire to succeed in school. In turn, this assumption results in creating circumscribed categories by which the experiences and performances of students are understood, preventing teachers and researchers from noticing and intentionally considering the full repertoires of their students' experiences and backgrounds, especially those students who speak "non-academic" varieties of any language (Enright, 2011). From a socially oriented view of literacy, "academic language" can be seen as one aspect of many students' communicative repertoires (Rymes, 2010) "that includes various codes, styles, registers, ways of speaking/writing that emerge or recede according to context, purpose, interlocutors, and topic" (Valdés, Poza, & Brooks, 2015 p. 68), which can, in turn, represent not one but many academic literacies. As such, social theories of academic literacy argue that while academic language is linguistically contextualized, all language, including everyday uses of language, is socially

26 Heritage Tutors in CA

contextualized. Therefore, everyday uses of language can also be mobilized in classrooms for academic purposes. Many contemporary scholars have recognized that while dichotomous understandings of academic language might be useful to identify the learning needs of students, they become "a bias towards an abstracted, idealized, homogenous spoken language which is imposed" (Lippi-Green, 2011, p. 67).

As such, Molle (2015) highlights the need to develop more productive and inclusive notions of academic literacy, particularly notions with the potential to reflect a literacy reality that encompasses *all* student literacies, and not just those of the mainstream. She underscores that among researchers there is consensus that academic language

> refers to the language used in school by which students process and produce knowledge; that it is key to students' academic success; and that academic language and everyday conversational language are not opposites but should be thought of as a continuum.
>
> *(Lippi-Green, 2011, p. 14)*

In explaining current notions of academic language, Molle also highlights that most research on academic literacy is informed by sociocultural approaches to academic language that consider context as primary. These approaches presume that students must be socialized into academic literacy (Lea & Street, 2006) by way of learning the practices of a discipline-specific discourse community "in which experts need to help novices gain greater control of a range of semiotic resources as well as an understanding of social and linguistic expectations for participation" (Colombi & Schleppegrell, 2002, p. 2). In other words, current notions of academic language give priority to understanding the specific demands of the language of school, providing explicit instruction on the interrelation of the social context and its implications for advanced literacy development. Lea and Street posit, however, that while socialization models of academic literacy recognize variations in language use across contexts, they presume that "disciplinary discourses and genres are relatively stable and that, once students have learned and understood the ground rules of a particular academic discourse, they are able to reproduce it" (2006, p. 369). According to the authors, this assumption is unfounded.

The notion that writing or academic literacy is a "vacant skill in the heritage learner's linguistic repertoire" is put into question by well-known linguist Glenn Martínez (2005), who notes that by the early 2000s, the field of heritage language education, most specifically in regards to Spanish, had moved from a *pre-process* or *process approach*—which highlighted writing skills as an "empty vessel" in the communicative repertoire of heritage speakers—to a *post-process approach*, highlighting functional approaches to writing that can guide students to recognize elements of the text akin to "academic language", or ways to participate in academic spaces (Colombi, 2003). While post-process approaches do shy away from the vision of the heritage student as "devoid of skills", they continue to prioritize professional and/or academic contexts, as Martínez states, which is problematic since the "professional or academic community" is still given special privilege, framing an "asymmetrical attention to the communicative practices of socially sanctioned discourse communities" (Martínez, 2005, p. 82). Thus, by showing how heritage students interweave textual features across a variety of linguistic repertoires to differing genres—a notion that is given center-stage in post-process approaches to academic literacy development—Martínez argues that the field is in need of a theory that can adequately handle the hybridity of the literacy practices enacted in heritage language communities and that could consider "how professional discursive practices are transformed into homely ones and how homely discursive practices are recast as professional ones in the lived experience of multicultural interaction and interchange" (Martínez, 2005, p. 83). In the same vein, and by highlighting the multiplicity and hybridity relevant in literacy academic development to which Martínez alludes, Villa (2004) had already posited that for heritage speakers of Spanish, writing development implies the consistent crossing of boundaries between Spanish and English, and that restricting academic literacy to one genre, one discourse, or one language interrupted heritage students' plight to continue writing as an act of *resistencia*. In fact, Villa affirms that spoken language has a crucial role in developing written literacy for heritage students and that writing, in fact, must "become an extension of the (oral) naming process, employing the printed (or electronic) word in addition to the written one" (Villa, 2004, p. 93).

To capture the rich flexibility present in the use of heritage written discourses in multiple settings, including academic ones, Molle (2015) and Lea and Street (2006) thus posit that there is an alternative model for language and literacy development which they refer to as the "academic literacies model". This model "is concerned with meaning making, identity, power, and authority, and foregrounds the institutional nature of what counts as knowledge in any particular academic context" (Lea & Street, 2006, p. 369). More direct attention is placed on the notion of literacy as a large set of contextually valued and concrete social practices (Street, 1984) and less direct attention is allotted to literacy practices used exclusively in school-related contexts. By subscribing to the notion of "literacy as practice" (Scribner & Cole, 1981), the academic literacies model asserts that the socially recognized and goal-oriented nature of all practices, including both school and out-of-school literacy practices, is subject to power dynamics. Thus, this model, by highlighting the tendency of schools to identify some practices as legitimate and others as deficient (Cook-Gumperz, 2006), recognizes the contested nature of literacy. The relevance of the academic context as a contested social context is therefore key to the academic literacies model, making it the model most appropriate for highly diverse academic contexts.

Additionally, in order to situate academic literacy within the framework of social literacy, many scholars have put forth the idea of "academic discourse as situated" (Antilla-Garza & Cook-Gumperz, 2015; New London Group, 1996).

28 Heritage Tutors in CA

This framework makes way for the exploration of literacy practices across academic contexts, highlighting that academic literacies in general are mobilized differently across classrooms and other non-classroom spaces. Further, situating academic discourse as practice considers the many literacy resources from which students draw (including both informal and formal literacy practices) to participate in academic spaces. Considering academic discourse as situated emphasizes that to acquire mastery of academic discourse practices in general, rather than a sole focus on the demands of "in-school" language, consideration of how students navigate these demands through the mobilizing of their own (heritage) literacy practices must be prioritized. As such, when conceptualizing academic literacy as a broad set of literacy practices influenced by students' interactions with academic texts, a "multiple literacies" perspective is embraced. This perspective considers academic literacies as only one aspect of an individual's repertoire of literacy practices, "with critical, personal, or community literacies also informing one's understanding of text and of the world" (Enright, 2011). As Enright states,

> The greatest advantage of these expanded notions of academic language and literacy is that they generally resist starting with firm categories and definitions, allowing a careful examination of the research context, participants, and activities to suggest locally defined understandings of which language and literacy practices do or do not "work" toward school success.
>
> *(2011, p. 86)*

Given the work outlined here and the different conceptualizations of academic literacy, it is crucial to highlight that these approaches, one which prioritizes the demands of school literacy context and the other which includes the everyday lived experiences of students for academic language learning, are not mutually exclusive but rather overlapping. In fact, a sole emphasis on students' existing practices for defining literacy risks an exclusionary effect for student minorities outside of the mainstream. Delpit (1995), for example, while believing the importance of giving (marginalized) students a voice in the debate about academic literacy, calls for the consideration of the fact that emphasizing explicit literacy instruction should apply to students who do not have access to what she calls "the culture of power", that is, the culture of school. The author posits that those students who belong to the culture of power standardized in schools, that is, students who come from a predominantly white, middle-class background, already have access to the culture of power and have adopted the academic discourses of school. Yet many students who are members of minority groups have not been provided access to this culture of power given their marginalization, thus making it the responsibility of educators to socialize their students into mainstream academic literacies. It is important, though, to highlight the differences underlying each notion surrounding differed understandings of academic literacy, since these variations point to an emphasized shift from a focus on academic forms of language to an exploration of academic literacy, that is, "from language features to language in use, from regularities in disciplinary expectations to the variability and unpredictability of classroom interactions [...] and from reading and writing to multimodal discourse" (Molle, 2015, p. 15). It is the educator's responsibility, then, to position their pedagogy at the appropriate point of the continuum, considering the lived literacy realities of their students.

Importantly, it is also the task of researchers and educators to find the most effective ways of teaching academic literacy to all students, including, and importantly, linguistically diverse students such as heritage speakers. As these notions around academic literacy continue to develop, many researchers insist on "pushing boundaries and expanding definitions" (Enright, 2011) to highlight current students' needs and to develop new, more flexible literacies required for success in a world where "the lines of the local and global are constantly shifting" (p. 87); that is, they are best served by literacies which will enable them to negotiate differences in patterns of meaning from one context to the another (Cope & Kalantzis, 2015). Thus, while still relevant for literacy instructions and development, we must also

move beyond traditional methods of literacy found in formal education (i.e., question-answer exchanges between instructors and students, multiple-choice activities and traditional exams), since they do not reflect the complete kind of reality and learning that (linguistically diverse) students experience in their everyday life.

(Zapata & Lacorte, 2018, p. 13)

"The Peer-Effect": Illustrating Heritage Language Practices for Pedagogy

The social approaches to language and frameworks for academic literacy I have detailed here are the guiding principles I have used for years as I have come to understand that opening up academic spaces for *all* literacies, including heritage literacies, is how I value and validate the lived literacy experiences of my students and create belonging in my classrooms. As I hope it is clear by now, the intentional incorporation of heritage language practices into my pedagogical practices is the way I communicate to my students that the academic spaces they occupy belong to them just as much as they belong to me; it is how I help them understand that their linguistic repertoires have a place in the larger set of academic genres they seek to acquire. As I will show throughout this book, the incorporation of heritage language practices in my research and pedagogical design has had strong positive impacts, not just for students' academic literacy development, but also for their overall academic trajectories. This is simple: a "literacy as practice" analysis is invested in understanding how a student's literacy plays out, as opposed to determining whether a student has literacy or not. Heritage language repertoires continue to be stigmatized due to their incorporation of

30 Heritage Tutors in CA

features such as language contact phenomena and rural lexical and morphological features. As such, it is imperative that the definition of "heritage language speaker" is framed around the socially situated relevance of students' repertoires, as opposed to their lack of contextual appropriateness, and that this happens as they walk into our classrooms and as we intentionally design our pedagogies. In this case, if we incorporate using everyday, translingual literacy practices as part of the learning process in academic contexts, we demonstrate to our students that these practices *do* belong in the academy, and thus, that they themselves, as heritage speakers, also belong. To me, the intentional pedagogical effort to communicate and recreate belonging in the heritage classroom must precede the introduction and acquisition of standard academic literacy. As I see it, if the field begins to recognize and leverage the wide range of linguistic and cultural resources that heritage students bring to all academic settings, researchers and educators can begin to emphasize the importance of successfully navigating the discursive norms of multiple language communities, including those considered standard, in a world that is becoming increasingly more diverse (New London Group, 1996). For ideas on how to mobilize such a pedagogical stance in the classroom, see Chapter 6.

A particular experience of belonging, as illustrated in this book and part of my pedagogical design in heritage language teaching and learning, comes from the creation of a non-classroom, pedagogical space where heritage students are given the opportunity to mobilize their everyday language and literacy practices as they embody language expert identities and directly participate in language maintenance efforts without the presence or direction of an instructor. A sense of belonging, as understood in this project, comes from the creation (and valuing) of opportunities for students to give back to their peer communities—that is, to other speakers of Spanish as a heritage language. In this case, a sense of belonging is illustrated by students' participation in the peer tutoring program for the Native Speakers Program[1] at UC Davis, a program that serves students who already have oral capabilities in the language of their heritage, considering them to be of intermediate level. The program features a collective effort to instill a sense of belonging within a campus community of undergraduate heritage speakers of Spanish.

When talking about what it means to be a peer tutor (to other Spanish heritage speakers), Concepción, a focal participant, invokes Francisco X. Alarcón, the late Chicano activist who founded UC Davis' programs for Spanish heritage speakers in the early 1990s:

Concepción: Eh: yo pienso que lo que más aprecio de mi trabajo es poder ayudar a los estudiantes a que desarrollen seguridad en ellos mismos. Y más que nada con el uso del español [...] Siento que muchos de ellos vienen sintiéndose inseguros de cómo hablar en español-

Um: I think that what I appreciate the most about my job is being able to help students develop self-confidence in themselves. And most of all in terms of their use of Spanish [...] I feel that a lot of them come feeling insecure about how to speak Spanish-

Lina: Entonces tú ves tu rol como mentora o tutora académica, pero en realidad parece, según lo que me cuentas, que va mucho mas allá de lo académico.

So you see your role as mentor or academic tutor, but in fact, it seems, based on what you are telling me, that it goes beyond academics.

Concepción: Yo pienso que sí. Por eso, yo pienso que Alarcón quiso añadir ese nombre de mentores, porque sí, somos tutores, pero siento que el trabajo que se hace, como, no nada más yo, yo lo veo en todos los demás tutores. Va más allá. Va mas allá del contexto académico.

I think so, yes. That's why I think Alarcón wanted to add that name, that of mentors, because yes, we are tutors, but I feel like the work we do, like, not just me, I see it in all other tutors. It goes beyond. Beyond the academic context.

In recognizing that as a peer tutor, she has the power to positively contribute to the identity of her peers and the level to which they can belong as heritage speakers of Spanish, Concepción is deeply engaged with her role in language maintenance. She has a clear understanding of how her language and literacy experiences are crucial to positively impacting her peer community. Further, she has a clear understanding of her own belonging to the community of peer tutors and students in the program. Her reference to the implications of her role as extending beyond academics ("va más allá") is a testament to Concepción's perspective that her language and literacy practices represent positive experiences of belonging for herself, other tutors, and the tutees with whom she works. Thus, the unique aspects of this setting (the peer tutoring program), as I will show throughout this book, provide insights into how heritage speakers of Spanish mobilize their full repertoires of language and literacy practices (beyond those conventionally considered "academic") for academic literacy development in Spanish and in the service of their belonging. The use of this empirical data to begin informing pedagogy in Spanish heritage language is transformative and urgent.

Demographic Growth of Latinxs in and out of the Academy

The present study took place in a language program designed for speakers of Spanish as a heritage language in a large public university in northern California. The multiplicity of educational and linguistic experiences is not only evident within the department that offers the program (as demonstrated by its curricular advancement for linguistically diverse students such as Spanish heritage language speakers), but within the university at large. According to Fall 2017 enrollment numbers at this institution, 35.08% of all university students were Asian/Pacific Islander, 26.18% were White/Caucasian, 21% were Hispanic/Latinx/Chicanx,

32 Heritage Tutors in CA

3.56% were African American, 0.82% were Native American/Alaska Native, 1.63% comprised other ethnic groups, and 11.73% were international (UC Davis Profile, 2017). Additionally, given the student enrollment numbers of those who identify as Hispanic/Latinx/Chicanx, it became what is known a "Hispanic-Serving Institution" (HSI) in May of 2018. A HSI designation is issued by the US Department of Education to educational institutions with enrollment numbers of Hispanic/Latinx/Chicanx students comprising 25% or more of the larger student body. The designation provides opportunities for federal funding to support student success and retention initiatives. Further, still today, this institution continues a general demographic change reflected in the state of California at large. According to Census data from 2017, 38.9% of California's population is Hispanic/Latinx, making them the state's largest ethnic group, and surpassing Non-Hispanic Whites (37.7%) (Census Bureau, 2017). The latest data from 2019 show that Hispanic/Latinxs comprised 39% of the total population in California, sustaining a steady increase. Further, the California Department of Education reports that in the academic year 2017–2018, out of six million enrolled children in kindergarten through grade 12, three million were Hispanic/Latinx, and only one million were Non-Hispanic White (California Department of Education, 2018). Though student enrollment numbers of Hispanic/Latinx students at the institution where this study took place still do not parallel those of the state, the Hispanic/Latinx population is continuing to rapidly increase both in and out of the academic institution.

The Spanish for Native Speakers Program

The Spanish for Native Speakers Program (*Programa de español para hispanohablantes*) at this institution began in the academic year of 1992, under the supervision of a well-known Chicano activist poet and lecturer in the Spanish Department, Francisco Alarcón. Due to the traditional lack of programs for heritage speakers in Spanish departments, this program stands as one of the earlier programs implemented in higher educational contexts across the US and the only one of its kind to implement a peer-to-peer tutoring program as key curricular component. The program is divided into three courses (SPA 31, SPA 32, and SPA 33) offered consecutively per quarter and fulfills the lower division requirements for the Spanish major as well as minor (in the non-native speaker track, the major requirements can take up to seven quarters). At its conception in 1992, only one section of 25 students was established as part of the Spanish for Native Speakers curriculum. However, as early as 1995, three more sections were created per course, and enrollment numbers grew from 25 in 1992 to 66 in 1995 and later up to 95 in 2011 (Blake & Colombi, 2013). The continued student enrollment increase following 2017 in all three program courses are evident in the course enrollment data (Table 1.2).

It is important to note that all students who enroll in this program have oral capabilities in Spanish and that it does not offer Spanish heritage courses to

TABLE 1.2 Program for Native Speakers Student Enrollment Numbers from Fall 2012 to Fall 2017

Term and Year	Course/Number of Sections	Number of Registered Students
Fall Quarter 2012	SPA 31/4	61
Winter Quarter 2013	SPA 32/4	98
Spring Quarter 2013	SPA 33/4	76
Fall Quarter 2013	SPA 31/3	62
Winter Quarter 2014	SPA 32/3	61
Spring Quarter 2014	SPA 33/3	65
Fall Quarter 2014	SPA 31/4	88
Winter Quarter 2015	SPA 32/4	98
Spring Quarter 2015	SPA 33/4	89
Fall Quarter 2015	SPA 31/4	68
Winter Quarter 2016	SPA 32/4	84
Spring Quarter 2016	SPA 33/4	90
Fall Quarter 2016	SPA 31/4	94
Winter Quarter 2017	SPA 32/4	102
Spring Quarter 2017	SPA 33/4	101
Fall Quarter 2017	SPA 31/4	101

beginning-level or receptive speakers. The program description as advertised in flyers is distributed cross-campus at beginning-of-the-year events such as the Chicane/Latinx "Bienvenida", a first-year student event, and the AB 540 and Undocumented Student Resource Fair. The materials highlight the specific linguistic profile that the program is designed for, as well as the program's objectives, which center around language maintenance for both personal and professional goals, as stated in its information flyer:

> WHAT IS IT? This three-quarter series is designed for students who grew up with Spanish as their home language and are comfortable speaking it. Leaning on all of their previous experience with the language, the program seeks to enrich and complement the students' linguistic repertoire by exposing them to other language varieties, including academic Spanish. […] By the end of the series, we hope that students will have gained increased confidence in the language and strengthened their identity as bilinguals, being able to interact with a more diverse group of speakers, pursue higher-level courses and/or apply this knowledge in their professional endeavors, inside or outside the United States.

Peer-to-Peer Tutoring by and for Heritage Students of Spanish

One of the most essential characteristics of the Spanish for Native Speaker Program as described is its adoption of Ugarte's peer tutoring curriculum (1997), which was the result of in-house pedagogical innovation between faculty members

34 Heritage Tutors in CA

and graduate students at the time in the University's Spanish and Portuguese Department. Following said curriculum and hired by the Department, an advanced student who has completed the heritage program hosts weekly one-on-one meetings with a currently enrolled student as part of the core program curriculum. As explained in a program flyer,

> The tutors, the most unique component of our program, are students that recently completed the series, serving as peer mentors who offer encouragement as well as academic support during weekly one-on-one meetings.

According to Blake and Colombi, two Spanish linguists involved in the implementation of this program, the tutors' mission is to "reinforce the academic process through personalized attention as well as to motivate students to appreciate Spanish in an academic context" (2013, p. 299). Importantly, at its conception, the tutoring model within this program was conceived to not only provide personalized academic support, but social support as well. The original model delineated the tutoring hour as beginning with five to ten minutes of "casual conversation" where tutors may establish a personable relationship with the student so that students can feel comfortable: "in order to achieve this [students feeling comfortable], tutors could ask the following questions: What do you like to do? What plans do you have for the future? Why are you interested in Spanish?" (Ugarte, 1997, p. 85, my translation). As a pedagogical tool, peer-to-peer tutoring is contextualized in this setting as a way to further "non-hierarchical dialogue amongst equals", where tutors may provide a bridge between the topics covered in class and students' personal experiences as related to navigating college as underrepresented, and, in most cases, first-generation students. In Ugarte's own words: "tutoring sessions provide students with an opportunity of using Spanish in a real-life context of human communication. They [tutoring sessions] go beyond academics; they are key in helping students develop their personal identities and facilitate Spanish teaching for native speakers" (Ugarte, 1997, p. 89, my translation).

Participant Selection and Background

Data collection, including participant recruitment for this project, was conducted throughout Fall Quarter, at the beginning of the 2016–2017 academic year. The intimate, small-scale tutoring group I was able to access as a course instructor made it easy to present my study to potential participants. I used a project flyer (see Appendix A) and communicated my investment in the value of the tutoring program when I presented my goals and the involvement tutors would have as potential participants. I talked about my project during two tutors' bi-weekly meetings, which are conducted in collaboration with other instructors and the Program Director.

Via a sign-up sheet I distributed, six of the total 11 tutors communicated their interest in participating in my study. After I secured their agreement in writing, I distributed an initial survey that included questions about tutors' linguistic and educational trajectories, as well as about their bilingual practices in everyday life. This survey was designed with the intention to gather concrete evidence about the tutor's a) transnational experiences, b) hybrid literacy practices and repertoires, c) perceived proficiencies, and d) academic experiences as first-generation students.

Regarding the design of my study, I was not particularly interested in recruiting a specific type of tutor. In reality, I was interested in tapping into the shared experiences of all tutors—specifically the trans/multilingual, unconventional educational experiences of first-generation students of Latinx descent—all experiences outside of the mainstream, and which many of the tutors may share. When I conducted the recruitment process, I expected to net a mix of experiences regarding time in the tutoring program. However, only two out of five new tutors signed up for the study. I can assume that this may be because of new tutors' perceived "lack of expertise" and/or desire to concentrate on learning their main responsibilities as new tutors (as opposed to being in the spotlight). Given the situational relevance of the tutor's role (and not the value of the longitudinal effect of working as a tutor), I did not consider the participant pool's homogeneity in terms of time in the program as an obstacle for analysis. Throughout the course of the study, one of the two new tutors who signed up to participate received no consenting tutees. Therefore, data collected for this individual is not included as part of the present study; only one tutor who was just beginning the program continued as a study participant. The remaining participants had been tutors in the program for at least one year.

Table 1.3 shows demographic as well as educational information for each participant, including other relevant information about their literacy practices, language use, and language ability perceptions. I also note the number of tutoring sessions analyzed for this project, per tutor (roughly, one tutoring session equals one hour). In the following section, I supplement this information with brief additional descriptions for each participant.

Concepción

As an undergraduate, Concepción was very involved in the McNair Scholars Program at this institution, where students from underrepresented groups are supported to pursue research as well as graduate degrees. From the start, she had a vision to pursue a post-graduate degree in Spanish after graduating from college. She was active in the department as an academic tutor for the Program for Native Speakers and often advocated within the department for legislation related to Spanish (e.g., Proposition 5812), including topics of relevance in her honor's thesis (titled *Las experiencias laborales de los tutores/mentores del Programa de Español para Hispanohablantes: Un cambio atípico para el desarrollo de una comunidad*[2]) which she completed under the supervision of the department's Chair. In the 2016–2017 academic year, she won the Outstanding Senior Award for Spanish, which is given to a graduating undergraduate senior who has made significant contributions to the dynamic intellectual life of the institution. In late Winter 2017, after having applied and been accepted to several master's level programs,

TABLE 1.3 Demographic and Educational Profile of Tutor Participants

	Concepción	Maité	Vanessa	Joaquín	Cristal	Esmeralda
Demographic						
Age	21	21	20	21	21	21
Sex/orientation	Female	Female	Female	Male	Female	Female
Family place of origin	Jalisco, Mexico	Sinaloa, Mexico	San Salvador, El Salvador	Guanajuato, Mexico	Oaxaca, Mexico	Chihuahua, Mexico (father); Sinaloa, Mexico (mother)
Birthplace	Jalisco, Mexico	Sinaloa, Mexico	San Salvador, El Salvador	Guanajuato, Mexico	Oaxaca, Mexico	Norwalk/La Mirada, CA
Place where raised	Sacramento, CA	San Diego, CA	San Fernando Valley, CA	Fairbaugh, CA	Oaxaca and Salinas, CA	Norwalk/La Mirada, CA
Age of most recent immigration to the US	10	13	8	18	14	N/A
Times emigrated back to country of origin	N/A	2 times	N/A	3 times	N/A	N/A
Educational						
Year in college	Senior	Senior	Sophomore	Junior	Senior	Senior
Major	Spanish and Chicanx Studies	Forensic Chemistry and Spanish	Neurobiology, Physiology, and Behavior	Biochemistry and Molecular Biology	Spanish	Spanish
Years of schooling completed in country of origin	4–5	7	1	6	8	N/A
Years of schooling completed in the US	11	7	13	8	7	16
First-generation student?	Yes	Yes	Yes	Yes	Yes	Yes
Years as tutor	3	3	1	2	3	3

Concepción earned acceptance into graduate school and expressed plans to pursue studies in Spanish linguistics. She expressed excitement about becoming a language instructor and beginning her experience as such.

Maité

Maité often talked about her struggles as a recent immigrant when she began college. She noted that her intentions to take Spanish courses were minimal, as she felt she needed to catch up academically with English and with content in the sciences as her major. It wasn't until her early years as an undergraduate that her academic college advisor suggested she take Spanish to fulfill her general education units. Maité initially enrolled in SPA 24, a writing composition designed for second language learners, and often complained to her friends that the class was easy and boring. After she heard from a friend of the Spanish for Native Speakers program, she enrolled in SPA 33 in the spring, completing only the last of the three courses of the series. Given her hard work and motivating energy, she demonstrated to her instructor that she did not need to take the first courses in the program to fulfill the requirements. In fact, her SPA 33 instructor suggested she apply to become a peer tutor. Since joining the tutoring cohort, Maité has remained very active in the department and, during weekly meetings, is vocal about the needs, experiences, and hopes of the tutors. She volunteers her time every year at the annual Día de los Muertos event that the department organizes and helps set up and take down the altar. She, along with Esmeralda, led the community-building events organized for the tutor cohort during the 2016–2017 academic year (outings, picnics, etc.)

Vanessa

Vanessa is the only tutor in the cohort not of Mexican descent. She immigrated with her mother from El Salvador at eight years old and often talked about her mother's in-home efforts to continue Vanessa's literacy development in Spanish. She discussed her mom reviewing the ABCs and reading to her in Spanish and considered her mother's efforts as the main reason—along with continuing with Spanish throughout high school—why she has strong literacy skills in Spanish. That said, Vanessa often expressed that she did not feel her Spanish was as strong as her English and often expressed anxiety when her students (tutees) asked a grammar question she was unable to answer. As a first-year tutor, Vanessa was active in the weekly meetings, curious about her development as an instructor, and demonstrated a keen ability to ask questions, use the resources available to her, and remain open-minded about her work with students.

Joaquín

Joaquín was studying to become a doctor. He was an active health peer educator through his work in student-led associations for Latinx health such as Clínica

38 Heritage Tutors in CA

Tepati, a volunteer-run health clinic in Sacramento. He had plans to study abroad in Oaxaca, Mexico, to work as a health volunteer and contribute to the health needs of communities there. Open about why he wanted to pursue medicine, Joaquín often told other tutors and instructors about the struggles he and his family have suffered due to his younger brother's disease. At a very young age, Joaquín's brother was diagnosed with leukemia. For many years, Joaquin's family rose money, organized community events, and fought his brother's cancer in all the ways they could. Recently, Joaquin's brother became cancer free. The implications of this journey for Joaquín, and his own experience as a transnational Latino youth, have deeply inspired him to pursue his academic goals. Joaquín often came into the tutoring room before business hours to do some of his own reading and schoolwork and preferred to see his students early in the morning. Despite all life has dealt Joaquín, his resilience remained admirable.

Cristal

Cristal's academic aspirations remained in the Spanish teaching field. From the beginning of her college journey, she showed interest in becoming a Spanish teacher and took many of the classes offered by the instructors of the program— she was a student, for example, in an upper-division course where I was Teaching Assistant (TA), and took several courses offered by a variety of professors in the program. Because she minored in Education, Cristal often completed internships at local elementary schools where she assisted teachers with Spanish instruction. Despite Cristal's involvement in the department and in the tutoring program, she expressed to some of her instructors that she suffered from depression and anxiety and that battling these conditions away from family represented a significant challenge in her life. She encountered a lot of empathy from her colleagues in the peer tutoring program and showed great empathy for her students despite her own challenges. Cristal had plans to graduate the year this study was conducted and had expressed hopes to continue with graduate school after taking a break. Recently she communicated to me that she has been accepted into the Spanish Linguistics Master's program at another large Californian university and had plans to begin coursework in the fall.

Esmeralda

Esmeralda is the only tutor in the study who grew up in the US without returning to her parents' country of origin (Mexico). As a first-year undergraduate and a first-generation student, she struggled to find community on campus, and could not rely on her family, who were unsupportive of her decision to leave home and pursue college. She often shared the many instances in which she seriously considered dropping out of school. During her second year, she began taking the program's courses and often stated that it was because of the Spanish-speaking peer tutor community in the Program for Native Speakers that she decided to stay in college. She switched from majoring in engineering to Spanish after working as a tutor and had plans to become a Spanish teacher following graduation. Esmeralda was strongly committed to the program and to her role as tutor and she often engaged in conversation about her bilingual identity, openly sharing her insights and experience as a first-generation, Spanish-speaking Californian Latina.

Data Collection

Video Recordings of Tutoring Sessions and Field Notes

For this project, video recording of tutoring sessions constitutes the bulk of data sources. After tutor recruitment, I conducted tutee recruitment throughout the first two weeks of Fall Quarter 2016. Tutees, or students enrolled in the first course of the program series (SPA 31), either accepted or declined consent for video recordings of two of their tutoring sessions (with the same tutor) throughout the quarter. I excluded tutees who were students in section 4 of the course (my session) to comply with ethical requirements regarding the recruitment of my own students. During the recruitment process, I visited tutors for tutee recruitment during the first five minutes of their session and sometimes spoke to one or more tutees, depending on the number of students in the tutoring room at a particular time. This recruitment process yielded two tutees for Cristal, two for Concepción, three for Joaquín, three for Maité, four for Esmeralda, and three for Vanessa. After I recruited enough tutor–tutee dyads, I began video recording their interaction using an iPad and directing the image towards the tutor–tutee dyad using a tripod. While I tried to record one tutoring session towards the beginning of the quarter and one towards the end, the decision to video record on a particular day was mostly based on convenience. Given that I wanted to gather examples of representative tutor–tutee interactions at any point in time, I did not make any decisions regarding when to record based on the course's syllabus or the content of the session, nor did I consider the time between recordings as relevant given that this is not a longitudinal study. The final video recording schedule resulted as detailed in Table 1.4. As I show in the following, I did not use all the video-recorded data and then made the decision to not include all videos in the data analysis. This mainly stemmed from technical difficulties with sound, specifically for days when there were too many students in the tutoring room and it was difficult to hear the specific tutor–tutee dyad. Therefore, the final videos used for data analysis are as follows. Table 1.4 includes the specific number of sessions per tutor, the number of hours of video collected per each tutor, and the total amount of video data used in this study.

During video recordings, I sat in a corner of the tutoring room attuned to the tutor–tutee interaction but taking field notes discreetly on my computer. Beyond capturing what was happening in the room, I recorded field notes on specific events related to the theoretical framework and the questions of interest

40 Heritage Tutors in CA

TABLE 1.4 Total Number of Sessions and Hours of Video Recording per Participant Tutor

Tutor	Tutoring Session Date and Duration; Total Video Sessions and Total Video Time
Concepción	Student #1 (Only session) November 7 (50 mins) Student #2 (First session) November 8 (42 minutes) (Second session) November 15 (37 mins) Total sessions: 3 Total video time: 2 hours, 9 mins (129 mins)
Joaquín	Student #1 (Only session) November 7 (39 mins) Student #3 (Only session) November 28 (45 mins) Total sessions: 2 Total video time: 1 hour, 24 mins (84 mins)
Esmeralda	Student #1 (First session) November 7 (12 mins) (Second session) November 21 (36 mins) Student #2 (Only session) November 7 (42 mins) Student #3 (First session) November 14 (57 mins) (Second session) November 16 (46 mins) Student #4 (Only session) November 9 (26 mins) Total sessions: 6 Total video time: 3 hours, 39 mins (219 mins)
Vanessa	Student #1 (Only session) November 7 (61 mins) Student #2 (First session) November 8 (41 mins) (Second session) November 15 (48 mins) Student #3 (Only session) November 17 (51 mins) Total sessions: 4 Total video time: 3 hours, 21 mins (201 mins)
Maité	Student #1 (First session) November 8 (28 mins) (Second session) November 15 (29 mins) Student #2 (First session) November 14 (46 mins) (Second session) November 21 (43 mins) Total sessions: 4 Total video time: 2 hours, 26 mins (146 mins)

(Continued)

Heritage Tutors in CA **41**

TABLE 1.4 (Continued)

Tutor	Tutoring Session Date and Duration; Total Video Sessions and Total Video Time
Cristal	Student #1
	(Only session) November 9 (45 mins)
	Student #2
	(First session) November 18 (49 mins)
	(Second session) December 2 (56 mins)
	Total sessions: 3
	Total video time: 2 hours, 30 mins (150 mins)
Total tutoring sessions analyzed	22
Total video hours analyzed	15 hours, 29 mins (929 mins)

to the study. Specifically, I noted the particularities of the interpersonal interactions between the tutor and the tutee, including ways in which tutors were being strategic about guiding the sessions, asking tutees to report their experience of the course content even though tutors knew the syllabi well. Because I stayed in the room during video recordings, tutors often asked me for assistance, especially during a particularly challenging grammatical point they were explaining to their students. This organically developed my role as that of "observer as participant" or as having a "peripheral membership role" (Adler & Adler, 1998) where, during some sessions, I interacted closely enough with the tutor–tutee dyad to establish an insider's identity but without wholly or consistently participating in the tutoring session.

Tutor Interviews

I also conducted semi-structured interviews with all tutor participants towards the end of the quarter after having completed the video recording process. These were not highly structured interviews, as I wanted to tap into some of the nuances of participants' positionings, personal strategies, and opinions regarding their varied experiences as academic peer-to-peer tutors for the program. At the same time, interviews were designed to allow me as the researcher to introduce and explore topics of interest to the study. These included participants' opinions about what constitutes being a tutor, their tutor strategies for community building, as well as academic and literacy development in the session, among other topics of interest.

The interview protocol was flexibly ordered and did not include any technical jargon that would create distance between the researcher and the participant roles. Overall, interviews centered on beliefs, experiences, resources, preparation, and writing of specific academic texts and tasks mediated to the tutee by the tutor, adopting rapport and neutrality as per Patton (2015). As such, while I remained neutral with regard to the content of what was stated (neutrality), I cared that the person was willing to share their information with me (rapport). For that purpose, I also used an unobtrusive recording mechanism (e.g., an iPad). For a complete view of the interview protocol, see Appendix B.

On Belonging in Language Learning: Positionality

My own relationship with the languages that I speak (Spanish as a native tongue and English as a second language) is an intimate one; my loyalties, belongings, hopes, and fears are all encompassed within my languages. It is with language that I swing back into and out of the communities to which I belong and the ones to which I strive to belong. I use my languages to become present, become vulnerable, act, participate, and grow. In other words, my languages reflect who I am. Thus, as I have entered into communities that reflect my language practices, I have felt a strong sense of belonging.

These sentiments of belonging through language learning, as I see my literacy reality reflected in my social reality, foreground my own positionality in relation to the data interpretation included in this book. Per ethnographic tradition (Erickson, 1986; Watson-Gegeo, 1992), it is crucial for the researcher to address how their position and experiences influence the ways in which data is collected and interpreted. This brief section dialogues with a particular set of personal experiences in my life that have shaped how I think of belonging through language and literacy learning. I consider my own influence as an intentional agent who has researched and written about other peoples' experiences from an insider's point of view, making transparent how my own experiences inform the analyses and theorizing processes herein (Qin, 2016).

Importantly, I have had the privilege of always feeling a sense of belonging within the various communities of speakers I have been part of, especially as related to the variety of educational trajectories throughout my life and the initial presence that English had in my early years in school. As a young teenager attending an English/Spanish bilingual school in Pereira, Colombia, I found that the lack of connection I had with most of my peers (due mostly to being the youngest of the class) was remedied by the admiration and resultant feeling of belonging that several of my teachers—young English-speaking, international educators, most of whom were Canadian—instilled in me. As I developed a fascination with the English language, my teachers invited me to engage in a variety of literacy practices that gave me a strong sense of belonging: listening to artists who sang in English, talking about topics that engaged my curiosity such as traveling, journaling, reading novels, etc. These practices were very distant from those of my peers, who were mostly interested in talking about the latest in fashion and shopping. At the same time, though mostly not to my knowledge, due to Colombia's social unrest throughout the late 1980s and early 1990s, political relationships became closer with the US and English was becoming mandatory in all of Colombia's public and private education. Speaking English, then, represented a child's future financial advantage, especially for families, such as mine, who envisioned their children going abroad to the US or Canada for their postsecondary education. Thus, my family was not too taken aback when I expressed my desire to leave Colombia and spend time abroad.

My departure from Colombia represented my quest for belonging. Now, when people seem puzzled and surprised that I immigrated to a small town in Nebraska from Colombia out of my own free will, I tell them jokingly that at the time I was really wanting to "see the world" and therefore landed in the cornfields of middle America. Even though it sounds jocose, it is true that I left my home country because I didn't have a complete sense of belonging in a place where I was mostly a Spanish monolingual; it was only in a place where I could engage with both of my languages and literacies that I felt I belonged.

Throughout my time as an undergraduate, I continued to shape my belonging while seeking my place as a bilingual, international student. Here I found joy in accessing temporary Spanish-speaking places in the classroom (I was a Spanish and French major), especially as I encountered other Spanish-speaking individuals with distinct—yet fascinating—linguistic and socio-educational trajectories compared to mine. I had access to belonging through English as I engaged with peers, host families, and colleagues, and later with Jeff, a bilingual Nebraskan whom I met my first year in college and who is now my husband of 15 years. His family quickly welcomed me, and I continued encountering myriad opportunities to develop a sense of belonging through engagement with Spanish/English literacy practices, and as I continued to strongly identify as a bilingual, bicultural individual.

I began my master's with the assumption that my experiences in belonging through language and literacy were also the type of experiences that other Spanish/English bilinguals have encountered throughout their educational trajectories. I was aware of the multiplicity of linguistic profiles across Spanish speakers in Nebraska, where I lived at the time, especially having taught Spanish for a couple of years. However, it wasn't until I worked for the Nebraska Department of Health and Human Services as head Spanish/English translator that I realized to what extent I had been deeply privileged throughout my life. My role in providing translation and interpretation for social service access across Spanish-speaking communities in Nebraska proved that the systems then in place gave strong prevalence to English as the language of power and that the language access needs of Spanish speakers were being largely ignored. My English monolingual colleagues often questioned why I was part of their team, believing that a Google Translation would do just as adequate of a job translating if not better than a bilingual person. The complex linguistic experiences of Spanish speakers were poorly understood at the state government level, and I began growing frustrated and feeling helpless in my employment. After a year and a half of working for the state, I returned to campus.

44 Heritage Tutors in CA

I developed the conviction that I needed to pursue more academic training to address the shortcomings of Spanish education for the heritage speakers I was observing at the institutional and societal levels. For years, I witnessed Spanish instructors dismiss the relevancy of the heritage speaker population and their contribution to our programs and instead choose to continue mobilizing traditional pedagogical models of Spanish as a foreign language, thus discouraging heritage students to pursue a sense of belonging throughout their Spanish education trajectories. Perturbed by this, I wrote a master's thesis (Reznicek-Parrado, 2013) that illustrated how Spanish instructors and faculty at the institution where I completed part of my postgraduate studies lacked sociolinguistic knowledge about the heritage speaker sociolinguistic and educational profile and therefore had little curiosity regarding students' pedagogical contributions and needs in the Spanish classroom. I discovered then the strong connection between Spanish language learning and social justice. During the process of writing my MA thesis, I completed a six-month student-teaching placement at a large school district in Mecklenburg County, North Carolina, where a track for heritage speakers had been recently created to meet the curricular needs of the rapidly increasing school population of Spanish heritage speakers. This experience was one of the most powerful and inspiring teaching experiences of my early career as an educator, though it was also a painful one. The Latinx youth with whom I worked were inspiring young people with stories of growth, trauma, and hope, as well as clear potential for the future. Unfortunately, their unique and complex relationship to Spanish was mostly ignored by educators who, despite their best intentions, possessed limited theoretical knowledge of responsible pedagogical models that could meet students' linguistic and educational needs. As a result, as I saw it, they were unable to create a learning experience where students could truly see themselves reflected. Instead, educators mobilized pedagogical frameworks that largely ignored the language and literacy practices of these students, exclusively emphasizing formal literacy. These pedagogies, rather than using students' linguistic repertoires in service of their learning, were incongruent with students' profiles, thus fostering educational inequities. During my time at this school in Charlotte, I fell in love with the tenacity and resiliency of the young students with whom I worked.

In all, my teaching interests as they relate to the heritage speaker population have gone hand in hand with my research interests. Both are motivated by the mission to improve Spanish education for this population as a social justice issue and the responsibility of creating learning opportunities in which students can see themselves reflected. Thus, I have significant investment in the educational well-being of the Spanish heritage speaker population, subscribing to socially responsible research frameworks and methodologies. As I discuss further in Chapter 6, I strive to continue this work in my role as founding Director for the Heritage/Bilingual Program at the University of Denver, where my course design centers on the incorporation of heritage language literacy practices such as those described throughout this book. It is my view that heritage programs exist

Heritage Tutors in CA **45**

primarily to create spaces for belonging to a student population that has been consistently excluded in spaces of teaching and learning in this country.

I continue to foster deep admiration for, and am consistently inspired by, so many heritage students of Spanish for whom the heritage learning journey is full of respect, curiosity, and at times pain and inadequacy. I wish to continue carrying the responsibility of furthering inclusive educational experiences that reflect speakers' stories, hopes, struggles, and futures. In other words, I wish to invest attention into how Spanish learning can be transformed into a process of belonging for heritage speakers, so we may all witness what happens when heritage students reclaim their language. I intend to carry this aspiration forth as I proceed in my roles as a researcher and educator.

In the next chapter, I introduce the first of two methods of data analysis by describing the ethnographic data that presents specific literacy practices mobilized during tutoring sessions by the six peer tutors introduced here. I explore what tutors are doing with language as they work collaboratively with their tutees, mobilizing hybrid and dynamic uses of language to complete academic tasks. Later, I describe tutors' translanguaging before detailing an analysis of the socially situated goals with which tutors mobilize such practices.

Notes

1 While founded as a language program for "native speakers" at its conception, the program described here is intentionally designed and exclusively enrolls heritage speakers of Spanish. Although the field has problematized the label "Spanish for Native Speakers" to refer to programs that serve speakers of Spanish as a heritage language, the program at this institution has adopted the label since its conception in 1992 and it is used as such in this project.
2 *Work-Related Experiences of Tutors/Mentors in the Heritage Speakers Program: An Atypical Change for Community Development.*

References

Adler, P. A., & Adler, P. (1998). Observational techniques. In N. K. Denzin & Y. S. Lincoln (Eds.), *Collecting and Interpreting Qualitative Materials* (pp. 79–109). Thousand Oaks: Sage.

Antilla-Garza, J., & Cook-Gumperz, J. (2015). Debating the world: Choosing the word: High school debates as academic discourse preparation for bilingual students. *Linguistics and Education, 31*, 276–285

Blake, R., & Colombi, M. C. (2013). La enseñanza del español para hispanohablantes: Un programa universitario. In D. Dumitrescu (Ed.), *El español en los Estados Unidos: E pluribus unum*. New York: Academia Norteamericana de la Lengua Española.

California Department of Education (2018). *2017–18 Enrollment by Ethnicity and Grade.* Retrieved from: https://dq.cde.ca.gov/dataquest/dqcensus/EnrEthGrd.aspx?cds=00 &agglevel=state&year=2017-18

Colombi, M.C. (2003). Un enfoque funcional para la enseñanza del ensayo expositivo. In A. Roca & M.C. Colombi (Eds.), *Mi lengua: Spanish as a Heritage Language in the United States.* Washington: Georgeton University Press, 78–95.

46 Heritage Tutors in CA

Colombi, M. C. (2015). Academic and cultural literacy for heritage speakers of Spanish: A case study of Latin@ students in California. *Linguistics and Education, 32*, 5–15.

Colombi, M. C., & Schleppegrell, M. J. (2002). Theory and practice in the development of advanced literacy. In M. J. Schleppegrell & M. C. Colombi (Eds.), *Developing Advanced Literacy in First and Second Language: Meaning with Power*. Mahwah: Lawrence Erlbaum.

Cook-Gumperz, J. (2006). *The social construction of literacy* (Vol. 25). New York: Cambridge University Press.

Cope, B., & Kalantzis, M. (2015). The things you do to know: An introduction to the pedagogy of multiliteracies. In B. Cope & M. Kalantzis (Eds.), *A pedagogy of multiliteracies: Learning by design* (pp. 1–36). London: Palgrave Macmillan.

Cummins, J. (1979). Cognitive/academic language proficiency, linguistic interdependence, the optimum age question and some other matters. *Working Papers on Bilingualism, 19*, 198–205.

Cummins, J. (1981). The role of primary language development in promoting eduational success for language minority students. In C. S. D. o. Education (Ed.), *Schooling and Language Minority Students: A Theoretical Framework*. Los Angeles: Evaluation, Dissemination and Assessemt Center, California State University.

Cummins, J. (2000). *Language, Power, and Pedagogy: Bilingual Children in the Cross-fire*. Clevedon, UK: Multilingual Matters.

Delpit, L. (1995). The silenced dialogue: Power and pedagogy in educating other people's children. *Harvard Educational Review, 58*(3), 280–299.

Enright, K. A. (2011). Language and literacy for a new mainstream. *American Educational Research Journal, 48*(1), 80–118.

Erickson, F. (1986). Qualitative research on teaching. In M. C. Wittrock (Ed.), *Handbook of Research on Teaching* (3rd ed.). New York: Macmillan.

Gee, J. P. (1992). *The Social Mind: Language, Ideology, and Social Practice*. New York: Bergin & Garvey.

Gutiérrez, K. D., Morales, P. Z., & Martínez, D. (2009). Remediating literacy: Cultura, difference, and learning for students from nondominant communities. *Review of Research in Education, 22*, 212–245.

Heath, S. B. (1982). What no bed time story means: Narrative skills at home and at school. *Language in Society, 11*, 49–76.

Hurtado de Vivas, R. (2005). La Educación Bilingüe y los Múltiples Beneficios de un Programa de Lenguaje Dual: Una Alternativa para el Inmigrante Latinoamericano en los Estados Unidos. *Docencia Universitaria, 6*(1), 137–150.

Kalantzis, M., Cope, B., Chan, E., & Dalley-Trim, L. (2016). *Literacies*. Cambridge, UK: Cambridge University Press.

Lave, J., & Wanger, E. (1991). *Situated Learning: Legitimate Peripheral Participation*. New York: Cambridge University Press.

Lea, M. R., & Street, B. V. (2006). The "academic literacies" model: Theory and applications. *Theory into Practice, 45*(4), 368–377.

Leeman, J. (2018). Critical language awareness and Spanish as a heritage language: Challenging the linguistic subordination of US Latinxs. In K. Potowski (Ed.), *Handbook of Spanish as a Minority/Heritage Language* (pp. 345–358). New York: Routledge.

Lippi-Green, R. (2011). *English with an Accent: Language, Ideology, and Discrimination in the United States*. London: Routledge.

Martínez, G. (2005). Genres and genre chains: Post-process perspectives on heritage language writing in a South Texas setting. *Southwest Journal of Linguistiscs, 1*(2), 79–90.

Martínez, D., Morales, P. Z., & Aldana, U. S. (2017). Leveraging Students' Communicative Repertoires as a Tool for Equitable Learning. *Review of Research in Education, 41*, 477–499.

Mills, K. A. (2011). *The Multiliteracies Classroom*. Bristol, New York and Toronto: Multilingual Matters/Channel View Publications.

Molle, D. (2015). Academic language and academic literacies: Mapping a relationship. In D. Molle, E. Sato, T. Boals, & C. A. Hedgspeth (Eds.), *Multilingual Learners and Academic Literacies* (pp. 13–32). New York: Routledge.

New London Group. (1996). A pedagogy of multiliteracies: Designing social futures. *Harvard Educational Review, 66*(1), 60.

Patton, M. Q. (2015). *Qualitative Research and Evaluation Methods* (3rd ed.). Thousand Oaks: Sage.

Qin, D. (2016). Positionality. In A. Wong, M. Wickramasinghe, R. Hoogland, & N. A. Naples (Eds.), *The Willey Blackwell Encyclopedia of Gender and Sexuality Studies* (pp. 1–2).New York: John Wiley & Sons, Ltd.

Reznicek-Parrado, L. M. (2013). *Pedagogía de hablantes de herencia: Implicaciones para el entrenamiento de instructores en el nivel universitario*. (Unpublished Master's Thesis), University of Nebraska-Lincoln. Retrieved from https://digitalcommons.unl.edu/modlangdiss/15/

Rymes, B. (2010). 19. Classroom Discourse Analysis: A Focus on Communicative Repertoires. In N. H. Hornberger & S. L. McKay (Eds.), *Sociolinguistics and language education* (pp. 528–546). Multilingual Matters.

Scribner, S., & Cole, M. (1981). *The Psychology of Literacy*. Massachusetts: Harvard University Press.

Street, B. V. (1984). *Literacy in Theory and Practice*. Cambridge, UK: Cambridge University Press.

Street, B. V. (1993). Introduction: The New Literacy Studies. In B. V. Street (Ed.), *Cross-cultural approaches to literacy* (pp. 1–21). New York: Cambridge University Press.

Street, B. V. (2005). Recent applications of new literacy studies in educational contexts. *Research in the Teaching of English, 39*(4), 417–423.

UC Davis Profile. (2017). Retrieved from https://www.ucdavis.edu/admissions/undergraduate/student-profile/

Ugarte, G. (1997). Tutorías de estudiante a estudiante: Un modelo que funciona para los estudiantes hispanohablantes. In M. C. Colombi & F. X. Alarcón. (Eds.), *La enseñanza del español a hispanohablantes: Praxis y teoría*. Boston: Houghton Mifflin.

U.S. Census Bureau. (2017). Quick facts California. Retrieved from https://www.census.gov/quickfacts/CA

Watson-Gegeo, K. A. (1992). Thick explanation in the ethnographic study of child socialization: A longitudinal study of the problem of schooling for Kwara'ae (Solomon Islands) children. *New Directions for Child and Adolescent Development, 58*, 58–66.

Valdés, G., Poza, L., & Brooks, M. D. (2015). Language Acquisition in Bilingual Education. In W. E. Wright, S. Boun, & O. García (Eds.), *The Handbook of Bilingual and Multilingual Education*. Hoboken: John Wiley & Sons.

Villa, D. (2004). No nos dejaremos: Writing in Spanish as an Act of Resistance. M. H. Kells, V. Balester, & V. Villanueva (Eds.), *Latino/a Discourses on Language, Identity & Literacy Education*. Portsmouth: Heinemann, 85–95.

Zapata, G. C., & Lacorte, M. (2018). *Multiliteracies Pedagogy and Language Learning: Teaching Spanish to Heritage Speakers*. London: Palgrave Macmillan.

2

HYBRID LITERACY PRACTICES IN A TRANSLINGUAL ACADEMIC SPACE

Methods of Inquiry

This book uses sociolinguistic ethnographic research methods that integrate the micro and macro levels of contextualized data (Watson–Gegeo, 1992) through emic inquires on human society and culture, including the beliefs, values, and attitudes that structure the behavior patterns of a group of people (Merriam & Tisdell, 2015). Specifically, I employ thematic analyses (Bernard & Ryan, 2010) of multiple interviews and tutoring session interactions of six focal participants who work as academic peer tutors in a program for Spanish heritage speakers at a large public university in California. Additionally, I use qualitatively driven linguistic analyses of data based on theories put forth by System Functional Linguistics (SFL) (Halliday, 1994; Martin & White, 2003), which are concerned with language as the product of socially situated interactions that are influenced by the experiences, tensions, empathies, contradictions, and conflicts of speakers engaged in socially collective activities (Eggins & Slade, 1997). This second analysis will be explained throughout Chapters 4 and 5.

All data analyses, including both the ethnographic and linguistic methods in this book, adopt an interpretivist qualitative approach toward empirical data, utilizing emic, iterative, and inductive analytical processes informed by theory. The combination of these two methodologies, one ethnographic and one linguistic, allows me to conduct research that critically understands tutors' literacy practices considering the social context in which they are mobilized. Thus, tutors' social experience takes center stage, explicitly the socially situated characteristics of the context of study in the data analysis. Further, the combination of ethnographic and linguistic methodologies enriches the analysis by asking two complementary questions in relation to this study. First, an ethnographic approach allows me to pay attention to the construct of language as practice by answering questions such

DOI: 10.4324/9781003191179-3

as what actions or tasks tutors are conducting to serve in their role. Second, a focus on the structure of language allows me to consider how grammar and discursive patterns occurring at the clause and turn-taking level mirror the language practices that tutors mobilize. Thus, the linguistic analysis I adopt guides my analysis at the micro level (i.e., the tutors' actual verbalized language), whereas the ethnographic method guides my analysis at the macro level (i.e., the tutors' use of language). This multi-level analysis engages in thick explanation (Watson-Gegeo, 1992) to achieve a holistic understanding of tutors' literacy practices.

Importantly, the ethnographic methodology I have adopted allows me to understand how tutors themselves interpret their experiences as language peers and how they construct their roles as language experts. I am not, therefore, determining causal relationships or predicting tutees' proficiencies based on their involvement in an academic activity such as the tutoring session.[1] For this analysis, I study six focal participants who represent a larger student population (i.e., speakers of Spanish as a heritage language). While analyses of focal participants are not quantitatively generalizable to other contexts of study, their rich descriptive nature capturing a particular place in time contributes to what educational ethnographer Stake refers to as "naturalistic generalization" (1995)—that is, our ability as researchers to develop inferences about the future based on an orderly account of the past. On this note, ethnographers Dyson and Genishi extend Stake's argument by stating that

> if a study gives readers a sense of "being there", of having a vicarious experience in the studied site, then readers may generalize from that experience in private, personal ways, modifying, extending, or adding to their generalized understandings of how the world works.
>
> *(Dyson & Genishi, 2005, p. 115)*

Thus, the present account and analysis of heritage language speakers as focal participants serve as a localized effort to generate emic understandings about this group of speakers with the intention of contributing to other etic systems of knowledge that have governed the field of Spanish heritage language studies.

Sociolinguistic Ethnography

As stated, the starting point in the analysis was ethnographic in nature, given that I needed a methodology that would allow me to dig deep into tutors' experiences of belonging in this student-led learning community (the tutoring room). Importantly, the interpretive approach of ethnographic work is useful for the present study as it assumes that reality is socially constructed; namely, that there is no single, observable reality. Rather, it posits that there are multiple realities and interpretations of events (Merriam & Tisdell, 2015). Thus, as a researcher, my role was not to "find knowledge" but rather to construct my participants' social experiences in collaboration with them.

50 Heritage Literacy Practices

To achieve said construction and in working with the data, I watched video recordings of tutoring sessions, read transcriptions and field notes, and noted observations. Next, as I completed open coding, I began to make annotations, observations, and particular queries of data that struck me as relevant for the analysis. I did this using NVivo, a qualitative analysis software. This process of open coding initially produced a series of categories related to the types of language and literacy events and practices I was observing across the data, such as "switching from Spanish to English", "telling a story", "asking questions to an expert", and the like. However, open coding also resulted in another group of categories related to the goals of the literacy practices I was observing. As such, it was most salient in the data that the tutors were using specific literacy practices in the service of contextually situated goals, which all reflected both academic literacy development and community building. Thus, throughout open coding, and as I observed that the goals outnumbered the literacy practices across the data, I developed a series of themes after interpreting and reflecting on the meanings of my initial codes. The result was an analysis of the observable literacy practices' goals. Thus, after concluding open coding and as I began to group recurring categories together and across the data, I began the process of axial coding (Charmaz, 2014; Corbin & Strauss, 2015; Strauss, 1987). Here, I relied on NVivo's exploratory visual mappings to understand the relevance of codes in relation to each other and the relationship across such codes. A Hierarchy Map, for example, allowed me to visually see that "community belonging" was one of my most heavily coded categories. For example, a matrix query (a type of query that shows which two codes are most commonly coded together) showed me that "use of both Spanish and English" was commonly coded with themes such as "tutor as expert". While the operationalization of themes is elaborated on in Chapter 3, axial coding resulted in the emergence of four themes, as shown in Table 2.1.

To illustrate, two salient themes were *tutor as expert* and *academic empathy*. I coded for tutor as expert every time the tutor adopted an instructor-like identity, passing on information about the design of the course or about any topic related to the content of the conversation as a fact, whether this was about task design, grammar, vocabulary, writing, etc. Further, I coded for academic empathy when tutors mobilized regard for their students' academic experiences, that is, expressing interest in hearing students' descriptions of their experience in the program (or in college), and provided students with emotional support around personal matters that affect academic life.

Yet, as mentioned, when I refined axial coding, I realized the codes that related to specific literacy practices significantly overlapped with the themes illustrated here and thus required additional detailed analysis. For that reason, I describe the particular types of literacy practices that were most common across the data, before detailing the thematic analysis of the socially situated goals with which tutors mobilized such practices (referred to in the themes illustrated in the table) in Chapter 3. Lastly, because linguistic hybridity, or the translingual

Heritage Literacy Practices **51**

TABLE 2.1 Definition of Themes

Theme	Definition
Academic Support	Any instance where the tutor supports learners in accessing and using pertinent information to manage learners' academic trajectories within and beyond the institution: what classes to take/when, the importance of visiting professors for office hours, where to get academic support, "unwritten requirements", steps to take if in dismissal, etc.
Tutor as Expert	The tutor taking the role of the instructor, that is, passing on information about the design of the course, or about any particular topic of content as a fact (grammar, content, writing, etc.)
Academic Empathy	Regard for students' academic experiences (i.e., "wearing their shoes"), including emotional support with personal matters that affect academics and regard for students' (academic) experience in the tutoring session
Belonging to Community	Overt reference to learning as a collective process (as applied to both the tutee and the tutor), including the creation of a "feels like home" environment; regard for students' lives outside of the program

resources with which tutors mobilized their literacy practices, was consistent throughout the data, I explain the composition of this hybridity in the first section of Chapter 3, then move on to more localized analyses of the linguistic features in tutors' literacy practices in Chapters 4 and 5. Significantly, the discussion across chapters overlaps due to the relevance of the academic context and community building across the data. All data chapters (2, 3, 4, and 5) address the larger mission of the present study: to illustrate how tutors' linguistically hybrid literacy practices mobilize highly structured functionally and semantically motivated language crucial in creating positive academic experiences for newly enrolled heritage students in a non-classroom, peer-to-peer collaborative academic context of language study such as the tutoring session. As previously mentioned, Chapter 6 engages with the pedagogical implications of the study's data.

Table 2.2 summarizes the types of analysis presented in the data analysis chapters.

Tutors' Language and Literacy Practices: Translanguaging in Context

During a typical day in the academic quarter, I walk the hallway of the first floor in Commons Hall[2] back and forth several times as I enter my office, walk to the copy room to prepare for a day's lesson, visit the administrators on the second floor for questions, and make small talk with colleagues and friends.

52 Heritage Literacy Practices

TABLE 2.2 Data Analyses Performed per Data Chapters

Types of Data Analyses Performed		
Chapter 2	Tutors' translanguaging: hybrid literacy practices	Open coding, axial coding, and thematic analysis
Chapter 3	Socially situated goals with which tutors mobilize translanguaging literacy practices	
Chapter 4	Tutors' development of an academic persona	Discourse analysis of the exchange; structure and mood of speech acts
Chapter 5	Development of a student-led academic community	Evaluative analysis using Appraisal Theory (Martin & White, 2015)

Every time I walk the hall, I peek into the Program for Native Speakers' tutoring room: Commons Hall 101. I see a typical scene: a room bustling with tutors and tutees talking and laughing, reading, consulting computer screens, comparing, and taking notes—overall seamlessly and simultaneously engaging in myriad language practices both in Spanish and English.

This typical scene depicts a specific situation in a specific socially situated context: two to four tutor–tutee pairs working through that week's tasks (as delineated by the program course's syllabus), all of them Spanish/English bilinguals and speakers of Spanish as a heritage language, many of them Californians with families from Mexico and other Central and South American countries, and most of them first-generation Latinx undergraduate students at a large public institution in the United States. The bustling of the room, primarily composed of utterances in Spanish and English (sometimes simultaneously, sometimes consecutively) is inherently socially situated. That is, it is because of *who* is participating in this space that one hears the language that is used in interaction.

As explained in Chapter 1, Scribner and Cole's seminal work on the relationship between literacy and cognition (1981) states that ignoring the socially embedded nature of reading and writing undermines the extent to which researchers can examine an individual's complex and complete literacy repertoires. Such undermining, according to the authors, can happen especially in educational programs composed of students with social experiences noted as outside of the mainstream (such as ethnically, racially, and linguistically diverse students). Indeed, "the socially organized and goal-oriented nature of language makes all practices, including literacy practices, subject to power relations" (Molle, 2015, p. 16). Traditionally, it is the case that in educational contexts, some literacy practices are recognized as more "legitimate" and others as more "deficient" (Cook-Gumperz, 2006). Scribner and Cole's conceptualization of literacy demonstrates the importance of bringing the socially situated nature of

Heritage Literacy Practices

TABLE 2.3 Transcription Conventions

-	Hesitation, self-interruption, or "false starts"
bolded word	Inter- or intra-sectional switch into English from Spanish or into Spanish from English
(())	Overlap in speech
@@	Laughter
(.)	Short pause (shorter than 2 seconds)
(…)	Untimed silence (longer than 2 seconds)
CAPS	Loud/emphasized utterance
:	Elongation of utterance
xxx	Unintelligible utterance
<transcriber's comments>	Additional paralinguistic information and other transcriber's comments

these practices to light to critically analyze the extent to which these so-called "deficient" practices actually exhibit genuine social value within the particular cultural contexts from which they emerge.

Because, for many students, school-like literacy tasks are not necessarily representative of the many productive literacy practices encountered in daily life outside of school (Scribner, 1984), research must explore the linguistic practice repertoires of under-represented students such as heritage speakers of Spanish. Thus, with the goal of socially situating the literacy repertoires of tutors, in the following section I discuss the results of the thematic analysis that emerged from tutor–tutee interactions. This chapter's aim is to examine what literacy practices are employed by tutors in the session and the significance of those practices. Second, in Chapter 3, I examine the goals tutors use to mobilize these same literacy practices through a description of the socially meaningful context in which they are mobilized. I note where specific literacy practices co-occur with specific socially situated and socially meaningful interactions. Chapter 3 also contextualizes the same recurrent themes with a description of tutors' translanguaging—the linguistically hybrid repertoires used in their interactions with their tutees.

Table 2.3 gives a list of transcription conventions used throughout this book.

Literacy Practices

The concept of "literacy practice" is crucial to understanding literacy as a social phenomenon. As previously stated, a literacy practice is defined as "a recurrent set of goal-directed activities with some common [socially situated] object, carried out with a particular technology and involving the application of particular knowledge" (Scribner, 1984, p. 202). Thus, a literacy practice is how people use language to "draw upon their lives" (Barton and Hamilton, 2000) and make sense of their social reality.

The literacy practices mobilized by tutors in this program for Spanish heritage speakers reflect their participation across sociocultural contexts which are mediated by specific tools and artifacts. These specific sociocultural contexts

54 Heritage Literacy Practices

are not separate; rather, tutors consistently and simultaneously mobilize literacy practices relevant to academic, informal, formal, and other contextual types of social participation while they participate in the tutoring room, most of the time through hybrid or translingual uses of language. In the following, I explain five literacy practices observed throughout the data: talking about social media, asking metalinguistic questions, searching the internet for academic information, guiding student answers, and personal storytelling.

Talking About Social Media

One specific context of tutors' sociocultural participation referenced internet viral phenomena, a literacy practice I call "talking about social media". These are instances when tutors reference particular internet viral phenomena in social media by talking about or replicating these phenomena in their interaction with the tutee. As I will show, tutors use this practice bilingually as they collectively interact, interrupting the one-to-one tutoring session to include other tutors and tutees in the room. The references they make to viral phenomena are shared by their tutees; thus, through this practice, tutors are inviting their tutees to somewhat or extensively shape this student-led academic community of learning in a dynamic, hybrid way:

Esmeralda: Uhm, la tesis es importante, no sé, ya sé que no todos tienen tesis oficialmente pero **I mean, we can put a thesis in there now** porque ahora sí se sabe. Um, eso es algo que podemos hacer con cual- entonces nada más **look at them, check and see which one has the highest score**

Uhm, the thesis is important, I don't know, I know that not everyone officially has a thesis but I mean, we can put a thesis in there now because now you do know. Um, that's something we can do with which- so just look at them, check and see which one has the highest score

Another tutor: We should do the mannequin challenge—

Esmeralda's student: <smiles>

Esmeralda: Yes! <excitedly raises hand> (.) I'm so sorry that was like so distracting but I- I really want to do that thing and be like ehh <poses> <chuckles>. Pero okay, um, **cualquiera que se elija, lo que voy a querer que hagas es** (.)

Yes! I'm so sorry that was like so distracting but I- I really want to do that thing and be like eehh. But okay, um, whatever you choose, what I will want you to do is (.)

Esmeralda's translanguaging, or deployment of her full linguistic repertoire in both Spanish and English, is illustrated as she works with a student, helping them prepare for a final assignment in which the student must choose an essay to revise. As Esmeralda engages one-on-one with her student, delineating specific advice related to how to select an essay and revise it, she engages simultaneously with the collaborative context of the tutoring room and joins another tutor's initiative to participate in doing a "mannequin challenge". The challenge, which consists of a short video of a group of people engaging in a particular scene (a meeting, a classroom, a restaurant, a dance, or just about anything) while being completely still and silent (like mannequins) as music plays in the background, was made popular by high school students across the country who posted a series of videoed, silent (and frozen) scenes of their classrooms in 2016 and 2017 on Twitter. What followed was a viral phenomenon, much like "planking" in 2010 (BBC News, 2011) or "the ice bucket challenge" throughout 2016 (*USA Today*, 2017). Notably, a social approach to literacy would explain the mannequin challenge as an illustrated literacy practice of young people who "display impressive network awareness in the ways they mobilize internet resources and cobble together creative and productive ad hoc online networks of collaborators to pursue shared creative and innovative purposes" (Lankshear & Knobel, 2011, p. 205). Indeed, tutor and tutee's collective knowledge and desire to replicate the mannequin challenge—not unlike many TikTok challenges today—require both of their engagement in multimodal—and often multilingual—literacy platforms.

As mentioned, the tutor who brought up the possibility of doing a mannequin challenge, and Esmeralda's response to it, illustrate the discussion of viral phenomena in social media as a literacy practice. As Esmeralda translanguages throughout her interaction with the student, reference to the mannequin challenge is made in English, which is loyal to the phenomenon's language of use. Once Esmeralda reengages with her student, she switches to Spanish as she crosses back into the context of participation related to the course's final assignment.

The crossing of sociocultural contexts of participation as indexed by tutors' referencing viral phenomena is again illustrated by Esmeralda in another instance. In this case, as the tutoring session begins, Esmeralda impersonates the recording of her own YouTube channel, where she will show her imaginary viewers how to properly execute French braiding. She uses the session's recording device (the iPad) as her channel's video camera, switching between impersonating the recording of her channel and expressing her motivations behind it across English and Spanish. Maité, another tutor who is also Esmeralda's roommate, joins in:

Esmeralda: ¿Empezastes Lina? <making reference to beginning the video recording> **Do we start my YouTube channel?** <looking at the camera>

Did you start, Lina? Do we start my YouTube channel?

Student: @@

Esmeralda: So today we're going to teach you guys how to French braid. So what you want to do is: you are going to get your hair @@

56 Heritage Literacy Practices

Maité: Please continue

Esmeralda: Divide it into three sections @@

Student: @@

Maité: Yo no sé cómo trenzarme el pelo (.) Lo bueno es que vivo con e la entonces ella me lo trenza

*I don't know how to braid my hair. The good thing is I live with her so she does it
for me*

Esmeralda: True (.) I should- I'm telling you, one day I'm going to start a
YouTube channel. Lina is just my outlet for me to practice ((now))

Student: @@

Esmeralda: This is a legit thing by the way, I wanted to have a YouTube channel
since I was like, maybe, uhh, thirteen?

Student: Yeah, me too

Esmeralda: Okay, anyways. <Esmeralda says student's name> **¿Cuál es tu
apellido?**

Okay anyways. What is your last name?

Esmeralda and Maité's translanguaging is relevant in this interaction. First,
Esmeralda addresses me (the researcher/instructor) in Spanish to confirm that
I set up and started the recording as usual before beginning recordings of the
tutoring sessions. Then, once she was certain that the camera was on, she looks
at her "audience" (the imagined consumers of her channel) and addresses them in
English, the language in which she chooses to narrate her braiding. As Esmeralda
conducts her imagined tutorial, Maité comments, in Spanish, that she is lucky
to have Esmeralda as her roommate, so Esmeralda can French braid Maité's hair
when she pleases. Maité, as she speaks, is not looking at the camera; rather, she
is addressing other students in the room who are conducting tutoring sessions,
most of them using Spanish for that purpose. Thus, Maité purposefully alter-
nates between languages to adapt to her audience, indexing particular social and
cultural contexts and demonstrating awareness of her different audiences, speaking in English when participating in the YouTube channel with Esmeralda, and
switching to Spanish when addressing (or talking with) the other students in the
tutoring room. As Esmeralda finishes her imagined YouTube channel recording,
she begins the day's tutoring session with her student. Here, she uses English
("okay, anyways") to transition from recording her presumed channel (the first
context of participation) into the tutoring session (the second context of participation), where she seamlessly adopts her instructor-like voice and switches to
Spanish to ask the student's last name as she completes the tutoring documenta-
tion. Thus, for both Maité and Esmeralda, their translanguaging was contingent

upon an awareness of the linguistic and cultural backgrounds of their particular interlocutors, showing that they can identify this particular genre, its discursive norms, and its audience. Importantly, the literacy skills both tutors demonstrate are the same skills that students are socialized into as they develop academic literacy, demonstrating that tutors are already mobilizing daily uses of language in similar ways they are expected to use language for academic purposes. Esmeralda and Maité's interactions here show how talking about social media and the following bilingual literacy practices reflect "the socially constructed and socially situated nature of academic language and literacy" (Martínez, 2010, p. 145) as illustrated in the tutoring room, an academic space itself.

Consulting an Expert: Asking Metalinguistic Questions

This next translingual literacy practice refers to instances where tutors initiate contact with an expert in the room (an instructor or another tutor) to clarify specific questions about a grammar activity. As I have previously mentioned (see Chapter 1), one of the main goals of the tutoring component of the Program for Native Speakers is the potential for tutors, as peers, to socially and academically support other peers. One of the main contributions of this program is the opportunity for students to use their personal and academic experiences and knowledge as first-generation, minority, and linguistically diverse students to guide other students with similar personal and academic experiences through successful navigation of the academic system by developing the skills and resources necessary to attain academic success. The tutors participating in this study consistently modeled what I call "invisible academic practices" which are those not traditionally taught explicitly in classrooms, but that may be especially crucial for the academic success of first-generation students who may lack access to the modeling of these practices at home and/or in their communities. These academic practices include finding the appropriate academic resources and support when needed, such as visiting their professors' office hours or a particular office on campus or having access to informational resources online. One of these academic practices involves knowing how and when to consult an expert when needed. As tutors exhibited "invisible academic practices", they modeled yet another practice—what I call "asking metalinguistic questions"—particularly as related to working through a grammar exercise and understanding metalinguistic information. It is important to highlight that, even though tutors often act as instructors or "experts" during a session, not knowing the answer to a question gives them the opportunity to embody peer identities, where tutors are both experts and learners. This provides tutees a greater sense of community where learning can happen gradually (and not automatically—such as what is expected of many formal classroom spaces). Thus, a common literacy practice engaged by tutors occurred when they consulted other "experts" in the tutoring room for help with grammar rules and explanations.

58 Heritage Literacy Practices

In this instance, tutors Cristal and Concepción, while working through metalinguistic problems with their students, consistently reached out to me (as the instructor) for help when they were unable to explain details of verb conjugations, for example, as well as the grammatical rules related to written accentuation in Spanish. For example, as Concepción worked through grammar exercises on the difference between the preterit and the imperfect, her tutee asked her whether sentences could use both tenses in one single sentence. As Concepción realized she was not sure how to respond to her tutee's question, she interrupted the session to turn to me as I sat in a corner of the room. She then addressed me for further clarification on whether a single sentence could take the two past conjugations. I approached the pair to explain:

Concepción: ¿Cómo? Tener ((uh))-

How? Having-

Student: Um imperfecto y el pretérito-

Um imperfect and the preterite

Concepción: El pretérito en la ((misma))

The preterite in the (same)

Student: ¿En una oración? Ajá-

In a sentence? Yeah-

Concepción: Yo pienso que cuando hablamos sí, pero-

I think that when we speak yes, but

Student: Mhm

Concepción: Si: estás como escribiendo a veces- bueno para mí yo pienso que es mejor como que seas consistente- con los tiempos que usas-

Yes, you're kind of writing sometimes. For me, I think it is best to be consistent with the tenses you use

Student: Ohh, mhm

Concepción: Pero podríamos (.) podemos (…) preguntar (.)

But we could ask

Student: Pensaba que en un tiempo dice eso y en otro le puedo poner en otro

I thought one tense says this and the other one you can use another one

Concepción: Hay que preguntarle a Lina- <looking at Lina> ¿te podemos hacer una pregunta?

I think we need to ask Lina, can we ask you a question?

Lina: SÍ claro que sí

Yes of course

Concepción: Para estos ejercicios, ¿pueden tener los dos tiempos?

For these exercises, can they have both tenses?

In the minutes following this interaction, I discussed with both Concepción and her student that beyond needing to know proper tense conjugations, they must be able to explain the use of either tense to their tutees. Thus, we worked through the problems, generated our own explanations using metalinguistic terms, and concluded that indeed one can use both conjugations if their use can be conceptually explained.

Across the data, Cristal also took advantage of my presence in the tutoring room to interrupt the tutoring session and extract additional information. The following case concerned the rules for written accentuation in Spanish, a topic to be included in the course's final exam. In the instance detailed next, Cristal was unable to explain why the word "examen" does not take a written accent, but "exámenes" does. Thus, she secured my attention to ask a metalinguistic question:

Student: ExAmen. No dices examEN, dices exAmen. ¿Y esta por qué no sigue la regla? ¿Por qué no decimos exaMEN? <repeats to herself> tuve un exa-MEN @@

ExAmen. You don't say "examen", you say "exAmen". And why doesn't this one follow the rule? Why don't we say "exaMEN?" "I had an 'exaMEN'"

Cristal: Esa es un poco complicada porque si yo la viera así por la x yo diría que no lleva <chuckles>

That one is a bit tricky because if I saw it I'd say that because of the x I'd say it doesn't take an accent

Student: EXAmen

Cristal: EXAmen. Pero um- <facing Lina> Lina, ¿me podrías explicar un poquito más sobre la complicación con eXAmen y exaMEN?

"EXAmen". But um, Lina could you explain a little more why it's "eXAmen" and not "exaMEN"?

Lina: ¿Cómo la silabificas?

How would you split it into syllables?

Cristal: Yo la silabifico como E y luego XA y luego MEN

I would do "E" then "XA" then "MEN"

Lina: Entonces si termina en s según la regla (.) el énfasis iría en la (.)

60 Heritage Literacy Practices

> *Okay if it ends in "s" according to the rule, the emphasis would be on-*

Cristal: Penúltima

> *The second to last*

Lina: <repeats> Penúltima y, ¿donde va el énfasis según la regla?

> *Second to last and, where would the emphasis go according to the rule?*

Student: ExAmen

Lina: ExAmen

Cristal: ExAmen

Student: ExAmen

Lina: So, ¿va en la? (.) ¿En la última o la penúltima?

> *So, does it go on the last or second to last?*

Cristal: En la penúltima

> *In the second to last*

Lina: Ajá. Decimos exAmen y no exaMEN. Entonces no viola la regla 2- digo la regla 1

> *Yes. We say "exAmen" and not "exaMEN". So it does not violate rule 2- I mean rule 1*

Student: <repeats> ExAmen, no exaMEN

Cristal: ¿Entonces no lleva acento?

> *So it doesn't take an accent?*

In the following minutes following this interaction, Cristal, her student, and I worked through the differentiation between "examen" and "exámenes", applying the rules of accentuation to both words to illustrate the difference. Cristal ultimately realized she was assuming that the word "examen" was written with an accent, which was contributing to her confusion. In all instances where tutors asked me metalinguistic questions, I joined their tutoring sessions and engaged with both tutor and tutee to explain a concept; this mirrored what often occurs in a traditional classroom when students engage in pair work. Once the tutor explicitly asked me for help and I joined the pair, both tutor and tutee were engaged in discussing and understanding the subject in question.

Similar to the illustrations of asking me (the instructor) metalinguistic questions, tutors consistently relied on each other, asking other tutors for help when working through specific grammar problems, most often when assisting tutees with the rules of accentuation in Spanish. A recurring example was asking others about basic information on monosyllabic words that change in meaning based on written accentuation. Tutors considered each other "experts" in such instances. In the following example, Esmeralda, while working with a student, asked Maité (who was working with a different student) a question related to the grammar activity on monosyllabic words with written accents:

Esmeralda: Tengo una pregunta <talking to Matié> Los que son palabras monosílabas con acentos es mí, tú, él, té-

I have a question. Monosyllabic words with an accent are "mí, tú, él, té"-

Maité: Sé

Esmeralda: Sé, ¿y cuál me falta? ¿Hay otra más?

"Sé", and what am I missing? Is there another one?

Maité: Mmm, antes usaban "solo" pero "solo" ya no

Before they used "solo" but not anymore

Another tutor: <looking up> Si y sí

Maité: Mhm. ¿Tuvieron ejercicios escritos no? Ejercicios- ¿actividades?

Did they have written exercises? Exercises, activities?

Across the data, tutors interrupted their sessions to call a question out to the room, and other tutors participated to provide the necessary information. Thus, given the collaborative nature of this space, students were provided multiple opportunities to closely observe tutors asking for help when working through metalinguistic problems, in whatever language, and mobilizing any type of (bilingual) language practice they see fit in relation to the context. Additionally, tutors modeled to tutees how to be intentional about accessing the human resources available to them—a skill that is relevant, once again, in attaining academic success.

Peer-to-Peer Academic Advising: Searching the Internet for Academic Information

Relatedly, the kinds of literacy practices seen in the data, as noted, are situated in a pedagogical context that draws from learners' full repertoires of language and literacy. Importantly, this unique context also supports learners' overall academic trajectories and not just their mastery of academic genres in Spanish. As such, another "invisible academic literacy practice" related to accessing the additional information required to complete a task at hand was tutors "searching the Internet for academic information" to mediate a particular conversation related to tutees' academic success. In this way, tutors also embodied academic advisers, where, because they were more experienced undergraduate students, and thus had the skills and information to guide their peers through finding and understanding the requirements of academic life. This practice refers to instances

62 Heritage Literacy Practices

where tutors answer tutees' questions about related academic information such as course requirements, course instructors, office hours, and the like.

Although this occurred throughout the data, a particular illustration of this literacy practice involves Vanessa, who, while discussing a student's professional aspirations to apply to dental school, pulled up the website for a particular dentistry school of interest to the student. Through this practice, they both studied specific course requirements for application and discussed in what courses the student should enroll in during the following quarter:

Vanessa: Y sabes, bueno (.) ¿sabes a cuál escuela quieres ir para la dentadura? ¿Para la licencia de la ((dent))–

And, you know, well, do you know what school you want to go for dentistry? For your (dentist) license?

Student: A UCLA

Vanessa: Okay te enseño una cosa <pulls up computer screen> ¿Ya sabes the **Pre–Health website**?

Okay let me show you something. Do you know about the Pre-Health website?

Student: Sí

Yes

Vanessa: Ok, ahí te da. Ahí pon <types> "escuelas de–" <continues> solo te quiero enseñar este **resource** <student navigates computer>

Ok, there it shows. You put down "schools of". I just want to show you this resource

Student: xxx

Vanessa: Sí, si vas hacia arriba. Aquí <points to screen> (…) A ver <takes hold of laptop from student, browses> (…) Hmm, ¿cómo me metí el otro día? Siempre me pierdo (…) Oh okay me voy a **pre–health requirements** <points to screen> y aquí me voy a- digamos para ti es **Dental School** y aquí te muestra eso <points to screen> y digamos **if you're aiming for UCLA** te requiere tres **quarters** de biología, tres **quarters** de **chemistry**. **So** aquí escoges digamos tus escuelas en que estás interesada y bueno ahí decides– bueno tengo que tomar esta porque cabe en todas las escuelas. O tengo que tomar **chemistry, physics**, economía, **genetics, statistics**. Y, ¿ves cómo **statistics** es solo para una escuela? Entonces ahí decides tú bueno la quiero tomar o no, porque no es para las otras. **It's awful, huh?**

Yes, you scroll up. Here. Let's see. Hmm, how did I get on last time? I always get lost. Oh, okay I go to "Pre-Health Requirements" and here I go to- let's say for you it is Dental School and then it shows you, let's say you're aiming for UCLA it asks for three questions of Biology, three quarters of Chemistry. So there you choose, let's say the schools you're interested in and then from there you decide, I have to take this course because it fits in all schools. Or I have to take Chemistry, Physics, Economy, Genetics, Statistics. And, you see how Statistics is only good for the one school? So then there you decide, I want to take it or not, because it is not good for other schools. It's awful, huh?

In this instance, Vanessa was providing her tutee with a necessary resource useful to navigate current course requirements and life after college, while also modeling how to extract this information from the internet, all while seamlessly going into English from Spanish and vice versa. Importantly, she finished the interaction with a switch to English ("it's awful, huh?") as she conveyed how potentially overwhelming it can be to navigate the ins and outs of applying to dental school and the specific coursework requirements involved in the process. After participating in this practice with her tutor, the student now had access to both the critical information and practice that positioned her to extract additional information as she continued to navigate her academic life. In all, tutors continually use their computers for informational resource extraction, sharing specific websites and online resources that students will be able to use for their own academic success.

Personal Storytelling: Esmeralda

This practice refers to tutors' recounting their own experiences in service of guiding their students toward understanding the expectations of a writing activity. Esmeralda's storytelling of specific experiences from her past is perhaps the best illustration of how tutors used the hybrid linguistic practices of their home communities to foster academic literacies. In this case, she used her own lived experiences to draw parallels with the content of a writing assignment with which her students were struggling. She used specific episodes from her struggles as a young bilingual growing up and navigating life in two languages. Esmeralda relied on her translingual storytelling to guide students into critically considering how to write a linguistic biography, which is one of the core course assignments. For this assignment, students must interview a Spanish speaker in their community and write a report that analyzes the complexity of language use within a particular bilingual individual's experiences.

Because students often struggle with generating questions that extend beyond simply asking an individual when and where they use a particular language, tutors must help students to think more critically about language use, which is one of the goals of the assignment. In order to guide students into a critical consideration of the relationship between language and use, Esmeralda used her own experience as a bilingual individual to illustrate the types of complex relationships an individual can have with their language(s) as a consequence of unique experiences solely relevant to individuals, such as heritage speakers, who speak more than one language from an early age. In the first instance to follow, as Esmeralda guided a student into deciding who to interview for the assignment,

64 Heritage Literacy Practices

Esmeralda explained the particularities of her experience with two languages as a young child. She included reasons why she would not qualify as an ideal candidate for an interview, as students must select an individual who uses Spanish more than English:

Esmeralda: Puedes preguntarle <al entrevistado> con respecto a eso. ¿Cuándo aprendieron- cuál idioma? ¿Sí me explico? Entonces, como para mí yo aprendí a hablar español, primero que nada. Y yo no- yo fui aprendiendo el inglés como a los tres o cuatro años porque yo tenía hermanas mayores y ellas hablaban inglés en casa. Pero personalmente, yo siempre utilizaba más frecuentemente el español y leía mucho en inglés e iba a la escuela y todo eso en inglés, pero todo lo demás lo hacía yo, yo misma en español. Y me recuerdo que como durante tiempo de, de almuerzo y de receso, todo eso hablaba en español. No estaba hablando en inglés con los otros estudiantes y por eso no tenía muchas amistades de pequeña. Al punto que cuando yo tenía catorce años, yo todavía tenía un acento al hablar inglés, aunque estaba muy desarrollada en el idioma, y como al escribir y el leer. Leía muy bien, escribía muy bien. Mi pronunciación nunca era buena porque nunca utilizaba el idioma frecuentemente hasta que empecé la preparatoria fue cuando hice amistades y OH estás amistades no hablan español y pues tenía que forzarme a hablar inglés más seguido y ya fue cuando perdí el acento el si- al hablar inglés. Pero pues me tardé un poco, porque, aunque empecé con el idioma muy joven no lo utilizaba tanto como usaba el español, ¿sí me explico? Entonces, es algo que obvio puedes preguntar. Si antes se p-hablaban más un idioma que otro y si eso ha cambiado para ellos. Porque quizás, quien quieras

entrevistar, antes hablaba más inglés que español y ahora habla más español que inglés

You can ask the interviewee about that. When did they learn which language? Do you know what I mean? So like, for me, I learned to speak Spanish before anything. And I started learning English at three or four years old because I had older sisters and they spoke English at home. But personally, I always used Spanish more frequently until I started high school and I started making friends and that's when I realized they didn't speak Spanish and so I had to force myself to speak English more frequently and that was when I lost my accent when I spoke English. But it took me a while, because, even though I started with the language so young I didn't use it as much as I used Spanish, do you know what I mean? So, that is something you could ask. If before they spoke a language more than the other and if this has changed for them. Because maybe, whoever you want to interview, before they spoke more English than Spanish and now they speak more Spanish than English.

The implementation of the linguistic biography as part of the course for heritage speakers is in part due to the opportunity that this assignment presents. Students must consider how bilingual individuals such as themselves share certain experiences, such as not speaking English until their entrance to formal schooling or their perception of "having an accent" in a particular language. Before telling a particular story to a student while working through a linguistic biography, we see here how Esmeralda contextualized her own position as a bilingual learner and the various experiences that marked her upbringing—instances which are highly relatable to her students, who, as heritage speakers of Spanish themselves, most likely share similar school-related contexts. Then, as illustrated next, Esmeralda shared two particular episodes in her life that illustrated the complexities of her emotional relationship with her languages. Esmeralda made explicit reference to how these stories could help the student shape the questions they were developing before conducting their linguistic interviews:

Esmeralda: También puedes preguntarle como **you know, the experiences that they had being bilingual,** um (.) me recuerdo que una vez en la secundaria andaba muy nerviosa, tenía una presentación para la clase de inglés, **you know,** yo para ese tiempo yo ya sabía que tenía un acento, la gente ya me lo había dejado saber de que hablaba de forma extraña en inglés. Y de tantos nervios que tenía, lo que sea, hice toda mi presentación en español sin darme cuenta. Entonces, **you know, we, we- I had a PowerPoint going on and I would read the slides, the- I was reading them in English** pero mientras yo hablaba de lo que estaba diciendo lo estaba diciendo todo en español **because I was so nervous that I automatically just went to that language to feel more comfortable. And, so that was a very funny day. I had to re-present the whole thing the next day in English**

You can also ask, you know, the experiences they had being bilingual. I remember once in high school I was so nervous, I had a presentation for English class, you know, back then I knew I had an accent, people had already told me that I spoke weirdly in English. And so, I was so nervous, whatever, I did the entire presentation in Spanish without realizing it. So, you know, I had a PowerPoint going on and I would read the slide, I was reading them in English but while I talked about what I was saying I was saying it in Spanish because I was so nervous that I automatically just went to that language to feel more comfortable. And so that was a very funny day. I had to present the whole thing again the next day in English

Not only did Esmeralda share personal stories from her early experiences in school, but also divulged some events of growing up as a bilingual teenager:

Esmeralda: Tu entrevista está muy formal, um recuerda que sí lo puedes hacer más personal **and like ask lik-** nomás como, cuál es tu preferencia de idioma por qué or **like** umm (.) sé que el ejemplo que le he dado mucho a mis estudiantes es que hay que recordar que emveces para cierta gente, yo soy un ejemplo de eso, uuhh un idioma tiene más emoción que otro.

66 Heritage Literacy Practices

Umm por ejemplo, el inglés es mucho más (.) **formal very distant to me, I am not emotionally connected in English** pero en español es mucho más emotivo. Um y el ejemplo pues que yo siempre di es que cuando rompí con mi primer novio me recuerdo que yo xxx como dos meses tocando **sad music in English like "Break Even" and all those break up songs all the time** verdad **but I didn't care. I was just like OH this is sad** y era lo único. Nada de emoción. Y umm hubo un día que caminé pues por la cocina y mi mamá tenía el radio prendido y escuché la canción de Enrique Iglesias, la de "Lloro por ti" **and I started crying**

Your interview is too formal, remember that you can make it more personal and like ask what language you prefer or why or like, I know one example I give my students is that you have to remember that sometimes for certain people, I am an example of that, one language has more emotion than the other one. For example, English is a lot more formal and distant to me, I am not emotionally connected to English but in Spanish it is a lot more emotional. And the example I always shared is that when I broke up with my first boyfriend, I remember it was like two months after and I would play sad music in English like "Break Even" and all those break-up songs all the time right? But I didn't care. I was just like oh this is sad, but that was it. No emotion. And then there was one day I was walking by the kitchen and my mom was playing that song by Enrique Iglesias called "Lloro por ti" and I started crying

Student: @@

Esmeralda: I was just like I MISS HIM and I- y est- **it was like** dos meses después de algo triste en inglés **and it didn't do anything** pero escuchándolo en español **again I'm more open with my emotions in Spanish than I am in English**

I was just like I miss him and it was like two months later after something sad happened in English and it didn't do anything but listening to it in Spanish again, I'm more open with my emotions in Spanish than I am in English

As Esmeralda translanguaged through these two personal stories, she used both English and Spanish in addition to referencing particular cultural products (the songs "Break Even" by popular Irish band The Script and "Lloro por ti" by Spanish singer Enrique Iglesias) to make her account relatable to her students who translanguage in the same way. Additionally, Esmeralda highlighted particular struggles such as internalizing a negative view of her English abilities as a young child, and her inability to emotionally connect with English—experiences that are also potentially relatable to her students who are also young, bilingual, Latinx heritage speakers of Spanish in the United States. By illustrating her own life as a bilingual individual, and the very particular life events that depict the dynamic (and complex) relationship she has with both English and Spanish, Esmeralda guided the student toward a better understanding of the assignment's expectations. Thus, she mobilized storytelling to mediate a particular academic task as she leveraged the linguistic richness in her repertoire.

Defining Norms of Academic Writing: Guiding Student Responses

Other literacy practices mobilized by tutors mirror traditional, mechanical writing exercises akin to the decontextualized "banking approach" devoid of a social context. While the problematic dichotomy of academic vs. non-academic language or standard vs. non-standard language is fueled by writing activities that do not trigger critical considerations of writing as a social act, students in the program described here continue to have to master these activities to pass the course and get a good grade. Thus, considering that, for better or worse, both mechanical writing exercises and critical understandings of personal experiences are expected of the academy at this level, I consider tutors' intentional support of peers as they acquire traditional literacy practices as relevant for the illustration of their role. What is most relevant in the following illustrations is the way that still, when tackling traditional conventions of academic Spanish, tutors mobilize hybrid heritage practices to guide their peers in understanding functional aspects of academic literacy.

As such, a traditional use of language for academic purposes involves the IRE discourse pattern, in which the teacher Initiates, the student Responds, and the teacher Evaluates or gives feedback on a student's responses. This teacher-centered, question–answer discourse pattern is still typical in most traditional instructional contexts (Cazden, 2001). In this way, the IRE pattern implies that there is only one correct answer, thus limiting the extent to which the classroom can be a place for negotiation of meaning. In the case of the present study, tutors continually mobilized what I call "initiating student responses", where they replicated a similar task-oriented practice as IRE. In this case, however, we saw that tutors relied on their shared linguistic and cultural background with their tutees to work through grammar activities that posed a particular challenge for them. For example, they relied on this shared background as they provided guidance on features of academic writing (diacritic accents, transition words, etc.) that involve consistent practice and instruction. Therefore, we see how tutors translanguage to guide students to the correct answers.

When working with their students, both Esmeralda and Maité continually guided responses to support students toward desired answers related to the content or grammar topic being covered in the session. Esmeralda, for example, relies on asking her students short questions to prompt their engagement with a given task, particularly when working through grammar exercises. In the following illustration, Esmeralda was reviewing a spelling activity, where the student had to learn how to differentiate between the homophones "has", and "haz", as well as "asta" and "hasta". The student was instructed to choose between these four words to complete the sentence "El catorce de febrero Romeo le llevó un _____ de flores a Julieta" where the correct response is "haz":

68 Heritage Literacy Practices

Student: El catorce de febrero, Romeo le llevó un (…) ¿has de flores a Julieta?

The fourteenth day of February, Romeo took a bundle of flowers?

Esmeralda: Bueno hay que empezar aquí. Has, h-a-s, TÚ has ido a tal lugar

Well, that's where we need to start. "Have", h-a-v-e, you have been to a place

Student: Mhmm

Esmeralda: ¿De qué verbo viene eso?

What verb does that come from?

Student: (…) ¿Ir? **Like** vas a-

To go? Like, you are going to

Esmeralda: No, porque dije has ido. Ido viene de ir, pero ¿has? ¿Sabes cuál es? Es uno de los tiempos perfectos. Entonces te voy a decir otros ejemplos de tiempos perfectos. Um, habría ido, habrás ido, has ido. ¿Sabes cuál verbo es cada uno de esos o no?

No, because I said "you have been". "Been" comes from to go, but have? Do you know which one it is? It's one of those perfect tenses. So I am going to tell you other examples of perfect tenses. Um, "would have been, will have been, have been". Do you know what verb is in each of those or not?

Student: No

Esmeralda: Es haber, de ahí viene

It's "haber", it comes from that

Student: <repeats to herself> ((Haber))-

Esmeralda: Entonces, **yeah, have you**. Entonces, si yo te digo ¿tú has ido? **Have you gone?**

So, yeah, have you. So, if I tell you, have you been? Have you gone?

Student: <student nods>

Esmeralda: Okay? Entonces (.) ¿Le llevó un haber de flores? ¿Viene de ese verbo o no? Bueno, primero, es un verbo @@ entonces, ¿queda ahí la palabra?

Okay? So, he brought her a "to have" of flowers? Does it come from that verb or not? Well, first, it is a verb, so would that work there?

Student: Le llevó un (.)

He brought her a (.)

Esmeralda: Cualquier verbo que quieras poner, ¿va a describir eso? ¿O no?

Would any verb you want to place there, would it describe it? Or not?

Heritage Literacy Practices **69**

Student: No

Esmeralda: Porque nec-, ¿qué es lo que necesitas si es algo de flores? ¿Qué se-qué se está usando?¿Qué, uh, tipo de palabra? Adjetivo, adverbio, verbo, sustantivo

Because you need, what do you need if it is something with flowers? What do you, what are you using? What, uh, type of word? Adjective, adverb, verb, noun

Student: Adjetivo

Adjective

Esmeralda: Perfecto, estás buscando un adjetivo o s- quizás sea un sustantivo por un tipo de flores

Perfect, you're looking for an adjective or even a noun since it is a type of flower

Student: Mhmm

Esmeralda: ¿Vale? (.) Entonces, has viene del verbo. Si yo te digo hasta mañana (.) ¿Qué es en inglés? Tradúzcamelo

Ok? So, "has" comes from the ver. If I tell you "hasta mañana" what is that in English? Translate it for me

Student: Uhm, hasta mañana xxx **until tomorrow**?

Um, "hasta mañana", until tomorrow?

Esmeralda: Bien

Good

Student: So, until?

Esmeralda: Until. ¿Funciona esa palabra ahí?

Until. Does that word work there?

Student: No

Esmeralda: Okay (.) ¿Qué es un asta? ¿Sabes qué es eso?

Okay. What is an "asta"? Do you know what that is?

Student: ¿Asta?

Esmeralda: Asta sin h

"Asta" without an "h"

Student: Asta como, como (.)

"Asta", like, like

Esmeralda: Moose have them, reindeer have them

70 Heritage Literacy Practices

Student: Ohhh

Esmeralda: Asta, entonces puedo usar esto o también otra descripción para asta es como un **shaft**, un tubo. ¿Queda eso?

"Asta", so I could use that or another definition for "asta" is like a shaft, like a tube. Would that work?

Student: No

Esmeralda: Okay. Entonces el único que queda es haz, h–a–z. Eso significa un **bundle**

Okay. So the only one missing is "haz", h-a-z. That means "bundle"

Student: Ahhh

Esmeralda: O un ramero

Or a bouquet

Student: H–a–s <spells>

Esmeralda: H–a–z <spells>

Student: H–a–z

Esmeralda: Bien, haz, entonces un haz de flores, fue lo que se le dio

Good, "haz", so like a flower bundle or bouquet, what was given

Student: <repeats> Haz

Esmeralda: Bien. ¿Número 6?

Good. Number 6?

Student: <repeats> Un haz de flo-, **oh okay** <nods and smiles>

A flower bouq-, oh okay

In the foregoing excerpt, Esmeralda posed a series of 11 questions, one right after the other, to guide her student into arriving at the correct answer. In doing so, she mobilized translanguaging in and out of Spanish as she illustrated contrastive analyses of Spanish to English in four key moments with four specific goals. First, she illustrates the use of the auxiliary "haber" (one of the homophones in the exercise) equating the use of "have" with the same use in English when she asks "have you gone". Second, she asks the student (through the use of an imperative clause) to translate "hasta" so the student is able to eliminate that as a possible answer through a comparison in meaning, since "hasta" means "until" and not "bundle", the word she is searching for. Third, she continues to teach her student to rely on meanings in English (first to think of the meaning of "asta" as "horn" or "antler" and then to extend the meaning of "asta" to "pole" or "tube"). Lastly, she explains the meaning of the answer included in the answer key—"haz" means "bundle". Thus, while guiding responses is the literacy practice that Esmeralda mobilized in this interaction, she relied on the semantic meanings of English to illustrate the appropriate use of homophones in Spanish, tapping her entire linguistic repertoire and modeling this process for her student through the use of 11 short, back-to-back questions in this short interaction.

Similarly, Maité guided student responses in another instance when she was walking a student through the notion of lexical chains, an important feature of functional academic writing used to avoid repetition of nouns by using synonyms, a concept taught several times across the courses in the Program for Native Speakers at this institution. As such, using lexical chains represents one of the most important expectations for the written productions of students in the program. In this case, Maité, while working with a student through a draft for one of the course's main writing assignments (a hypothetical letter written to the school Chancellor who has announced a possible cancellation of the Spanish for Native Speakers Program), used a series of short, back-to-back questions to guide the student away from overusing the word "personas":

Maité: ¿Cuál es un sinónimo de personas?

What is a synonym for people?

Student: ¿Otros individuos?

Other individuals?

Maité: Okay. ¿De qué otra manera se puede decir personas?

Okay. How else could you say "people"?

Student: ¿Individuos?

Individuals?

Maité: Ajá. ¿Qué otro sinónimo hay?

Yes. What other synonym is there?

Student: ¿Otra gente?

Other folks?

Maité: Gente okay.

Folks, okay.

Maité prompted her student to generate other options for referring to "people" in their letter since the student used it redundantly throughout the draft. After the student generated "individuos" as a synonym for "personas", Maité continued to prompt them by asking the question "how else could you say 'personas'?" a second time. The student, then, produced a second synonym, "gente", and

72 Heritage Literacy Practices

ended with two other lexical options as he worked through this lexical chain. Thus, both Esmeralda and Maité mobilized the shared knowledge between them and their tutees (Esmeralda relying primarily on her translanguaging and Maité relying on her previous experience as an undergraduate writer herself) to inform and guide student responses.

Tutors' Literacy Practices: Summary

As illustrated in this section, tutors consistently mobilize specific literacy practices drawn from a variety of sociocultural contexts of participation. These acts are performed in service of their tutees' academic success, given the fact that many mirror the academic literacy and other practices deemed necessary for successful academic achievement (for example, "asking metalinguistic questions", "searching the internet for academic information", and "guiding student responses"). Further, tutors' literacy practices are embedded and situated across their participation in online contexts such as social media—particularly discourses representative of out-of-school contexts—and in academic contexts of participation, among others, that are deeply bilingual (including, especially, Esmeralda's personal storytelling). Thus, tutors' translanguaging, or the literacy practices they mobilize, reflect the "situated, dynamic, contextualized, and mutually constituted [nature] across the normative tasks and activities that [they] accomplish in different spaces" (Pacheco, 2015, p. 136), illustrating the socially situated nature of the practices they mobilize and their relevance in academic contexts.

Since tutors' literacy practices described in this section are the product of specific, socially situated interactions with their students, it is equally important to further analyze the nature of this particular social context of participation. In the next chapter, I examine the socially motivated goals tutors use to mobilize these literacy practices, highlighting the contributions of these literacy practices to tutees' academic development and community building. For a discussion of the pedagogical implications of the data, see Chapter 6.

Notes

1 To see an analysis that does present causal relationships between the tutoring session and academic writing development in students within this same program for Spanish heritage speakers, see Reznicek-Parrado, Patiño-Vega, and Colombi (2018).
2 Names of places are fictionalized for IRB purposes.

References

Barton, D., & Hamilton, M. (2000). Literacy practices. In D. Barton, M. Hamilton, & R. Ivanic (Eds.), *Situated Literacies: Reading and Writing in Context* (pp. 7–15). London and New York: Routledge.

BBC News. (2011). Who, what, why: What is planking? Retrieved from http://www .bbc.com/news/magazine-13414527

Bernard, H. R., & Ryan, G. W. (2010). Chapter 3: Finding themes. *Analyzing Qualitative Data: Systematic Approaches*. Thousand Oaks: SAGE Publications.

Cazden, C. (2001). *Classroom Discourse: The Language of Learning and Teaching*. Portsmouth: Heinemann.

Charmaz, K. (2014). *Constructing Grounded Theory* (2nd ed.). London: Sage.

Cook-Gumperz, J. (Ed.) (2006). *The Social Construction of Literacy* (Vol. 25). New York: Cambridge University Press.

Corbin, J., & Strauss, A. (2015). *Basics of Qualitative Research: Techniques and Procedures for Developing Grounded Theory* (4th ed.). Thousand Oaks: Sage.

Dyson, A. H., & Genishi, C. (2005). *On the Case*. New York: Teachers College Press.

Eggins, S., & Slade, D. (1997). *Analyzing Casual Conversation*. London: Cassell.

Halliday, M. A. K. (1994). *An Introduction to Functional Grammar* (2nd ed.). London: Edward Arnold.

Lankshear, C., & Knobel, M. (2011). *New Literacies: Everyday Practices and Classroom Learning*. Maidenhead: Open University Press.

Martin, J. R., & White, P. R. R. (2015). *The Language of Evaluation: Appraisal in English*. New York: Palgrave.

Martínez, R. A. (2010). Spanglish as literacy tool: Toward an understanding of the potential role of Spanish-English code-switching in the development of academic literacy. *Research in the Teaching of English, 45*(2), 124–149.

Merriam, S. B., & Tisdell, E. J. (2015). *Qualitative Research: A Guide to Design and Implementation*. San Francisco: Jissey-Bass.

Molle, D. (2015). Academic language and academic literacies: Mapping a relationship. In D. Molle, E. Sato, T. Boals, & C. A. Hedgspeth (Eds.), *Multilingual Learners and Academic Literacies* (pp. 13–32). New York: Routledge.

Pacheco, M. (2015). Bilingualism-as-participation: Examining adolescents' bi(multi) lingual literacies across out-of-school and online contexts. In D. Molle, E. Sato, T. Boals, & C. A. Hedgspeth (Eds.), *Multilingual Learners and Academic Literacies* (pp. 135–165). New York: Routledge.

Reznicek-Parrado, L. M., Patiño-Vega, M., & Colombi, M. C. Academic peer-tutors and academic biliteracy development in students of Spanish as a heritage language. In S. Pastor Cesteros & A. Ferreira Cabrera (Eds.), *L2 Spanish academic discourse: New contexts, new methodologies / El discurso académico en español como L2: nuevos contextos, nuevas metodologías. Journal of Spanish Language Teaching, Special Issue, 5*(2), 152–167.

Scribner, S. (1984). The practice of literacy: Where mind & society meet. *Annals of the New York Academy of Sciences, 433*(1), 5–19.

Scribner, S., & Cole, M. (1981). *The Psychology of Literacy*. Massachusetts: Harvard University Press.

Stake, R. E. (1995). *The Art of Case Study Research*. Thousand Oaks: Sage.

Strauss, A. L. (1987). *Qualitative Analysis for Social Scientists*. Cambridge, UK: Cambridge University Press.

USA Today. (2017). Ice Bucket Challenge: 5 things you should know. Retrieved from https://www.usatoday.com/story/news/2017/07/03/ice-bucket-challenge-5-things -youshould-know/448006001/

Watson-Gegeo, K. A. (1992). Thick explanation in the ethnographic study of child socialization: A longitudinal study of the problem of schooling for Kwara'ae (Solomon Islands) children. *New Directions for Child and Adolescent Development, 58*, 58–66.

3

TRANSLANGUAGING FOR ACADEMIC LITERACY DEVELOPMENT AND COMMUNITY BUILDING

Hybridity in Heritage Language Development: Going Beyond "Academic Language"

Traditionally, the ways in which educators have assessed whether language students are acquiring academic literacy or "the language of school" are couched in notions of language learning from a monolingual perspective; that is, we think we know students are "making progress" if they acquire the skills to successfully communicate in strictly monolingual contexts, usually through the exclusive use of standard repertoires. The issue with a monolingual-centered end goal in literacy development, however, and especially when working with multilingual students such as heritage speakers, is its blunt disregard for achievements students may have accomplished in additional languages they speak, as well as the varied linguistic skills they may already possess (interdialectal competencies, language brokering experiences, cross-cultural knowledge, etc.). We need, thus, alternative models of framing academic literacies in order to better evaluate language development, especially in academic spaces of heritage language teaching and learning both in the K–12 as well as in the higher education context.

Likewise, multilingual students in language courses are often traditionally labeled according to the linguistic skills they do not yet have —"English learner", "emergent learner", "heritage language learner", etc. But what happens when the educational framework incorporates students' lived experiences to develop new theoretical frames of reference? Might students' academic literacy development benefit? As Bailey and Orellana (2015) state, instead of framing the multilingual student as lacking specific literacy skills, educators and researchers should focus on the commonalities that students have. For example, most multilingual students, such as heritage speakers, live in communities where "flexibility and diversity in language practices is the norm" (p. 54). If students have, since

DOI: 10.4324/9781003191179-4

birth, been exposed to multiple and varied uses of language, why not take these language practices into account when measuring their language development? Why not utilize these to develop new pedagogies in language learning as well as academic literacy learning?

Indeed, translanguaging and other hybrid language practices, which comprise a distinct component of heritage students' linguistic repertoires, are largely hidden and traditionally ignored by second language and heritage language educators. Such disregard for students' language practices is especially true in how seldom they are incorporated into pedagogical models for diverse spaces of language teaching and learning. However, intentionally including everyday language practices of multilingual students in language pedagogy is imperative:

> Examining the characteristics of [adolescent] development that interact with students' everyday language practices alongside the more commonly held expectations inherent in academic content standards and curricula for literacy may reveal new ways for researchers and educators to support the literacy of multilingual adolescents, and to view these adolescents' linguistic competencies in more hopeful and pedagogically strategic ways.
>
> *(Bailey & Orellana, 2015, p. 55)*

Because traditional ways of conceiving academic language can be detrimental to the academic development of linguistically diverse students, as Flores (2015) explains, the mere notion of "academic language" is rejected by many educational linguists and other researchers who engage with diverse spaces of language teaching and learning. According to Flores, the concept of academic language is fundamentally flawed, as it masks the fact that bilingual learners already engage with complex linguistic tasks before arriving in the classroom. As Flores posits, bilingual and multilingual students already consider, for example, the important relationship between language and identity as they explain how their name should be pronounced, when they reflect on the importance of understanding cultural contexts when translating, or as they debate words that vary in meaning depending on the context in which they are used, etc. Flores highlights that traditional, dichotomized conceptions of what is "academic" and what is "nonacademic" "presupposes that Latino children inevitably come to school without a strong foundation in the academic forms" (2015), establishing a deficit perspective as the norm.

This book counteracts the implications of traditional notions of "academic language" as simply language that is decontextualized, as well as dichotomized notions of "language appropriate for school" versus "language not appropriate for school". Instead, "academic literacy", as understood in this book, follows Molle's (2015) suggestion to develop more productive and inclusive notions of academic language, particularly notions that reflect a literacy reality encompassing *all* literacies, and not just those of the mainstream (for a more complete

76 Literacy and Community Development

discussion of academic literacy and its implication for heritage literacy development, see Chapter 1). "Academic literacy", as I conceive it, implies the erasure of dichotomized divisions of language usage and the subsequent visible deep ties between oral language and written literacy which are crucial for understanding how everyday language practices can serve as a resource for academic literacy. The goal of this chapter is to bring these practices into view.

Tutors' Linguistic Hybridity

As shown in the data presented throughout the second and fifth chapters, tutors consistently mobilize what I term "linguistic hybridity" as they engage in specific literacy practices while working with their tutees in the tutoring room. In this analysis, linguistic hybridity refers to the notion of translanguaging, or "speakers' construction and use of original and complex interrelated discursive practices that cannot be easily assigned to one or another traditional definition of language" (García & Wei, 2014, p. 22). The notion of translanguaging—beyond the traditional concept of bilingualism which presents the bilingual mind as having two autonomous and separate linguistic systems—is useful in that it allows for the conception of language use as practice. As such, it highlights the use of language as it is readily observable in social interaction. Thus, translanguaging emphasizes the socially meaningful aspect of tutors' bilingual literacy practices, taking into consideration that when they translanguage, they are in fact engaging in multiple discursive practices to "make sense of their bilingual worlds" (García, 2009a, p. 45). Further, the notion of translanguaging, rather than offering an "additive" or "subtractive" lens for framing bilingualism, instead views it as dynamic, framing individuals' linguistic and literacy practices as complex and interrelated, emerging not in a linear manner nor functioning separately through two or more linguistic systems (García & Wei, 2014). Instead, this notion conceives the bilingual individual as having one large literacy repertoire from which they strategically choose specific features to communicate effectively in socially situated interactions.

In educational settings, as well as contexts of academic literacy learning, translanguaging refers to "building on bilingual students' language practices flexibly in order to develop new understandings and new language practices, including those deemed as 'academic standard' practices" (García & Wei, 2014, p. 92). Thus, a translanguaging pedagogical framework incorporates an understanding of how students engage with academic language through particular linguistic practices, many of which are conceived of as "informal" or "vernacular", as speakers engage with and adopt standardized language and formal academic literacy practices. Such an approach can build on students' strengths and not exclusively emphasize students' knowledge gaps (an emphasis that takes center stage when pedagogies solely focus on formal registers and standard academic language). This is especially important in educational contexts where the standard language often reflects the literacy repertoires of a privileged majority, and where many of the repertoires used by those positioned as minorities—the non-White speakers of minoritized languages, such as heritage speakers of Spanish—are left out. It is thus important to consider the political implications of adopting a translanguaging framework in contexts of language teaching and learning. As explained by Heller (1999), in traditional models of literacy teaching and learning, language is considered from the external viewpoint of the political state and is given linguistic reality that is illusory since named languages have been socially constructed. In the translanguaging model, on the other hand, named languages such as "English" or "Spanish" are recognized as having social, but not linguistic, reality (Otheguy, García, & Reid, 2015). As highlighted by García and Kleyn (2016), taking up a theory of translanguaging means that we start to teach bilingual students from a different and better place. It means

> that we start from a place that leverages all the features of students' repertoires, while also analyzing along with them when, with whom, where, and why use some features of their repertoire and not others according to the social norms of languages as used in schools.
>
> *(García & Kleyn, 2016, p. 15)*

In order to leverage heritage students' literacy repertoires, educational contexts can be structured in ways that allow full use of students' repertoires and their many features. In the present analysis, conceptualizing the tutoring room as the context of study is one illustration of an academic space where students translanguage as they negotiate the acquisition of additional registers in academic literacy. Tutors navigate these registers while they engage in academic literacy practices, using their complete linguistic repertoires as part of the learning process. Further, and as seen in the data presented throughout, tutors consistently translanguage as they deploy elements from English while using Spanish as well as when they deploy elements of non-traditional "academic" Spanish while using features of standard Spanish, or the language deemed necessary as per the course's curriculum. While Esmeralda uses English the most of all tutors (perhaps because she is the only tutor who grew up in California exclusively), translanguaging is apparent throughout all transcriptions for all tutor participants. In the data set as a whole, instances of using English with Spanish were the most heavily coded instance throughout open coding (289 coding references out of 877 total references). On the other hand, codes for deploying language not traditionally conceived of as "academic" with "standard" Spanish included 53 coding references in total.

Tutors' Translanguaging

The data included in this section is an illustration of the way tutors use specific aspects of their semiotic repertoires to participate in a non-traditional, bilingual, academic space. It is one way of understanding how both languages are simultaneously used to convey information and it positions me as the data analyst to

78 Literacy and Community Development

bilingually analyze the discourse. This analysis continues to understand bilingual linguistic practices as fluid, dynamic, and framed within social practices. The present analysis echoes previous work that shows the use of Spanish to English or English to Spanish as one way bilingual Latinxs use hybrid repertoires to accomplish meaning-making practices (Zentella, 1997). The particular discursive and pragmatic uses of tutors' change of named language also highlight the linguistic practice as a reaction and appropriation of a particular socially situated interaction, highlighting speakers' ability to control changing languages as a way to appropriate the literacy practices best suited to their bilingual interactions as well as their social reality as bilingual individuals.

Changes of named languages occurring in response to external factors, as noted, happen when speakers mention cultural references of a particular language, as well as when contextual changes occur—as in when speakers refer to topics, objects, or items that are related to a particular language. In the data, we see an illustrative example of these changes in language in two instances. First, Maité, who had been working as a tutor for one year, switches from Spanish to English as she concludes a tutoring session with a student referring to the course's timeline, which was interrupted by a short week when Thanksgiving is celebrated and no classes are held. Then, as she refers to the software and visual mode of the final presentation the student was assigned, she refers to it in English. As seen in the following interaction, she uses English to refer to "Thanksgiving Break" and "PowerPoint slides" even though the rest of the interaction is in Spanish:

Maité: Y um después de eso vamos a tener **Thanksgiving Break** WOO, y um vamos a empezar con las presentaciones entonces (.) ¿supongo que es como con **Powerpoint slides**? No estoy segura.

And then um we are going to have Thanksgiving Break WOO, and um we are going to start with the presentations so, I guess it will be just like with the Power Point slides? I am not sure.

In another instance, Esmeralda intentionally uses both Spanish to English as she quotes and paraphrases while reading a student's text (in Spanish) out loud, but comments on it in English:

Esmeralda: <Esmeralda reads out loud from students' computer screen> Una vez nosotros cuando <facing student> **Sorry, that's the part- (.) excuse me.** <Continues to read out loud> Una vez cuando nosotros teníamos xxx-

One time when we were- sorry, that's the part- excuse me. One time when we had-

Other types of elements from Spanish into English used by tutors included reformulations and automated speech, such as Cristal's use of 'I mean' in a Spanish conversation about the preterit:

Cristal: Apenas está haciendo la acción (.) **I mean** SÍ está en el pasado ((pero))

You're just doing the action. I mean, yes it is in the past.

Student: Mhm

Another example is the stylistic use of "*Mira*, you see?" Cristal, who joined the tutor cohort for the first time several months earlier, uses this phrasing in the exchange transcribed next to emphasize the contrast in pronunciation as she works with a student on the concept of prosody in the following interaction:

Student: <repeats pronunciation> di fi CIL

Cristal: no lo dirías

You wouldn't say that

Student: <talks to herself> estuvo di FI cil- ((estuvo))

It was diFFIcult

Cristal: di FI cil

Student: <repeats> di FI cil

Cristal: Mira, **you see?**

Look, you see?

Student: Ohh.

Other ways in which tutors mobilized translanguaging between Spanish and English in the interaction are also used for elaboration. During a tutoring session, both Vanessa and Joaquín, brand new tutors in the program, elaborate on the topic they are discussing with their tutees by using English. Vanessa goes into English to more efficiently engage her student in a discussion of why the sentence "en el canal cinco daban un partido" (*on channel five they showed a game*) utilizes a plural verb conjugation even though it has a singular subject:

Vanessa: Cinco es uno, pero cuando piensas en un canal, un canal

Five is one, but when you think of a cannel, a channel

Student: Hmm

Vanessa: ¿Quién está-? xxx ¿quién está (haciendo) ese canal? Es- digamos, **when you think of a channel, a channel kinda doesn't run itself, but there is people behind it, right?**

Who is- who is doing the channel? It's- let's say, when you think of a channel, a channel kinda doesn't run itself, but there is people behind it, right?

80 Literacy and Community Development

Student: Yeah

Vanessa: There's- there's a LOT of people, you cannot just be like **esta persona hace que todo el canal corra. Entonces es muchas personas,** so you are- **el canal cinco es una organización y cuando en cuando piensas en una organización ¿es una persona o varias personas?**

There's- there's a lot of people, you cannot just be like this person makes the whole thing work. So it is a lot of people, so you are- the channel is an organization and when and when you think about an organization, do you think of one or several people?

Student: Varias

Several

Vanessa launches into and exits out of English (from Spanish) to elaborate her explanation to her tutee. The use of translanguaging for elaboration is also combined with its use for emphasis by Esmeralda, who, in this example, employs English to both elaborate that the student should not place too much attention on their text's grammar in a draft assignment and to emphasize that the student should not be overly concerned about a particular grade for grammar on a first draft:

Esmeralda: Lo único que te voy a decir ahorita- porque es la única regla que tengo. Como son borradores no revisaré nada de gramática, **I won't be checking your grammar**. Nomás reviso contenido.

The only thing that I am going to tell you- because it is the only rule I have. Since they are drafts I am not going to review grammar. I won't be checking your grammar. I only review content.

Student: Oh en el borrador

Oh in the draft

Esmeralda: Entonces no es súper importante, **don't (just) panic**. So nomás repasaré como si está bien your format **and stuff like that**, pero no corregiré la gramática.

So it is not super important, don't (just) panic. So just I will review if your format and stuff like that is good, but I won't check grammar.

Lastly, translanguaging occurred in response to lexical needs, or when a tutor quickly relies on English when an equivalent or similar Spanish work fails to momentarily come to mind. In the following example, Joaquín switches to English when referring to technical words of academic writing such as "topic" and "primary source". We assume he does not often generate these words in Spanish since he most frequently uses them in English:

Joaquín: Acuérdate que tú haces un informe muy- (.) el **topic** del- del final es umm esto es un informe lingüístico. Entonces es como un **research paper**. Una persona que sabe eso- que sabe español entonces va a ser tu **primary source**

Remember that you make a report that is- the topic of- at the end is um, this is a linguistic report. So it's like a research paper. A person that knows- that knows Spanish is going to be your primary source

The foregoing examples illustrate how tutors' translanguaging reflects the socially situated nature of the way they deploy English with Spanish and vice versa, and that they use this literacy practice to leverage their bilingual repertoires as a resource for further academic literacy development.

Tutors' translanguaging, or the hybridity of their literacy practices, is also illustrated in the use of academic language along with language not traditionally mobilized in academic spaces, according to functional iterations of what has traditionally been understood as "academic". As explained in Chapter 1 and the beginning of this chapter, problematizing the very notion of "academic language" is crucial in the construction of equitable pedagogies that can intentionally leverage heritage language practices with notions of "formal" or "standard" language within literacy development. To highlight tutors' linguistic hybridity and the various linguistic repertoires involved in their translanguaging, as well as to identify effective ways of incorporating heritage language practices into pedagogical frameworks, I find it useful to categorize examples of language not traditionally common in academic spaces used by peer tutors during tutoring sessions. Importantly, tutors' use of these linguistic elements is crucial in how they successfully mobilize the socially situated goals of their literacy practices, as I show in the second part of this chapter. As a first illustration, tutors used lexical items such as the use of "grado" as a semantic extension for *grade*:

Maité: okay muy bien (…) y ya te dio un **grado** para esto

Okay um very good, and she already gave you a grade for that

Concepción: ¿y les van a dar un mejor **grado**?

And they will give them a better grade?

Vanessa: El **grado** de tutoría sí, hasta el final

The tutoring grade, yes, until the end

Esmeralda: Si sé que te- que te baja el **grado**, pero lo que yo sé te lo baja después de la tercera falta no después de la primera

82 Literacy and Community Development

Yes I know that- that it lowers your grade, but what I know is that it lowers it after your third absence and not your first

Other items such as the lexical borrowing "chansa" for *chance* are used during an interaction between Joaquín and Concepción:

Joaquín: Si quieres indicarle haber si te da otra **chansa**

If you want you can tell her to see if she will give you another chance

Concepción: Okay so ojalá y les den **chansa** de que lo entreguen más tarde

Okay so hopefully and they give you a chance to submit later

Importantly, dialectal features of tutors' regional varieties of Spanish included mostly morphological variations of referential varieties of Spanish spoken in the US, specifically those varieties of recently arrived immigrants, including, in its majority but not limited to, Mexican and Central American immigrants (Escobar & Potowski, 2015). As such, we see in the data morphological features, such as the insertion of –s for the second person in the preterit, in Cristal's question:

Cristal: ¿Entonces puedes decir el uso de los automóviles al igual que o tanto como o- (…) so ya le **agarrastes**?

So you can say the use of cars as well as or as much as- so, you got it?

Archaic verbal forms, such as in "haiga" for the present (perfect) subjunctive third person form of the auxiliary verb "haber", were also present in the data, such as in Joaquín and Esmeralda:

Joaquín: Él prepa- él preparaba. Entonces para que **haiga** concordancia

He was pre- he prepared. So that there is agreement

Esmeralda: Entonces la contaminación de los automóviles verdad. Causa que **haiga** problemas

So car pollution, right. It causes that there be problems

When considering the pedagogical implications of using linguistic elements not traditionally used in academic spaces and in regard to Spanish curricula for heritage speakers, Villa (1996) highlights that the lack of dialectal variation in the Spanish as heritage language classroom does not represent language as it is used in the speech community. It therefore fails to capture "the linguistic dynamics of human communication, which is in constant development" (Villa, 1996, p. 193). This dynamic is clearly exemplified in the ways that tutors use regional and informal registers in their linguistic repertoires when they work with students in an academic space, alongside uses of language deemed more "formal" or "academic". This type of translanguaging is the most accessible; that which "reduces negative affective reactions and serves as an unsurpassed base for further development of language skills" (Villa, 1996, p. 195).

Considering tutors' translanguaging in the foregoing data, it is my view that pedagogical design in Spanish should model real-life communication across the US and throughout the entire Spanish-speaking world. Doing so would extend and enhance students' ability to make and negotiate meaning in social interaction and the skills to adapt to contextual variations calling for different registers—all for which students' linguistic repertoires, including features of regional varieties, can be leveraged for the purposes of developing "the language of school"[1]. Thus, I suggest that tutors' translanguaging within their repertoires, as shown in this work, is an important component of both tutors' and tutees' Spanish academic literacy development, as they represent the cultural pluralism necessary for Spanish revitalization.

Tutors' Literacy Practices for Academic Development and Community Building

Considering the relevance of tutors' consistent translanguaging throughout all tutoring sessions for academic learning, in this section, I examine the goals tutors use to mobilize hybrid literacy practices by describing the socially meaningful context in which they are used. I do this via thematic analysis (Bernard & Ryan, 2010) of video recording transcriptions, including all tutoring sessions for every tutor program participant, where particular literacy practices co-occur with particular socially situated and socially meaningful interactions.

As I studied the sessions' transcriptions, I created a list of coding categories for the types of interactions I was observing, including both literacy practices and other types of interactions (e.g., tutor demonstrating empathy to student, use of English and Spanish, tutor using additional resources in the session, tutor using metalinguistic vocabulary, etc.). As I reviewed these codes, I searched for overarching themes or descriptions that could more systematically encompass the original list of codes. Lastly, I developed a final list of themes that represented strong trends across the data.

The final themes that illustrate the goals of literacy practices and emerged from thematic coding are mapped as follows.

I refer to the tutoring session (situated in the tutoring room) as "peer-to-peer collaborative academic language learning" given its strong interactional (i.e., collaborative) nature. Another contributing factor of such labeling is that despite the session being situated outside the classroom, it does represent an academic context of participation that is designed to support a formal, academic curriculum grounded in academic literacy. The two branches immediately extending from the center illustrate data that describe the linguistic practices of tutors, or what I call "linguistic hybridity". This term refers to instances of translanguaging in tutor–tutee interactions.

FIGURE 3.1 Illustrative view of tutors' socially centered literacy practice goals.

The remaining branches of the diagram, situated at the far left and the right of Figure 3.1, describe the goals with which tutors mobilized particular literacy practices. They are organized in two overarching themes: "Academic Literacy Development" and "Community Building".

Academic Literacy Development

The codes included in this section describe the development of academic literacy as one of the main goals of the particular practices mobilized by tutors during a tutoring session. These practices function under the definition of academic literacy following what Lea and Street call "the academic literacies model" that is "concerned with meaning making, identity, power, and authority" as well as "viewing the process of [acquiring literacy] as complex, dynamic, nuanced, situated, and involving both epistemological issues and social processes, including power relations among people, institutions and social identities" (2006, p. 396). Thus, critically for this analysis, "academic literacy" is not simply understood as a process of acquisition and acculturation into the academic genres of educational contexts and specific subject areas (such as, for example, the argumentative essay in a Spanish course). Rather, this work's notion of "academic literacy" also includes considerations of larger institutional requirements as well as contextual variation across professors, course requirements, assignment requirements, and the like. By considering the relationship of epistemology and language variation (Lea & Street, 2006) not just in the subject area but also in specific and larger contexts of academic participation (i.e., the tutoring session, courses across the curriculum, office hours, peer-to-peer collaborative enterprises, etc.), we are able to frame academic literacy as contested and negotiated, supporting "discussions of larger forces that shape learning environments in schools" (Molle, 2015, p. 15).

Academic Support

Beyond contributing to specific writing skills around particular course writing assignments, tutors also consistently were vigilant in understanding that tutees' academic literacy is pertinent to students' overall academic success. According to the present thematic analysis, "academic support" is defined as:

Any instance where the tutor supports learners in accessing and using pertinent information to manage their academic trajectories within and beyond the institution: what classes to take/when, the importance of visiting professors for visiting hours, where to get academic support, "unwritten requirements", steps to take if in dismissal, etc.

To illustrate, I describe three separate instances during which Esmeralda and Vanessa mobilize the theme of Academic Support in the data. They provide information regarding the successful navigation of the Learning Management System (LMS) to access instructor feedback, determine the absence policy of the course, and, lastly, navigate what courses tutees should take based on particular professional aspirations shared by tutor and tutee. Some of these instances, explained in Chapter 2, also illustrate separate uses of the literacy practices "peer-to-peer academic advising" and "consulting an expert".

In the first instance, Esmeralda, along with me, walks the tutee through accessing instructor feedback. The ability to access the instructor's comments on Canvas (the LMS used by the course) is a basic yet crucial academic skill that students must cultivate to complete future drafts of a writing assignment and therefore demonstrate writing progress. It is one of the most heavily graded aspects of the course. In the interaction featured next, Esmeralda explains the final assignment's composition to the student, which will be a reflection on the student's best essay. While doing so, she explains that, in order to determine which essay to reflect upon, the tutee must study the instructor's feedback on previous essays. Here, as Esmeralda realizes that her student does not actually know how to access this feedback, she turns to the student's laptop and starts navigating Canvas. Esmeralda knows the student must find a particular section on the assignment's rubric that says "View Feedback", but she is unable to locate it. Once Esmeralda realizes she is unable to find the necessary link on Canvas, she turns to me and asks me, an expert, for help, mobilizing one of the literacy practices described in the previous section. In the following exchange, both Esmeralda and I guide the student toward finding the section for feedback and what action to take given that she does not have the appropriate software to actually read annotated versions of her drafts:

Lina: Entonces se abre ese, lo bajas y en ese- **wait (.)** entonces ¿no

tienes Acrobat Reader? ¿No tienes este? <points to screen>

So then you open that one, you download and there- wait. So you don't have Acrobat Reader? You don't have that one?

Esmeralda: The PDF reader?

Student: <shakes head>

Lina: Ajá

Uh huh

86 Literacy and Community Development

Esmeralda: Okay, **use a school computer, the s– the school computer will have the Adobe PDF Acrobat thing**

Besides suggesting that the student should use a school computer lab, Esmeralda also indicates that in the next session, her student must print out annotated versions of her essays to closely study the instructor's feedback and decide which essay is best to revise for the final course assignment.

It is crucial to note here that navigating the course's LMS directly affects the student's academic literacy development; without access to instructor feedback, the student would be unable to understand what aspects of her literacy need development or to build an understanding of the instructor's expectations and norms for the genre or assignment. By modeling "consulting an expert" to the instructor (a literacy practice detailed in Chapter 2, with the instructor in this case, me), Esmeralda is directly offering academic support to her student—support without which the student's academic literacy development would be negatively impacted.

In another instance, Vanessa and her student spend some time discussing what courses the student should take for the following quarter, given that the student hopes to apply to dental school after graduating. Besides modeling "consulting an expert" by accessing resources online, as an NPB (Neurology, Physiology, and Biology) major and a sophomore who has taken many science courses, Vanessa also issues very specific advice to the student regarding what courses she should take:

Vanessa: ¿Cuál es tu- cuál es lo que estás tomando ahorita, ese

workload? *¿Quién es tu maestra?*

What is your- what is it that you are taking now, that workload? Who is your instructor?

Student: <Says name of instructor>, es güerita-

She's white-

Vanessa: ¿Con lentes grandes? Fue profesora- instructora, a mí me tocó

también y dije **I want her to be my professor**. *Oh muy bien. Es buena instructora. Sí, entonces bueno, hay que hacerle caso. Yo tomé a <says name of different instructor>*

She wears large glasses? She was my professor- instructor, I had her too and I said I want her to by my professor. That's good. She's a great instructor. Yes, okay well, you have to listen to her. I took <instructor's name>

Student: <nods>

Vanessa: Es rápido. **I felt like he was, really fast.**

He's fast. I feel like he was, really fast.

Student: Sí, mi compañera tiene a <instructor's name> también

Yeah my friend has <instructor's name> also

Vanessa: Es buen profesor pero <pretends as if writing quickly on board> es súper **fast writer** pero a lo mejor eso sería mejor.

He's a good professor, but he is a super fast writer but maybe that would be better.

Right before this interaction, Vanessa and her student also discuss a particular course they have both taken with an instructor in the Chicana/o Studies department. When they mention the instructor's name, another tutor in the room chimes in and says she loved the course she took with this instructor. Vanessa notes that students often want to take the instructor's courses in question given his popularity.

We see here that Vanessa is providing her student an "insider" or experienced knowledge of which instructors have favorable or unfavorable reputations among students. This informational advice increases the student's likelihood of enrolling in a course that will offer her relevant and positive experiences, thus contributing to the student's academic success, motivation, and sense of belonging in that course. This, once again, is the sort of information students are often unaware of or lack access to acquire—especially those unfamiliar with the norms of the institution such as first-generation students. The result is a default reliance on their instincts when choosing a particular instructor for a class. Vanessa, thus, relies on her own experience as a student with the same academic interest as her tutee to provide academic support.

Lastly, in another instance, Esmeralda works with a student concerned about a course grade, noting that despite having one absence, her grade has decreased substantially. After re-explaining the absence policy of the course to her student, Esmeralda encourages her to visit her instructor and discuss why one absence has so significantly affected her grade:

Esmeralda: Yeah ok so then go ahead- **pregúntale, nomás dile. Um y luego también-**

Yeah okay so then go ahead- ask her, just tell her. Um and then also-

Student: xxx

Esmeralda: Yeah no, either way debería estar también en su syllabus, si

pierden más de eso like-

Yeah no, either way it should be in her syllabus, if you lose more than that like-

Student: Yo no sabía que te baja tanto por una clase

I didn't know it went down so much after one class

88 Literacy and Community Development

Esmeralda: Entonces, de la forma que ahorita está es que no- este la primera

clase no te afecta si tienes excusas. Pero ya la tercera falta más adelante te baja **half a letter grade each time which is why** *estás viendo que bajó hasta cin- hasta och-* **whatever it is. It's half a letter grade**. *Pero sí, déjale saber de esto*

So, the way it is now is that it doesn't- like, the first class does not affect you if you have an excuse. But then the third absence later on costs half a letter grade each time which is why you are seeing it go down to five- to eight- whatever it is. It's half a letter grade. But yes, let her know about this

Despite Esmeralda's inability to fully explain why the student's grade has decreased more than it should have per the course's absence policy, she urges her student to discuss the impact with her instructor, noting the possibility that it could be a mistake, and that the instructor can correct it. This, in fact, is a recurring issue among the students enrolled in our course for Spanish heritage students, since any absence is actually counted against them per the course's absence policy and is not corrected until the end of the course. Having been an instructor for this course, I know students often have questions about this policy, but it is not until they come and speak to me directly that I am able to explain how the system reflects their absences within their grades. By encouraging the student to speak directly to her instructor, Esmeralda is urging her tutee to mobilize a particular academic practice important for students' success—establishing and maintaining close contact with instructors regarding, for example, attendance policies. Therefore, both the re-explanation of the absence policy as well as the instruction to contact the instructor directly represent an instance of 'academic support". This support is relevant to the student's academic literacy development as she navigates academic contexts of participation such as reading and understanding the course's syllabus and initiating a conversation about her grade and progress in the course with her instructor of record.

Tutor as Expert

In order to provide academic support as a contribution to their students' academic literacy development, tutors consistently position themselves as experts with the purpose of mediating particular academic tasks when working with their students. "Tutor as expert", as defined by the present thematic analysis, includes any instance which follows this definition:

> The tutor taking the role of the instructor, that is, passing on information about the design of the course, or about any particular topic of content as a fact (grammar, content, writing, etc.).

As the definition states, "tutor as expert" was noted as more commonly utilized when tutors were directly working with students on a written assignment,

Literacy and Community Development **89**

specifically when students were acculturating to a particular feature of academic writing as required by the courses' curriculum.

To illustrate this theme, I will share the following instance during which Teresa is revising an essay with her student, noting the strategies she uses to position herself as the expert, much like an instructor would.

Maité: Stats?

Student: Mm?

Maité: ¿Es lo que estabas haciendo en la mañana?

Is that what you were doing this morning?

Student: Sí

Yes

Maité: ¿Sabes cómo se dice **stats** en español?

Do you know how to say "stats" in Spanish?

Student: ¿Estatísticas?

Maité: Huh?

Student: ¿Estatísticas? Esta–

Maité: ESTADÍSTICAS

STATS

Student: –dísticas

Student: Estadística. Es lo que dije, estadísticas

Stats. That's what I said, stats

Maité: Dijiste "estatísticas". Y ahí hay video de que dijiste "estatística" @@ <points to screen>

You said "estatísticas". And there's a video that you said "estatística"

Student: Primero pero después, a ver–

First but then, let's see–

Maité: Cuando estaba tomando esa clase me acuerdo que le hablé a mi mamá un día en la mañana bien enojada–

When I was taking this class I remember that I told my mom one day when I was really mad–

Student: <mumbles> Estadísticas–

Stats–

90 Literacy and Community Development

Maité: Y dije estatísticas porque estaba enojada y no estaba pensando, y me dijo no mensa, se dice "estadísticas". Eehh- **I'm like okayyyy.** Y me dijo yo te voy a quitar tu- tu trabajo de tutora @@

> *And I said "estatísticas" because I was mad and I wasn't thinking, and she said no silly, you say "stats". Eeehh- I'm like okayyy. And she said I'm taking your tutor job*

Before Maité begins to work with the student's text, she engages in conversation with him about a midterm he has just completed before coming to the session. When the student incorrectly pronounces the midterm's subject, saying "*está istica" and mirroring the English pronunciation, Maité promptly corrects him. Prior to correcting him, however, Maité prompts the student to pronounce the word, sensing that he may be pronouncing it incorrectly. The sense that Maité has about her student's pronunciation of the word "estadística", as we see, is directly based on her own history of incorrectly pronouncing the word (imitating the English spelling), as she illustrates in the brief personal narrative she shares towards the end of this interaction. Thus, Maité uses the literacy practice of "guiding student responses" (see Chapter 2) to correct her student. She does so while positioning herself as the expert in the interaction but relies on her own learning trajectory to prompt this particular pronunciation mistake. At the end of this interaction, we see the student uptake the correct word pronunciation when he repeats (under his breath) the word "estadísticas" as Maité is sharing the story of how she learned to pronounce the word correctly.

Later in the same interaction, Maité is discussing the correct use of commas in declarative clauses with her student, once again positioning herself as the expert:

Maité: El bilingüismo. Aquí no ocupas coma. No se- no se lee <reads out loud> el bilingüismo (…) no solo es un fenómeno en las Américas (…) sino casi en todo el mundo entero (…) <begins sentence again> El bilingüismo no solo es un fenómeno en las amer- un fenómeno en las américas sino en el mundo entero <ends reading> Entonces no ocupas poner una coma

> *Bilingualism. Here you don't need a comma. You don't- you don't read "Bilingualism (…) is not only a phenomenon in the Americas (…) but in the entire world (…)" "Bilingualism isn't a phenomenon in the Amer- a phenomenon in the Americas but in the entire world". So you don't need a comma*

Student: Oh okay

Maité: En la mayoría de las veces cuando tienes um oración, coma, oración, coma, la oración es como un sándwich <uses air quotes> y estamos diciendo que lo que está en el medio si no estuviera ahí <referencing the use of comas> todavía tendría uh- sentido la oración

> *The majority of times when you have um, sentence, comma, sentence, comma, the sentences is like a sandwhich, and we are saying that what is in the middle if it wasn't there the sentence would still make sense*

Literacy and Community Development **91**

Student: Pero que- ¿qué no es como la de inglés?

But, it isn't like English?

Maité: Sí, por ejemplo, si tuvieras eso entonces sería-

Yes, for example, if you had that then it would be

Student: Not only dadada but (…) and there's two commas?

Maité: Well take- quita lo que está en el medio. <reads outloud> El bilingüismo sino en todo el mundo entero <ends reading>. Normalmente cuando tienes algo en comas en el medio **it's 'cause it's not really necessary to have it there. Like the sentence should still make sense if you didn't have this in the middle**

Well take- take what is in the middle. "Bilingualism but in the entire world". Normally when you have something in between commas in the middle it's 'cause it's not really necessary to have it there. Like the sentence should still make sense if you didn't have this in the middle

Student: Oh, okay

Maité does not identify that her student's confusion regarding comma use in this declarative clause could be due to his assumption that the clauses he has written are comparative (which would take commas). Yet she illustrates the use (or lack) of commas in declarative clauses by using the metaphor of a sandwich, stating to her student that "if you take the commas out"—or the lettuce, per the metaphor—the sentence should still make sense. She then reads the remaining clause as if the middle clause was removed, illustrating to the student that the remaining sentence does not stand on its own, and therefore, does not take commas (as a declarative statement).

Even though the student expresses agreement at the end of this interaction, it is still unclear whether, moving forward, he will continue to properly use commas in declarative clauses, as I do not have the students' written productions as evidence. However, a pivotal outcome of this interaction is the academic skill Maité presents to her tutee through the practice of guiding his response. This demonstrates the ability to illustrate a grammatical concept through the use of a metaphor for illustrative purposes, or "defining norms of academic writing", another literacy practice explained in Chapter 2. Additionally, Maité's switch to English at the end of the interaction, used to emphasize the main point of her argument, which includes that it is "not really necessary to have it [the comma] there" and that "the sentence should still make sense if you didn't have this [the comma] in the middle", better illustrates this particular notion to the student, who—as evidenced in his first draft—shows a lack of acquisition of this particular skill. Regardless of whether the student does or does not acquire an enduring knowledge of the standard use of comas during this interaction, as Maité positions herself as an expert, she offers

92 Literacy and Community Development

the student academic support that an instructor in a traditional classroom setting—who may be unwilling to use English and who would not interact with a student one-on-one as a tutor and tutee do—would not be able to offer.

Community Building

When discussing the pedagogical goals of utmost importance in heritage language pedagogy, one of Martínez's main arguments is that appropriate language instruction can be a powerful engine for the improvement of heritage language communities (2016). However, he posits that the inclusion of standards-based pedagogical models in isolation from the community context may potentially devalue the linguistic repertoires and practices of the heritage language student community, especially their community-based learning identities. As the author explains, the heritage language research agenda has revealed "a profound embeddedness of the community in heritage language education" (Martínez, 2016, p. 43).

This section illustrates how the tutoring room is the locus for the development of a particular student-led learning community which is invested in the improvement of its members. That is, data shows that tutors are consistently invested in their students' academic (and personal) well-being. This positions the teaching and learning environment of the tutoring room as an opportunity to build a community of heritage language speakers who share particular practices and experiences, creating a sense of belonging for its members. By providing an opportunity for community building, the tutoring room represents a pedagogical opportunity for students (both tutors and tutees) to participate in language maintenance and language revitalization activities in their own communities (as they engage in translanguaging and Spanish academic literacy with other heritage speakers) and to mobilize agency in promoting positive attitudes outside of the classroom.

Academic Empathy

Besides providing students with tools for academic success and positioning themselves as experts, tutors also position themselves as learners. In doing so, they contribute to students' overall experience as college students who are members of a large, public campus, rather than solely as members of a particular Spanish course. "Academic empathy", as defined by the present thematic analysis, includes any instance which follows this definition:

> Regard for students' academic experiences (i.e., wearing their shoes), including emotional support with personal matters that affect academic life and regard for students' (academic) experience in the tutoring session.

In the following instance, Joaquín works with a student who is struggling to come to terms with his less-than-desirable performance in the course. This student, as Joaquín explained to me in an interview, had consistently shared with Joaquín that he was struggling to find friends and that he often felt alone. As Joaquín stated, one Sunday the two ran into each other at one of the campus dining rooms and ate together. During this time, Joaquín asked his student more about his personal experience as a college student, and the two discussed possible solutions to his loneliness. In the following interaction, Joaquín demonstrates academic empathy when he makes an effort for his student to consider that while the course has almost finished, there is still room for improvement in his final grade:

Joaquín: Yeah porque el ejercicio cuesta bastante. No me acuerdo qué

está en el sílabo. Está escrito, es diez por ciento de tu clase, de tu grado

Yeah because the activity is worth a lot. I don't remember what is in the syllabus. It's there, it is 10% of your course, of your grade

Student: So lo más que pue- todavía puedo agarrar una A

So the most I can- I can still get an A

Joaquín: A menos

A minus

Student: Pero esto ya se acabó

But it's over

Joaquín: Haste cuenta que yo te doy diez por ciento también de tu grado

Assume that I give you 10% too for your grade

Student: Hmm pero todavía falta xxx fue mi culpa

Hmm but I am still missing xxx it was my fault

Joaquín: Nunca sabes cómo te puede ir al final

You never know how it can go in the end

Student: Huh?

Joaquín: Nunca sabes cómo te puede ir al final. Con que le sigas dando ganas y termines fuerte. **Finish strong**

You don't know how you will do in the end. As long as you keep trying and you finish strong. Finish strong

As Joaquín encourages his student, he offers him empathy to not give up and to consider that much can happen in the last weeks of the academic quarter, including the fact that the student will receive full credit for his tutoring attendance, which has been impeccable, therefore improving his final grade. In this sense, Joaquín is also mobilizing "peer-to-peer academic advising", another literacy

94 Literacy and Community Development

practice explored in Chapter 2. Additionally, at the end of the interaction, Joaquín uses English to emphasize his intention of encouragement, elaborating on the sentiment of not giving up at the end of the interaction and illustrating Joaquín's translanguaging for the explicit purposes of cultivating community building and utilizing academic empathy, as he uses both languages (also spoken by the student) to support a peer.

Belonging to a Community

Beyond being experts, tutors also embody the kind of empathy that a peer, ally, or friend might offer. In doing so, tutors consistently put forth the message that the tutoring room is, above all, a place where tutors and students, as like-minded individuals, belong. It is a place, that is, that can offer a safe and nurturing community. Across the data, tutors and students connect to such an extensive degree that they empathize with each other around various shared issues such as financial difficulty, food preferences, and academic challenges, for example.

Here, I frame "belonging to a community" as:

> Overt reference to learning as a collective process (as applied to both the tutee and tutor), including the creation of a "feels like home" environment; regard for students' lives outside the program.

In the following interaction, Concepción and her tutee have just finished their last session before Thanksgiving. Before the student departs the tutoring room, they talk about their plans for the break, and then commiserate about the financial hardship of being a college student and the distinctive pleasure of enjoying a homecooked meal:

Concepción: Vas a estar bien, ya mero terminamos

You will be okay, we're almost done

Student: I know (.) y de todas maneras la otra semana ni es una completa

I know and anyways next week isn't even a whole week

Concepción: Va a ser el día de Acción de Gracias (.) ¿Vas a ir a casa o te quedas?

It's going to be Thanksgiving. Are you going home or are you staying?

Student: No, SÍ me iba a quedar, pero mi amiga me dijo okay um, mi papá va a venir ¿quieres venir con nosotros? Okay pues @@ yo no quería pagar un avión porque muchos- un **ticket** de avión pues todos (.) quieren hacer eso, pero yo no tengo dinero para eso, yo me quedo aquí no los miro hasta-

No, I was going to stay, but my friend told me okay um, my dad is going to come do you want to come? Okay well I didn't want to pay for an airplane ticket because

a lot- an airplane ticket because everyone wants to do that, but I don't have money
for that, so I will stay here and I will not see them until-

Concepción: The ((struggle))

Student: Hasta el uh huh–

Until uh-

Concepción: Yeah it's hard, bueno pues que te diviertas y comes mucho

Yeah it's hard, well I hope you have fun and that you eat a lot

Student: Sí, me voy a traer la comida pa' atrás porque ni cocino acá

Yes, I'm going to bring food back because here I don't really cook

Concepción: Ay sí, el domingo fui a visitar a mi mamá y había hecho tortillas
de harina **and I was just like uuh** <pretends to be smelling and enjoying
an object>

Oh yes, on Sunday I went to visit my mom and she had made flour tortillas and I
was like uuuh

Student: Cuando mi abuelita estaba– estaba, no me acuerdo qué semana era
estaba todavía aquí y ella estaba– es de México entonces pues visitó a mi
papá y hizo también torti- a tortillas de- sí dijistes de harina, ¿verdad? Sí,
entonces- entonces cuando vinieron y eso era como que dos semanas que
mi abuelita nos visitó me trajo mi mamá- um mi tort-mis tortillas entonces
me hacía mis burritos con frijoles con queso fresco

When my grandma was- was, I don't remember what week it was that she was still
here and she was- she's from Mexico so well she was visiting my dad and she also
made torti- um flour you said flour tortillas right? Yes so- so when they came and
that was like two weeks that my grandma visited and brought my mom- um, my
tortillas so she made me burritos with beans and queso fresco

Concepción: @@

Here, Concepción has less guidance to offer to the student in terms of particular
skills for academic development and success, while providing more direction while
positioning herself as another like-minded individual who shares the types of
experiences that the student describes. When the student references being unable
to purchase an airplane ticket to visit her family due to lack of funds, Concepción
makes reference to a well-known saying among peers who struggle with financial hardship: "the struggle". She chooses to reference "the struggle" in English
to again position herself as someone who can, both personally and linguistically,
relate to her student—deepening the tutor–tutee collaborative relationship.

After discussing the implications of financial hardship, Concepción makes
reference to her mother's home-cooked comfort food, and how much it means

96 Literacy and Community Development

to her to be able to enjoy *tortillas de harina* (or flour tortillas). This then prompts the student to engage in telling her tutor a personal story (mirroring Esmeralda's personal storytelling as a literacy practice) about a similar situation in which her mother brought her homemade tortillas and how much she enjoyed accessing her grandmother's cooking, especially as she did not do much cooking herself while in college. The two connect interpersonally through very specific extra-academic experiences before parting for the break.

Often, first-generation students who are underrepresented across the academic campus have a challenging time finding like-minded peers who face the same struggles while in college. Indeed, Esmeralda has shared her own experience as a first-year engineering major, struggling not just with the academic demands of her major but also with the lack of support from her family, who had not wanted her to leave their hometown to attend college. Esmeralda often refers to finding her "family" in the tutoring room after taking courses in the program Spanish for Native Speakers and working as a tutor, framing her work as a peer tutor as the experience that encouraged her to remain a student and not drop out of college. The types of relationships, friendships, and possibilities for student academic success that develop in a collaborative space, such as the tutoring room, host implications for the teaching and learning of Spanish as a heritage language at this institution.

Considerations for Student Impact

In conceiving academic discourse as situated practice, this section explored the varied linguistic resources from which tutors draw to participate in the development of Spanish academic literacy through specific socially situated goals. The goal of this exploration is to show what kinds of translingual literacy practices tutors mobilize as they work with their tutees. I reveal that tutors' positioning of translanguaging within academic practice (that is, as a linguistic tool to mobilize literacy practices in an academic setting for academic purposes) is the most cohesive way in which they are transforming the relationship between everyday linguistic practices and academic knowledge (Martínez, 2016). Tutors are creating educational experiences through a sense of belonging where their language and literacy practices are reflected and thus, modeling equitable pedagogies. Further, this chapter conceptualized literacy as practice, delineating the socially situated goals from which tutors draw as they mobilize literacy practices that leverage sessions in support of their tutees. The series of literacy practices explored in Chapter 2, which recur in this chapter's data as well, demonstrates the interrelated relationship of the various sociocultural contexts of participation in which these young people exist. By highlighting the goals tutors use to mobilize these literacy practices, as well as the hybridity apparent in their linguistic repertoires, I suggest that tutors consistently contribute to both their students' academic literacy development and their social experience as members of a like-minded community by using a rich range of linguistic and literacy resources in both Spanish and English.

Literacy and Community Development **97**

While more research is needed to explore the true impact of the tutors' literacy practices on tutees' academic literacy development, analysis of tutors' translanguaging practices helps us better understand how heritage speakers mobilize their linguistic repertoire to access academic language, thus generating knowledge about similar literacy practices of other Spanish heritage speakers in comparable programs. This emerging knowledge can then inform pedagogical frameworks that better leverage students' linguistic resources for learning. With such an approach, researchers and educators can move toward more equitable instruction for speakers of Spanish as a heritage language, as we develop educational experiences for students in which the full range of their linguistic resources is used in the service of their learning. Ideas on how to develop approaches that place heritage language practices at the forefront of heritage language teaching and learning are shared throughout Chapter 6.

In the next chapter, I continue exploring the data through a second methodological framework rooted in discourse analysis. As I will show, this analysis continues to highlight the impactful role that tutors, as they translanguage in their interactions with tutees, play within this bilingual, peer-to-peer collaborative academic experience.

Note

1 For an example of an instructional text that promotes linguistic variation—including stigmatized varieties widely spoken in the US and the Spanish-speaking world—into the teaching of Spanish grammar, see Powtowski and Shin (2019).

References

Bailey, A., & Orellana, M. F. (2015). Adolescent development and everyday language practices: Implications for the academic literacy of multilingual learners. In D. Molle, E. Sato, T. Boals, & C. A. Hedgspeth (Eds.), *Multilingual Learners and Academic Literacies* (pp. 65–86). New York: Routledge.

Bernard, H. R., & Ryan, G. W. (2010). Chapter 3: *Finding Themes. Analyzing Qualitative Data: Systematic Approaches.* Thousand Oaks: SAGE Publications.

Canagarajah, A. S. (2013). *Translingual Practice: Global Englishes and Cosmopolitan Relations.* Abingdon, Oxon: Routledge.

Escobar, A. M., & Potowski, K. (2015). *El español de los Estados Unidos.* Cambridge: Cambridge University Press.

Flores, N. (2015). *Is it Time for a Moratorium on Academic Language?* https://educationallinguist .wordpress.com/2015/10/01/is-it-time-for-a-moratorium-on-academic-language/

García, O. (2009a). *Bilingual education in the 21st century: A global perspective.* Malden, MA and Oxford: Wiley/Blackwell

García, O., & Kleyn, T. (2016). *Translanguaging with Multilingual Students. Learning from Classroom Moments.* New York and London: Routledge.

García, O., & Wei, L. (2014). *Translanguaging: Language, Bilingualism and Education.* New York and London: Palgrave MacMillan.

Heller, M. (1999). *Linguistic minorities and modernity: A sociolinguistic ethnography.* London: Longman.

98 Literacy and Community Development

Lea, M. R., & Street, B. V. (2006). The "academic literacies" model: Theory and applications. *Theory into Practice*, *45*(4), 368–377.

Martínez, G. (2016). Goals and beyond in heritage language education. In M. Fairclough & S. Beaudrie (Eds.), *Innovative Strategies for Heritage Language Teaching: A Practical Guide for the Classroom* (pp. 39–55). Washington, DC: Georgetown University Press.

Molle, D. (2015). Academic language and academic literacies: Mapping a relationship. In D. Molle, E. Sato, T. Boals, & C. A. Hedgspeth (Eds.), *Multilingual Learners and Academic Literacies* (pp. 13–32). New York: Routledge.

Otheguy, R., García, O., & Reid, W. (2015). Clarifying translanguaging and deconstructing named languages: A perspective from linguistics. *Applied Linguistics Review*, *6*(3), 281–307.

Potowski, K., & Shin, N. (2019). *Gramática española. Variación social.* New York: Routledge.

Villa, D. J. (1996). Choosing a "standard" variety of Spanish for the instruction of native Spanish speakers in the U.S. *Foreign Language Annals*, *29*(2), 191–200.

Zentella, A. C. (1997). *Growing Up Bilingual: Puerto Rican Children in New York.* New York: Wiley-Blackwell.

4

THE PEER AS THE EXPERT

Tutors Mobilizing Academic Personas

The Relevance of Casual Talk in Heritage Academic Spaces

Following the social literacy framework that guides this book (explained at length in Chapter 1), it is imperative to remember that such theory considers the lines, which have been and continue to be drawn explicitly in most formal academic spaces, separating language as "informal" and "formal" to be truly imaginary. Especially in diverse contexts of teaching and learning, where students bring a variety of linguistic repertoires and ways of expressing themselves that are tied to their personal stories as multicultural individuals, the translanguaging and transgression of prepackaged linguistic borders throughout academic spaces are seen as necessary to observe the linguistic dynamism that can ultimately contribute to academic literacy development. "Formal" academic literacy for heritage students, as I see it, can only come from a place of linguistic freedom and belonging. In other words, we can only hope our students adapt and adopt formal literacies if we first truly explore and make space for the casual, "informal", and, in the case of heritage students, translingual interactions they are most accustomed to mobilizing in order to problematize the very idea of adopting "standard" language norms. This is the reason, in my view, why it is essential to study autonomous, non-traditional academic spaces outside the classroom such as the Spanish heritage program tutoring room described in this book.

The interpersonal underpinnings of tutors' language use, especially as it represents casual, unstructured, and unsupervised talk, are especially pertinent to this analysis, as the bulk of data comes from video transcriptions of tutoring sessions. I understand "casual talk", or what we also know as "informal talk", as a *functionally* motivated, semantic activity. Such language is used to accomplish specific, socially situated tasks through which interlocutors negotiate interpersonal relations. For the present analysis, I identify these socially situated tasks through a systematic analysis of identification utilizing the completed ethnographic analysis. Despite the institutional

DOI: 10.4324/9781003191179-5

100 The Peer as the Expert

implications that still govern the context of study of this book (i.e., tutors and tutees are interacting in an institutional setting following institutional norms), I draw from linguists Eggins and Slade's (1997) definition of casual talk since I find it useful to describe the type of discourse in which tutors and tutees engage unsupervised "informal" talk that responds to social and contextual factors. Eggins and Slade explain that in casual conversation there is an undeniable paradox—while casual talk is the type of talk through which we feel most relaxed, most spontaneous, and most ourselves, it is also a critical site for the social construction of reality: "[Casual conversation] is the only place where we are free to be ourselves and yet, at the same time, we are hardly free at all. We are in fact very busy reflecting and constituting our social world" (Eggins & Slade, 1997, p. 17). Casual conversation, as a way that participants relate to each other in informal settings, is also useful as a tool to uncover the meaning of individuals' interpretation of their experiences, the construction of their worlds, and the meanings they attribute to their experiences. With the combination of ethnographic and linguistic analysis, therefore, this book analyzes casual conversation as a productive way to understand heritage students' use of language and literacy in light of their social experience as students in an academic setting.

Beyond the Classroom: The Tutoring Room as Locus of Study

While this book studies academic literacy, it is intentionally located beyond the traditional classroom setting for various reasons. Firstly, scholarship in Spanish heritage language pedagogy has mostly been carried out in traditional formal teaching contexts, where instructors and/or researchers have studied how students can be socialized into the literacy practices of academic contexts; this often involves top-down methodologies and largely ignores the social implications of learning that extend beyond the classroom. Indeed, especially in higher education contexts, standard language ideologies that place colloquial or informal languages as "irrelevant" are still maintained (Valdés et al., 2006; Achugar & Pessoa, 2009). As such, US Spanish varieties of language, which tend to have greater amounts of features not traditionally deemed as "formal" or "academic", are devalued and considered in need of being "fixed" (Loza & Beaudrie, 2021). Additionally, previous studies which highlight students' experiences for learning often use interviews to extrapolate data (Vergara & Ibarra, 2015; Potowski & Carreira, 2004); few, however, focus on situated discourse as it happens to analyze interaction (such as in Showstack, 2012). The analysis presented here thus offers a unique opportunity to study what truly happens and not what is reported in educational exchanges, providing an even richer analysis.

The literacy standards for the field of Spanish as a Heritage Language Pedagogy (as developed by Valdés [1995] and discussed in Beaudrie, Ducar, and Potowski [2014]) largely involve speaker-oriented goals, such as maintaining the heritage language, expanding the speaker's bilingual range, and the transfer of literacy skills from English to Spanish. However, the field has just begun to (re)imagine Spanish pedagogy (both for second language as well as heritage learners) in ways that are responsive to heritage students' social reality. This includes students' personal trajectories, academic challenges, linguistic practices, and other relevant aspects of the student demographic. As suggested by Loza and Beaudrie (2021), the relevance of critical language awareness (CLA) as a tool to address criticality, social change, and linguistic inclusivity is gaining ground within the field's most recent pedagogical frameworks. As such, the authors highlight the imperative need to "contest and correct the discriminatory practices and discourses that disparage Spanish heritage language students and their bilingual varieties" (2021, p. 236). Additionally, Beaudrie and Vergara (2021) suggest that the field must include an additional standard—to facilitate heritage students' CLA development—in every aspect of their pedagogy—in order to achieve equity that involves "reflecting [with students] upon the long-unquestioned beliefs and ideologies regarding language and language teaching that have shaped the educational and institutional context centering Spanish" (2021, p. 236). As the authors note, tenets of CLA are increasingly becoming central to contemporary research and pedagogical practice in heritage language education.

To contribute to the field's CLA "critical turn", and while new frameworks bring heritage language practices as relevant for literacy and academic development, this book sheds light on the role of heritage speakers' language and literacy practices in the shaping of a non-classroom academic learning experience. I hope to echo the imperative need to respond to the longstanding theoretical viewpoint of literacy and linguistic hybridity as resources for teaching and learning, which can "inform any learning community [...] particularly in ethnically, racially, and linguistically diverse learning communities where difference as resource is not an organizing principle of instruction" (Gutiérrez, Baquedano-López, & Tejeda, 1999, p. 288). As the analysis will show, when students belong through literacy in academic spaces, they can actively see themselves reflected in spaces of teaching and learning. Other pedagogical implications of this analysis are discussed in Chapter 6.

The Peer-to-Peer Collaborative Academic Learning Space

As another way to illustrate the benefit of translanguaging spaces for academic heritage language learning, this chapter presents the discourse analysis component of tutor–tutee interactions. The section's title refers to the combination of two main facets related to the analysis presented. Firstly, it refers to "academic learning space" to emphasize tutors' participation and shaping of a space that is explicitly academic (i.e., the tutoring room). While this context is not part of the traditional classroom and does not include instructor presence most of the time, perhaps applying the misleading label of "informal space", the explicit goal of the tutoring session is to support and mediate the academic tasks that are informed by the program's formal curriculum—the one with which students engage within the classroom. Further, as I mention throughout the book, the social approach to literacy as the theoretical framework guiding this study conceptualizes academic literacy as situated practice, thus considering the use of academic literacies across non-traditional academic contexts, especially outside

102 The Peer as the Expert

of the traditional classroom. Secondly, the title refers to the collaborative nature of the study's context, in which tutors "go beyond academics" to shape a peer community wherein tutees can feel supported, not just academically but also personally, as they navigate life on campus.

As discussed in the thematic analysis of Chapter 3, there are two overarching goals inscribed in the types of literacy practices that tutors mobilize in the session: academic literacy development and community building. In light of this analysis, this chapter presents the discourse analysis of the lexico-grammatical resources inscribed in particular tutor–tutee exchange structures that reflect how tutors deploy an academic persona—that is, the ways in which they use language in an academic context for an academic task. In Chapter 5, I will explore the discursive resources signaling evaluative stances, which index tutors' and tutees' interpersonal experience as they participate in the same academic tutoring community. To do so, I use Appraisal Theory (Martin & White, 2005), which comes from the Systemic Functional Linguistics tradition (Halliday, 1994) as well as methodologies by Achugar (2009) and Eggins and Slade (1997). Importantly, this unique discourse analysis is useful in illustrating the specific interpersonal, "informal", or "casual" resources that tutors use in the language of the session to shape their belonging in this student-led community of learning.

An Appraisal analysis can reveal how interpersonal meanings are constructed in texts. In other words, it explores, describes, and explains the ways language is used in socially situated contexts to evaluate, adopt stances, construct interpersonal textual personas, and manage interpersonal positionings and relationships. As White (2015) explains,

> [Appraisal] explores how speakers and writers pass judgements on people generally, other writers/speakers and their utterances, material objects, happenings and states of affairs and thereby form alliances with those who share these views and distance themselves from those who don't. It explores how attitudes, judgements and emotive responses are explicitly presented in texts and how they may be more indirectly implied, presupposed or assumed. As well, it explores how the expression of such attitudes and judgements is, in many instances, carefully managed so as to take into account the ever-present possibility of challenge or contradiction from those who hold differing views.

In contexts of academic writing, Appraisal analyses have been employed to identify different uses of evaluative language to construct different types of authorial voices and/or personas (as in Hood, 2010; Hood & Martin, 2007; Achugar, 2009; Mori, 2014). In this work, as in other work adopting Appraisal Theory (Oteíza, 2009; Achugar & Oteíza, 2009; Macken-Horarik & Isaac, 2014), the term "Appraisal" is used as an all-encompassing word to include every evaluative use of language, including those by which speakers (or writers) adopt particular positions or stances and by which they negotiate them with their interlocutors (White, 2015). Following

Achugar (2009), this book holds that specific positionings in texts (or dialogue in interaction) allow speakers to construct identities by intentionally choosing orientations or stances toward the content at hand, or toward other participants. These stances are thus displayed through language which indexes positionings aligning or contesting the typical ways of being a member of the community. In order to illustrate such actions through language, it is useful to first analyze the exchange structure and mood of the speech event (Halliday, 1994), then match participants' evoked evaluations through an analysis of evaluative language.

The structure of the exchange refers to the separation of the interactive discourse into clauses and their coding following clausal *mood* types (such as "declarative", "interrogative", "imperative", "exclamative", and "minor"), *modalization* (*probability* or *usuality*), and *modulation* (*obligations* or *capability*). Additionally, every clausal mood type is of one polarity (*positive* or *negative*) and fulfills a subject and speech function (*statement, question, answer, acknowledgment, contradiction, disclaimer*, etc.). The analysis of mood choices in interaction can thus reveal tensions between equality and difference as individuals enact and construct relations of power through conversation (Eggings & Slade, 1997).

Secondly, in order to develop an analysis of evaluative language, the analysis followed the three main semantic regions involved in the Appraisal System, which encode affective involvement and shifting alignments within conversation: appreciation, affect, and judgment, as seen in Figure 4.1.

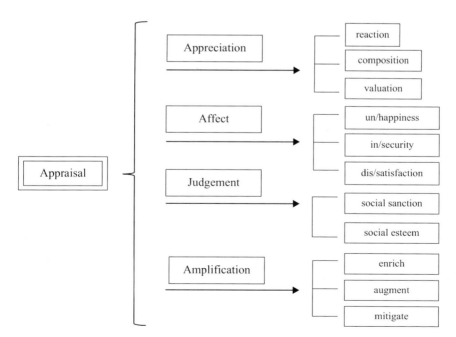

FIGURE 4.1 An Outline of Appraisal Resources. (Source: adapted from Eggins & Slade, 1997, p. 138).

104 The Peer as the Expert

To illustrate, the following are descriptions and illustrations of appreciation, affect, and judgment from the data.

Appreciation refers to how speakers evaluate a text, a process, or any semiotic/natural thing (object, individual, situation, context, etc.) in terms of its *composition* (its balance and complexity), including their *reaction* to it (whether it catches their attention), or its *value* (how innovative or authentic it is).

Cristal's student: Está más fácil así. [valuation]

> *It is easier that way.*

Esmeralda: La tesis es importante. [valuation]

> *The thesis is important.*

> *I don't know my students' teachers. That's really hard to remember [reaction]*

Vanessa–student interaction:

V: ¿No crees que va a ser mucho [tomar clases de] química y matemática?

> *Don't you think it's going to be a lot (to take) Chemistry and Math?*

S: Sí, va a ser difícil. [valuation]

> *Yes, it is going to be difficult.*

V: Espero que esto te ayude.

> *I hope this helps.*

S: Sí, sí, me ayuda bastante, gracias. [reaction]

> *Yes, yes, it helps me a lot.*

Esmeralda: Siempre he considerado yo el inglés más como idioma muy formal. [composition]

> *I've always considered English to be more of a very formal language.*

> El inglés es mucho más formal, **very distant to me** *[...]* El español es mucho más emotivo. [composition]

> *English is much more formal, very distant to me. Spanish is a lot more emotional.*

> Juanes y Maná son dos grupos que son muy así en español, y me gustan pero no me incitan el querer hacer algo progresista como Macklemore lo hace. [reaction]

> *Juanes and Maná are two groups that are very much like that in Spanish, and I like that but they don't make me want to want to do something progressive like Macklemore does.*

Maité–student interaction:

The Peer as the Expert   **105**

M: ¿dónde trabajas?

> *Where do you work?*

S: En la Forever 21

> *At Forever 21*

M: **Oh, how fun!** [reaction]

Maité: Pero, a mí [la clase de] veinticuatro- **like, if you don't think this is challenging**, veinticuatro es peor. [valuation]

> *But, for me, (Spanish) 24 like, if you don't think this is challenging, 24 is worse.*

Affect expresses positive or negative feelings as *happiness* or *unhappiness, satisfaction* or *dissatisfaction*, or *security* or *insecurity*:

Cristal's student: Es que yo pues todas las quiero- en todos les pongo el acento y

> me confunden todas. *[insecurity]*

> *It's just that I want to all- on all of them I place the accent and they all confuse me.*

Esmeralda–student interaction:

E: ¿Qué significa la (palabra) que tú escribiste, con la "h"?

> *What does it (the word) mean that you wrote, with an h?*

S: Cuando no quieres hacer algo, cuando **like** "rehusas" hacerlo

> *When you don't want to do something, like, when you refuse to do it*

E: Exacto. **"Refuse" is the English word,** "rehusó". [security]

> *Exactly. "Refuse" is the English word, "refused".*

Esmeralda's student: I don't want an A minus. Quiero una A. [dissatisfaction]

Esmeralda: Emocionalmente Enrique Iglesias **can make me** cry. [unhappiness]

> *Si voy a cantar* **because I'm in a happy mood I'm most likely going to**

start rapping in English. *[happiness]* **Again, I'm more open with my emotions in Spanish than I am in English.** *[security]*

> *Emotionally Enrique Iglesias can make me cry. If I am going to sing because I'm in a happy mood I'm most likely going to start rapping in English. Again, I'm more open with my emotions in Spanish than I am in English.*

Cristal–student interaction:

C: ¿Cómo te fue en el borrador?

> *How did it go with the draft?*

106 The Peer as the Expert

S: Mejor. Me puso cinco de cinco. [satisfaction]

Better. They gave me five out of five.

Instances of *Judgment* express evaluations about the ethics, morality, or social values of people's behaviors, and can be subdivided into *social esteem* and *social sanction*. Judgments of social esteem concern "normality" (how unusual someone is), "capacity" (how capable they are), and "tenacity" (how determined they are). Judgemnts of social sanction center on "veracity" (how truthful someone is) and "propriety" (how ethical someone is). The following examples illustrate this type of positioning:

Vannessa: Es buen profesor, **but super-fast writer.** [social esteem; normality]

They're a good professor, but super-fast writer.

Concepción: Lo que escribiste luego contradice todo lo que me dijistes anteriormente. [social sanction; veracity]

What you wrote then contradicts everything you had told me previously.

Esmeralda: You know Spanish-speaking people, cada vez que hay una "ese"- **they make the "eh" noise in front of it. So my mom says** "espray" y cosas así **all the time.** [social esteem; capacity]

You know Spanish-speaking people, every time there is an "ese" they make the "eh" noise in front of it. So my mom says "espray" and things like that all the time.

Mi hermana lo hace por floja, por cierto [social esteem; capacity]

My sister does it because she is a wimp, by the way.

Maité—student interaction:

M: Especialmente porque la población de las clases de veinti- veintitrés veinticuatro son personas, um–

Especially because the course's population of twenty- twenty-three, twenty-four year-olds are people, um

S: ¿No hispanohablantes?

Not Spanish-speaking?

M: Uh huh
S: **Aw, yeah** [social esteem; normality]

Further, attitudes can be raised or lowered through the system of *graduation*, one way in which amplification can happen in casual conversation. A speaker can raise or intensify a particular evaluation through *force*, and they can soften or mitigate such an evaluation through *focus*:

Cristal's student: Después de mil años ya entendí. [force]

After one thousand years, finally I get it.

Vanessa: It's not an easy A so it makes you work pero es muy muy muy interesante. [force]

It's not an easy A so it makes you work but it is very very very interesting.

Esmeralda: [Mi mamá y mi papá] no tienen esa táctica [de hablar inglés]. Tienen un poco lo que es oral pero no necesariamente completamente. [focus]

[My mom and my dad] don't really have that skill [of speaking English]. They can orally express a little but not really completely.

As mentioned, before achieving an analysis of evaluative language, however, it is necessary to identify the exchange structure and mood of the speech event. The following section will present such an analysis.

Constructing an Academic Persona: Analysis of Tutor Lexico-Grammatical Resources

This first analysis provides the interpretation of the lexico-grammatical resources inscribed in specific interactions indexing the construction of an "academic persona"—that is, the structure of the exchange and the modality of moments in which tutors mediate an academic task with their tutee while mobilizing an expert identity. Data for this section emerges from the themes "academic support" and "tutor as expert" from the analysis presented in Chapter 3. As mentioned, unique interactions were analyzed by dividing the clauses and coding for mood, using the basic mood classes in Eggins and Slade (1997, p. 75), as shown in Table 4.1.

As contextualized within Appraisal Theory, and with the interpersonally oriented analysis of casual conversation presented, each mood class is defined by a function in the interaction. Declarative clauses, for example, are used to initiate conversational exchanges by putting forward information for negotiations. Thus,

TABLE 4.1 Basic Mood Classes with Illustrations from the Data

Basic Mood Classes	
Mood Type	Example from the Data
Declarative	Me siento realizada
Imperative	Subraya donde debería de ir el golpe
Wh-interrogative	¿Cómo has estado?
Polar interrogative	¿Sigue la regla o no la sigue?
Exclamative	¡Qué bonito que hayas ido al evento de SPEAK!
Minor	So entonces / Ajá / Okay

108 The Peer as the Expert

they construct the speaker as taking on an active, initiatory role in the talk. Further, polar interrogatives are used to initiate an exchange by requesting information from others, thus constructing the speaker as dependent on the response of other interactants. As noted by Eggins and Slade (1997), polar interrogatives are not entirely common in casual conversation among friends or family members, where much of the information exchanged is already, in most cases, shared (an exception is the aforementioned example "¿Sigue la regla o no la sigue?" or *Does it or does it not follow the rule?* of a polar interrogative, since the tutor does provide metalinguistic information that the tutee needs). Wh- interrogatives, on the other hand, wield a much broader use and are typical of almost all contexts of interaction between tutors and tutees (and not just informal ones), as they are used to elicit additional circumstantial information, challenge prior talk, or achieve commands. Regardless of their interactional use, wh- interrogatives provide a means of decreasing the dependency relation that compliance with commands requires.

Further, imperative clauses function to make commands, setting up a particular compliant response. Given the contextual characteristics of the setting where tutors and tutees interact, imperatives are often used to indirectly negotiate action; this includes their utilization in step-by-step processes related to a grammar activity (as in the steps to follow the rules of accentuation, for example). Exclamative clauses, on the other hand, are used to encode a judgment or evaluation of events. Tutors often employ exclamative clauses to react to particular non-task-oriented events such as their tutees' weekend plans, break plans, or particular life events that happen outside of the tutoring session (such as Maité's reaction to her tutee working at Forever 21—"How fun!"). Thus, tutors seldom use these types of clauses to challenge the interlocutor (another common use of exclamative clauses). Lastly, minor clauses—clauses which have no mood structure—function either as a prelude to negotiation ("So entonces" or *so then*) or as a closure ("Yeah"). Within negotiation, they generally encode follow-up reactions or contributions that do not prompt negotiation status. Most minor clauses, therefore, position the speaker as a compliant supporter of prior interaction.

Specifically, mood is measured through *modality*, which refers to a range of different ways speakers can temper or qualify their messages. Halliday (1994) notes two types of modality: *modalization* and *modulation*. In *modalization*, the tempering of the message is achieved through reference to degrees of frequency (using such words as "usually", "sometimes", "seldom", "often", etc.) or probability ("may", "will", "probably", "certainly", etc.)—tempering the amount of security with which we utter a fact—while in *modulation*, the qualification of the message is with reference to degrees of obligation ("should", "must", etc.), inclination ("gladly", "willingly", "regrettably", etc.), or capability ("is able to", "capably", "can", etc.)—tempering the directness with which we wish to act upon another.

Lastly, two other components help illustrate interpersonal positions in association with mood: subject and polarity. The subject is the pivotal participant in

The Peer as the Expert **109**

the clause and with or without whose presence there could be no argument or negotiation. Polarity of mood, on the other hand, is not marked if positive and is marked with a [−] if negative.

The following two illustrative sections show a complete analysis of mood in the data. Both apply the previous thematic analysis of how tutors build their academic persona, or how they position themselves as experts. These two exchanges were chosen given that they both result in tutees' certain acknowledgment of comprehension of the topic at hand. Illustrations of complete clause division and tables with coding sheet analysis for both sections follow the initial transcription of the interaction.

Providing Academic Support

The following interaction occurs near the end of the quarter as Cristal, a tutor, reviews material for the final exam with her student. The student has been expressing anxiety about being unprepared for the test, especially in terms of the spelling section and specifically regarding orthographic accentuation. Cristal uses a worksheet to practice several words, including the use of the grammatical rules on identifying when and where to include written accents previously learned in class.

The two work through several words together, applying the rules learned in class to several sets of words:

Student: Chávez (.)

Cristal: ¿Pero dices ChaVEZ?

> *But do you say ChaVEZ?*

Student: ChaVEZ, no

Cristal: CHAvez, right?

Student: Ajá. Entonces digo ChAvez −

> *Uh huh. So I say ChAvez-*

Cristal: ((Mhm)) −

Student: Cesar Chávez. ¿En la e? ¿Sí, no?-

> *Cesar Chávez. On the e? Yes, no?*

Cristal: No, ChavEz. ¿Cuál se-? [unint]

> *No. ChavEz. Which one do you- ?*

Student: ChAvez. Cha. (…)

Cristal: <nods>

110 The Peer as the Expert

Student: Entonces si termina en dic- en la última (sílaba) no lo sigue (la regla) entonces va en Cha, en la a

So, if it ends in it- on the last one (syllable) it does not follow it (the rule) so it goes on Cha, on the a

Cristal: Mhm (.)

Student: Chávez

Cristal: Mhm

Student: (.) ChavEz, pero no digo Cesar ChavEZ. Entonces por eso no va en la- va en la a –

ChavEz, but I don't say Cesar ChavEz. So that's why it does go on the- it goes on the a

Cristal: Mhm –

Student: Porque no lo sigue. –

Because it doesn't follow it

Cristal: Yeah. –

Student: Cesar ChaVEZ. Con palabras más así como de dos sílabas es más fácil para mí como con palabras más largas porque me confundo. Okay, entonces fácil. Fa-cil.

Cesar ChaVEZ. With words like that like with two syllables is easier for me like with words that are longer because I get confused. Okay, so "easy". Ea-sy.

<Cristal and Student begin working through specific words. Approximately four minutes go by>

Cristal: ¿So ya miraste? –

So, did you see?

Student: Okay yeah –

Cristal: Pero sub- subrayas el- el xxx-

But underline the- the-

Student: Okay

Cristal: -de acuerdo con la regla es lo que dice

Following the rule, what does it say

Student: Okay y luego sílaba-

Ok and then the syllable-

The Peer as the Expert **111**

Cristal: Ajá –

Student: Termina en: (.) en um vocal y la regla dice que las que terminan en vocal deben de llevarlo en la penúltima

It ends in- um a vowel and the rule says that those that end on a vowel should have the accent on the second to last

Cristal: Mhm

Student: Entonces aquí, síla- y digo silaBA. No digo silaBA. –

So here, "sila-" and I say "silaBA". I don't say "silaBA"

Cristal: No, dices siLAba –

No, you say "silaba"

Student: Aha –

Cristal: So dices SIlaba.

So you say "SIlaba"

Student: –laba

Cristal: So entonces –

So then

Student: Sílaba (.) entonces lo rompe y lleva en la i. En la i

"Sílaba" so it breaks it and has it on the i. On the i

Cristal: Mhm. Pero ya mirastes que el golpe lo debería –

Mhm. But you see that the emphasis should be-

Student: Debería ir allí –

Should go there

Cristal: De caer allí, pero no cae ahí –

Should go there, but it doesn't go there

Student: ¡Oh! –

Cristal: Eso es lo que- (.) @@

That's what-

Student: @@ Después de mil años ya entendí

After a thousand years I got it

Cristal: Después de mil años ya entendí

112 The Peer as the Expert

After a thousand years I got it

Student: Ya, ya entendí –

Yes, I got it now

Cristal: Ayy –
Student: Eso es más fácil

That's easier

Cristal: So yeah
Student: Uh!
Cristal: xxx
Student: Ah, me siento realizada

Ah, I feel fulfilled

While reviewing the transcription of the interaction is useful to illustrate what was said between the pair, it is also useful to transcribe casual interactions while marking mood types for each clause. Following is such an analysis of the complete same interaction, including additional moments not illustrated in the preceding transcript.

Turn	Speaker	Text
1	Student:	(i) Aha. (ii) Entonces digo ChAvez. – [STATEMENT]
2	Cristal:	(i) Mhm – [ACKNOWLEDGMENT]
3	S:	(i) Cesar Chávez. (ii) ¿En la e? [QUESTION] (iii) ¿Sí, no? [QUESTION]
4	C:	(i) ChAvez. (ii) No ChavEz. [STATEMENT] (iii) ¿Cuál se-? [QUESTION]
5	S:	(i) ChAvez. (ii) Cha-, (iii) entonces si termina en la última no lo sigue (iv) entonces va en Cha en la a. – [STATEMENT]
6	C:	(i) Mhm – [ACKNOWLEDGMENT]
7	S:	(i) Chávez. – [STATEMENT]
8	C:	(i) Mhm – [ACKNOWLEDGMENT]
9	S:	(i) ChavEz, (ii) pero no digo Cesar ChavEz. (iii) Entonces por eso no va en la va en la a – [STATEMENT]
10	C:	(i) Mhm – [ACKNOWLEDGMENT]
11	S:	(i) porque no lo sigue. – [STATEMENT]
12	C:	(i) Yea. – [ACKNOWLEDGMENT]
13	S:	(i) Cesar Chávez. (ii) Con palabras más así como de dos sílabas es más fácil (iii) para mí como con palabras más largas (iv) porque me confundo. [STATEMENT] (v) Okay, (vi) entonces fácil. (vii) Fa-cil. (vii) ¿Dice que en la última, verdad? – [QUESTION]
14	C:	(i) Mhm – [ACKNOWLEDGMENT]
15	S:	(i) La tarea está fa-cIl. (ii) La tarea estaba facIl. (iii) No. – [STATEMENT]

(Continued)

The Peer as the Expert **113**

Turn	Speaker	Text
16	C:	(i) Mhm – [ACKNOWLEDGMENT]
17	S:	(i) FA-cil –
18	C:	(i) Okay. – [ACKNOWLEDGMENT]
19	S:	(i) Entonces en la a. – [STATEMENT]
20	C:	(i) Okay. – [ACKNOWLEDGMENT]
21	S:	(i) ¿Sí verdad? (ii) ¿En la a fácil? [QUESTION]
22	C:	(i) So te voy a dar algo más para los acentos. – [STATEMENT]
23	S:	(i) Ajá. – [ACKNOWLEDGMENT]
24	C:	(i) Um okay. (ii) Como por ejemplo si, si te dice como escribe usando tus propias palabras las dos principales reglas de la pronunciación y la acentuación español. (iii) Da por lo menos 2 ejemplos de la palabra (iv) que siga cada regla. – [STATEMENT]
25	S:	(i) Mhm – [ACKNOWLEDGMENT]
26	C:	(i) Que sigan cada regla, okay. – [STATEMENT]
27	S:	(i) Mhm – [ACKNOWLEDGMENT]
28	C:	(i) ¿Como cuáles son las dos reglas que te acuerdas? [QUESTION]
29	S:	(i) Ah de la primera regla (ii) es que si termina en vocal o n o s lleva – (iii) ehm [ANSWER, HESITATION] (iv) ¿como se dice el énfasis? [QUESTION]
30	C:	(i) El énfasis – [ANSWER]
31	S:	(i) va en la úl – no, penúltima sílaba. – [STATEMENT]
32	C:	(i) Penúltima sílaba. – [ACKNOWLEDGMENT]
33	S:	(i) Y si la segunda es (ii) si termina en en consonante (iii) ¿o esa también es n o s? – [QUESTION]
34	C:	(i) Excepto – [ANSWER]
35	S:	(i) Excepto n o s. –
36	C:	(i) n o s. –
37	S:	(i) Okay. (ii) Lleva en la última – [STATEMENT]
38	C:	(i) Mhm – [ACKNOWLEDGMENT]
39	S:	(i) el énfasis. xxx
40	C:	(i) Mhm. (ii) Y luego por ejemplo, si te dicen (ii) separa las siguientes palabras en sílabas – [STATEMENT]
41	S:	(i) Mhm – [ACKNOWLEDGMENT]
42	C:	(i) subraya – [STATEMENT]
43	S:	(i) Ajá – [ACKNOWLEDGMENT]
44	C:	(i) la sílaba donde debería llevar el golpe – [STATEMENT]
45	S:	(i) Oh – [ACKNOWLEDGMENT]
46	C:	(i) no el acento escrito – [STATEMENT]
47	S:	(i) Donde debería. – [STATEMENT]
48	C:	(i) el golpe – [STATEMENT]
49	S:	(i) últimO, (ii) último. – [STATEMENT]
50	C:	(i) o acento prosódico según las dos reglas principales de la acentuación en español. (ii) Ponle acento escrito a las palabras que lo necesiten. – [STATEMENT]
51	S:	(i) Mmm – [ACKNOWLEDGMENT]
52	C:	(i) Y las palabras que llevan acento escrito son las que no siguen las reglas. – [STATEMENT]
53	S:	(i) Oh okay. – [ACKNOWLEDGMENT]

(*Continued*)

114 The Peer as the Expert

Turn	Speaker	Text
54	C:	(i) ¿Okay? (ii) So entonces como cultural, (iii) si tienes cultural, (iv) como por ejemplo es, − cul-tu-ral − (v) esa es la forma que deberías de separar las sílabas − [STATEMENT]
55	S:	(i) Aha − [ACKNOWLEDGMENT]
56	C:	(i) ¿cierto? − [QUESTION]
57	S:	(i) cul-tu-ral [unint]. −
58	C:	(i) ¿De acuerdo a las reglas dónde lleva el-? − [QUESTION]
59	S:	(i) El −
60	C:	(i) Porque te-, porque ves que lleva, (ii) debes de subrayar − [STATEMENT]
61	S:	(i) Aha − [ACKNOWLEDGMENT]
62	C:	(i) el golpe. − [STATEMENT]
63	S:	(i) Ajá − [ACKNOWLEDGMENT]
64	C:	(i) ¿So entonces cómo harías eso? [QUESTION] (ii) Cultural.
65	S:	(i) Cultural. (ii) − C: Cul-tu − (iii) Termina en consonante (iv) entonces dice que en la última. [STATEMENT]
66	C:	(i) ¿So entonces dónde debes de subrayar el golpe? [QUESTION]
67	S:	(i) Aquí. − [ANSWER]
68	C:	(i) Mhm −
69	S:	(ii) Cul-tu-ral. [STATEMENT]
70	C:	(i) ¿Sigue las reglas o (ii) no las sigue? [QUESTION]
71	S:	(i) Cultural. (ii) ¿Sí? [QUESTION] (iii) Sí. [ANSWER]
72	C:	(i) ¿Entonces (ii) lleva acento escrito? [QUESTION]
73	S:	(i) No [ANSWER]
74	C:	(i) Pero (ii) ya subrayastes el golpe − [STATEMENT]
75	S:	(i) Ajá − [ACKOWLEDGMENT]
76	C:	(i) so (ii) estás bien [??]. −
77	S:	(i) Ah okay. −
78	C:	(i) Y luego como composición. [STATEMENT]
79	S:	(i) En la o lleva acento. [STATEMENT]
80	C:	(i) Lleva acento en la o, pero − [STATEMENT]
81	S:	(i) Ajá − [ACKNOWLEDGMENT]
82	C:	(i) debes de subrayar el golpe. (ii) ¿Te acuerdas? [QUESTION]
83	S:	(i) Com-po-si-ción, (ii) okay. [ACKNOWLEDGMENT]
84	C:	(i) ¿Dónde debe de llevar el golpe? [QUESTION]
85	S:	(i) ¿El golpe? [QUESTION]
86	C:	(i) De acuerdo a las reglas. [STATEMENT]
87	S:	(i) Oh de acuerdo a la, (ii) si termina en la penúltima. [STATEMENT]
88	C:	(i) ¿Entonces cuál es la que debes de subrayar? [QUESTION]
89	S:	(i) ¿Donde lleva en- sí? [HESITATION]
90	C:	(i) So eso es lo que te ayuda más − [STATEMENT]
91	S:	(i) Sí, ajá. − [ACKNOWLEDGMENT]
92	C:	(i) como por ejemplo, que subrayes (ii) en donde debe de decir la regla. − [STATEMENT]
93	S:	(i) Oh. − [ACKNOWLEDGMENT]
94	C:	(i) Como por ejemplo, la regla dice − [STATEMENT]
95	S:	(i) Ajá − [ACKNOWLEDGMENT]
96	C:	(i) que debe de llevar el golpe − [STATEMENT]

(Continued)

The Peer as the Expert **115**

Turn	Speaker	Text
97	S:	(i) en, en sí. – [REITERATION]
98	C:	(i) en este de acá. (ii) Pero cuando pronuncio la palabra –
99	S:	(i) sI-cion –
100	C:	(i) no digo –
101	S/C:	(i) composIcion –
102	C:	(i) digo –
103	S/C:	(i) composición [STATEMENT]
104	C:	(i) Entonces rompe la regla –
105	S:	(i) Oh – [ACKNOWLEDGMENT]
106	C:	(i) entonces debe de llevar aquí. [STATEMENT]
107	S:	(i) Oh es más fácil así [EXCLAMATION]
108	C:	(i) Y luego puedes decir como por ejemplo, ferrocarril. – [STATEMENT]
109	S:	(i) Mhm – [ACKNOWLEDGMENT]
110	C:	(i) Ferrocarril está dividido en estas sílabas, ¿cierto? [QUESTION]
111	S:	(i) Fe-rro
112	C:	(i) Fe-rro-ca –
113	S:	(i) -rril
114	C:	(i) rril.
115	S:	(i) Según la regla el énfasis – [STATEMENT]
116	C:	(i) Según la regla debe de llevar el énfasis(.) – [QUESTION]
117	S:	(i) en la- [HESITATION]
118	C:	(i) aquí cierto. (ii) Entonces um (iii) de de acuerdo a la regla debe de llevar el acento allí (iv) y cuando dices ferrocarril, (v) sí dices ferrocarril. – [STATEMENT]
119	S:	(i) Ajá ferrocarril. – [ACKNOWLEDGMENT]
120	C:	(i) ¿So entonces sí la sigue? – [QUESTION]
121	S:	(i) Mhm sí. – [ANSWER]
122	C:	(i) ¿Entonces no lleva acento escrito cierto? (ii) ¿Y luego qué hay de líder? [QUESTION]
123	S:	(i) Líder termina en consonante. [STATEMENT]
124	C:	(i) Lí-der. Termina en consonante (.) [REITERATION]
125	S:	(i) Entonces um – [HESITATION]
126	C:	(i) ¿Entonces de acuerdo a la regla dónde debe de llevar el golpe? [QUESTION]
127	S:	(i) Allí. [ANSWER]
128	C:	(i) Entonces subrayas el golpe. – [COMMAND]
129	S:	(i) Ajá – [ACKNOWLEDGMENT]
130	C:	(i) ¿Cierto? (ii) ¿Pero cómo la dices? [QUESTION]
131	S:	(i) No digo li-dEr, (ii) digo líder. [STATEMENT]
132	C:	(i) Mhm. (ii) Entonces la rompe – [ACKNOWLEDGMENT/ STATEMENT]
133	S:	(i) allí. – [STATEMENT]
134	C:	(i) y va allí. – [STATEMENT]
135	S:	(i) Oh. – [ACKNOWLEDGMENT]
136	C:	(i) So básicamente eso es lo que te están pidiendo que hagas. [STATEMENT]
137	S:	(i) Está más fácil así. [EXCLAMATION] (ii) Es que yo pues todas las quiero (iii) en todos les pongo el acento (iv) y me confunden todas. [STATEMENT]

(Continued)

116 The Peer as the Expert

Turn	Speaker	Text
138	C:	(i) So entonces −
139	S:	(i) Oh! − [EXCLAMATION]
140	C:	(i) así es, (ii) así es con todas las palabras − [STATEMENT]
141	S:	(i) Oh sí. (ii) Eso está más fácil − [EXCLAMATION]
142	C:	(i) que te pidan así. (ii) So entonces uh −
143	S:	(i) A ver hispanohablantes. − [STATEMENT]
144	C:	(i) Mhm − [ACKNOWLEDGMENT]
145	S:	(i) his-pan-o-ha-blan-tes. (ii) Termina en s en la penúltima dice. (iii) Hispano-a, hispano-a-blan-tes. (iv) Hispanohablantes, (v) sí la sigue. − [STATEMENT]
146	C:	(i) Mhm −
147	S:	(i) Oh! [EXCLAMATION]
148	C:	(i) ¿So ya miraste? − [QUESTION]
149	S:	(i) Okay yeah. − [ACKNOWLEDGMENT]
150	C:	(i) Pero subrayas el- el [unint] de acuerdo con la regla (ii) es lo que dice. [STATEMENT]
151	S:	(i) Okay y luego sílaba- [STATEMENT]
152	C:	(i) Ajá − [ACKNOWLEDGMENT]
153	S:	(i) Termina en, en una vocal (ii) y la regla dice (iii) que las que terminan en vocal (iv) deben de llevarlo en la penúltima. (v) Entonces aquí, síla- (vi) y digo sílaba. (vii) No digo silAba. − [STATEMENT]
154	C:	(i) No dices silAba − [ACKNOWLEDGMENT]
155	S:	(i) Aha − [ACKNOWLEDGMENT]
156	C:	(i) so dices sílaba. (ii) So entonces − [STATEMENT]
157	S:	(i) Sílaba. (ii) Entonces lo rompe y lleva en la i. [STATEMENT]
158	C:	(i) Mhm. (ii) Pero ya miraste (iii) que el golpe lo debería − [STATEMENT]
159	S:	(i) debería allí. − [ACKNOWLEDGMENT]
160	C:	(i) de caer allí, (ii) ponlo (iii) okay. − [ACKNOWLEDGMENT]
161	S:	(i) Oh! − [EXCLAMATION]
162	C:	(i) Eso es lo que- (.)
163	S:	(i) ¡Después de mil años ya entendí! [EXCLAMATION]
164	C:	(i) Después de mil años ya entendí. [EXCLAMATION]
165	S:	(i) Ya, ya entendí. − [STATEMENT]
166	C:	(i) Ayy − [EXCLAMATION]
167	S:	(i) Eso es más fácil. [STATEMENT]
168	C:	(i) So yeah. [unint] −
169	S:	(i) Ah, me siento realizada− [STATEMENT]
170	C:	(i) So (ii) así puedes hacerla como − [STATEMENT]
171	S:	(i) Oh −
172	C:	(i) con todas las palabras. − [STATEMENT]
173	S:	(i) Oh my God. − [EXCLAMATION]
174	C:	(i) Primero como subrayar −
175	S:	(i) como donde debería según la regla donde (ii) y luego lo pongo (iii) y si no suena como, (iv) oh. − [STATEMENT]
176	C:	(i) Mhm. (i) Y si no, y si no, pues no. − [ACKNOWLEDGMENT]
177	S:	(i) Ajá − [ACKNOWLEDGMENT]
178	C:	(i) Ajá. − [ACKNOWLEDGMENT]

(Continued)

Turn	Speaker	Text
179	S:	(i) Oh okay. −
180	C:	(i) Okay.
181	S:	(i) Yo no sé después de tantos años. (ii) Ya entiendo. [STATEMENT]

If the foregoing clause mood type analysis were condensed to quantify who in the interaction produces more or fewer clause types, the summarized data would be as given in Table 4.2.

Grammatical analysis of mood for Cristal's interaction with her student shows that turn-taking is almost balanced. This implies that, despite the tutor's role as expert, she does not take the floor entirely and consistently gives way to the student's concerns, questions, and process.

While Cristal does not position herself as an expert in terms of quantity of speech (that is, she does not guide the student by doing most of the talking),

TABLE 4.2 Analysis and Summary of Mood Choices in Cristal's Interaction

Mood (Clause Type)	Cristal	Student
Number of clauses	122 (48%)	135 (52%)
Declarative full	37	63
Polar interrogative full	7	6
Tagged interrogative full	—	2
Wh–interrogative full	10	1
Imperative	8	—
Minor	37	43
Subject		
Most frequent subject choice	tú 27	yo 15
	palabra 14	acento 10
	regla 7	regla 8
	golpe 7	palabra 6
	sílaba 4	Chávez 6
	yo 3	golpe 5
	acento 3	énfasis 3
	énfasis 2	sílaba 3
	Various third-person singular 13	Various third-person
	Third-person singular 1	singular 8
Language		
Percentage of language used in the interaction	Spanish (119 clauses, 97.5%) English (3 clauses, 2.5%)	Spanish (all clauses, 100%) English (0 clauses, 0%)
Modalization		
	2	5
Modulation		
Obligation	4	—
Capability	—	4

118 The Peer as the Expert

she mediates an "instructor–student"-like interaction, or an expert positioning, by shaping the interaction so that the student produces the highest number of minor clauses—clauses which have no mood (such as "uh huh", "okay" and other formulaic language). As minor clauses encode follow-up reactions without negotiation status, when used in this interaction, they indicate that the tutee does not challenge the tutor's role of expert as they work through words and discuss whether these should use a written accent or not. Instead, the tutee engages with the tutor as an apprentice.

Alternately, full declarative clauses, where the structural element of the subject occurs before the finite element of the clause, are used to initiate conversational exchanges and to construct the speaker as taking an active, initiatory role. Since it is the student who produces the highest amount of full declarative clauses, we can assume that she feels comfortable and is intentional about taking charge of her learning process throughout the session. This is also corroborated by the first few sections of this segment where the student is assertive about wanting to spend time in the session reviewing material for the final exam. It is also interesting to note that both the tutor and the student use almost the same number of polar interrogatives. Again, this attests to the student feeling empowered to directly ask the tutor yes/no questions regarding the task at hand.

The student-oriented approach of the tutor embodying an expert identity is also exemplified in the various subjects used throughout the interaction. In Appraisal Theory, the subject is considered a pivotal participant in the clause, as it represents the person or thing that the proposition is concerned with, and without whose presence there could be no argument or negotiation. We see here that Cristal's most frequent subject is "tú", thus demonstrating her intentional attention diversion towards the student, as in utterances such as "¿ya mirastes?" (*did you see?*) or "para que puedas (tú) practicar" (*so that you can practice*) as well as "te va a ir muy bien" (*you are going to do well*). Per Cristal's guidance, the tutee's involvement with the task at hand (written accents) is illustrated by the student's most frequently used subject—namely, "acentos" (*written accents*).

Importantly, while Cristal and her student mostly continue using Spanish throughout the interaction, they also translanguage into English, mostly to use certain discourse markers as minor clauses, follow up, and uptake each other's turns. Also, Cristal translanguages across a variety of registers of Spanish, as illustrated by her use of an s-insertion in the second person preterite—for example, "mirastes"—and her otherwise consistent use of forms more commonly used in formal contexts. That said, the pair's use of Spanish reflects the attention given to the academic task, which is closely annexed to the formal curriculum, carried out almost exclusively in Spanish.

Cristal and her student's modality also illustrate Cristal's student-oriented approach. As noted, Cristal produces the most instances of [modality; obligation], but only when guiding the student through specific moments that are crucial in the student's understanding of Spanish's rules of accentuation (as in "debes de subrayar" or "*you should underline*"). Cristal does not modalize with

The Peer as the Expert **119**

obligation outside of the step-by-step process of writing accents, thus communicating to her student that it is acceptable to risk making mistakes as they both work through the set of words. The student, on the other hand, mostly produces instances of [modality; capability] as she illustrates how capable she is of following the rules that Cristal has guided her through ("es más fácil así" or *it is easier that way*). The student's modalization, mostly in terms of frequency, also relates to her process from feeling overwhelmed and confused at the beginning of the session ("me confunden todas [siempre]" or *they all confuse me always*) to feeling accomplished and ready to ace the final exam ("después de mil años [ya entendí]" or *after a thousand years I got it*).

Further and according to Achugar (2009), stance construction through mood is also supported by the actions realized via the exchange structure of the conversation. Power differences/social roles are supported by concrete choices in speech functions, as demonstrated in Table 4.3.

As we see in the summary of the exchange structure, Cristal and her student are very much aligned in the number of times they acknowledge each other. The similar number of statements they both produce shows the freedom with which the student "repeats to herself" or "repeats out loud" steps in the activity they are working through, as opposed to her primarily focusing on asking questions for Cristal to answer. The student resorts to working through the steps in the form of statements, producing only six questions across the interaction. Cristal does produce the greatest number of questions, specifically as she guides the student through the steps in the grammar exercise. Finally, the student produces the greatest number of exclamations, mostly towards the end of the interaction when she expresses excitement and fulfillment at understanding how to apply the rules while expressing her readiness to take the exam: "¡Después de mil años ya entendí!" (*After a thousand years, I got it!*)

TABLE 4.3 Summary of the Exchange Structure in Cristal's Interaction

Participants	Speech Function
Cristal	Acknowledgment (18)
	Statement (34)
	Question (12)
	Answer (2)
	Reiteration (1)
	Command (1)
	Exclamation (2)
Student	Acknowledgment (25)
	Statement (32)
	Question (6)
	Answer (6)
	Reiteration (1)
	Exclamation (8)

120 The Peer as the Expert

Taken together, the different components of this exchange structure's mood analysis show how Cristal uses a variety of interpersonal lexico-grammatical resources to mobilize an overt and intentional student-oriented academic persona as she works with her tutee. We see that, after working with her tutor, the student expresses feeling accomplished and more prepared to complete the grammar section on accents in the final exam. This demonstrates how Cristal contributes to her tutee's academic experience.

Metalinguistic Knowledge

In this second interaction—an extended version of the verbal exchange analyzed thematically in Chapter 2—Esmeralda and her student are reviewing grammar activities for the week. Esmeralda is helping a student work through a spelling activity on homophones. The student must choose between the words "has", "haz", "asta", and "hasta" to fill in the sentence, "El catorce de febrero Romeo le llevó un_____ de flores a Julieta" (*on February 14 Romeo took Juliet a _____ of flowers*) (the correct word according to the answer key being "haz", translating to "bundle"). The following interaction illustrates how Esmeralda guides the student through a grammar exercise using explicit metalinguistic information, as well as the question-and-answer approach, explained in Chapter 2:

Student: El catorce de febrero, Romeo le llevó un (…) ¿has de flores a Julieta?

The fourteenth day of February, Romeo took a bundle of flowers?

Esmeralda: Bueno hay que empezar aquí. Has, h-a-s, TÚ has ido a tal lugar

Well, that's where we need to start. "Have", h-a-v-e, you have been to a place

Student: Mhmm

Esmeralda: ¿De qué verbo viene eso?

What verb doe that come from?

Student: (…) ¿Ir? **Like** vas a-

To go? Like, you are going to-

Esmeralda: No, porque dije has ido. Ido viene de ir, pero ¿has? ¿Sabes cuál es? Es uno de los tiempos perfectos. Entonces te voy a decir otros ejemplos de tiempos perfectos. Um, habría ido, habrás ido, has ido. ¿Sabes cuál verbo es cada uno de esos o no?

No, because I said "you have been". "Been" comes from to go, but have? Do you know which one it is? It's one of those perfect tenses. So I am going to tell you other examples of perfect tenses. Um, "would have been, will have been, have been". Do you know what verb is in each of those or not?

Student: No

The Peer as the Expert **121**

Esmeralda: Es haber, de ahí viene

It's "haber", it comes from that

Student: <repeats to herself> ((Haber))-

Esmeralda: Entonces, **yeah, have you**. Entonces, si yo te digo ¿tú has ido? **Have you gone?**

So, yeah, have you. So, if I tell you, have you been? Have you gone?

Student: <student nods>

Esmeralda: Okay? Entonces (.) ¿Le llevó un haber de flores? ¿Viene de ese verbo o no? Bueno, primero, es un verbo @@ entonces, ¿queda ahí la palabra?

Okay? So, he brought her a "to have" of flowers? Does it come from that verb or not? Well, first, it is a verb, so would that work there?

Student: Le llevo un (.)

He brought her a (.)

Esmeralda: Cualquier verbo que quieras poner, ¿va a describir eso? ¿O no?

Would any verb you want to place there, would it describe it? Or not?

Student: No

Esmeralda: Porque nec-, ¿qué es lo que necesitas si es algo de flores? ¿Qué se- qué se está usando? ¿Qué, uh, tipo de palabra? Adjetivo, adverbio, verbo, sustantivo

Because you need, what do you need if it is something with flowers? What do you, what are you using? What, uh, type of word? Adjective, adverb, verb, noun

Student: Adjetivo

Adjective

Esmeralda: Perfecto, estás buscando un adjetivo o s- quizás sea un sustantivo por un tipo de flores

Perfect, you're looking for an adjective or even a noun since it is a type of flower

Student: Mhmm

Esmeralda: ¿Vale? (.) Entonces, has viene del verbo. Si yo te digo hasta mañana (.) ¿Qué es en inglés? Tradúzcamelo

Ok? So, "has" comes from the ver. If I tell you "hasta mañana" what is that in English? Translate it for me

Student: Uhm, hasta mañana xxx until tomorrow?

Um, "hasta mañana", until tomorrow?

122 The Peer as the Expert

Esmeralda: Bien

Good

Student: So, until?

Esmeralda: Until. ¿Funciona esa palabra ahí?

Until. Does that word work there?

Student: No

Esmeralda: Okay (.) ¿Qué es un asta? ¿Sabes qué es eso?

Okay. What is an "asta"? Do you know what that is?

Student: ¿Asta?

Esmeralda: Asta sin h

"Asta" without an "h"

Student: Asta como, como (.)

"Asta", like, like

Esmeralda: Moose have them, reindeer have them

Student: Ohhh

Esmeralda: Asta, entonces puedo usar esto o también otra descripción para asta es como un **shaft**, un tubo. ¿Queda eso?

"Asta", so I could use that or another definition for "asta" is like a shaft, like a tube. Would that work?

Student: No

Esmeralda: Okay. Entonces el único que queda es haz, h-a-z. Eso significa un **bundle**

Okay. So the only one missing is "haz", h-a-z. That means "bundle"

Student: Ahhh

Esmeralda: O un ramero[1]

Or a bouquet

Student: H-a-s <spells>

Esmeralda: H-a-z <spells>

Student: H-a-z

Esmeralda: Bien, haz, entonces un haz de flores, fue lo que se le dio

Good, "haz", so like a flower bundle or bouquet, what was given

The Peer as the Expert **123**

Student: <repeats> Haz

Esmeralda: Bien. ¿Número 6?

Good. Number 6?

Student: <repeats> Un haz de flo-, oh okay <nods and smiles>

Once again, transcription of Esmeralda's interaction with the student can illustrate the interpersonal meanings inscribed in the session while noting clause division and mood type:

Turn	Speaker	Text
1	Student:	(i) El catorce de febrero, Romeo le llevó un (.) "hasta" de flores a Julieta? [QUESTION]
2	Esmeralda:	(i) Bueno (ii) hay que empezar aquí, (iii) "has", "h-a-s", (iv) "tú has ido a tal lugar" [STATEMENT]
3	S:	(i) Mhmm [ACKNOWLEDGMENT]
4	E:	(i) ¿De qué verbo viene eso? [QUESTION]
5	S:	(i) (...) ¿Ir? (ii) Like (iii) vas a- [QUESTION]
6	E:	(i) No, (ii) porque dije (iii) has ido. [ANSWER] (iv) Ido viene de ir, (v) pero ¿has? (vi) ¿Sabes cuál es? [QUESTION] (vii) Es uno de los tiempos perfectos. [ANSWER] (viii) Entonces (ix) te voy a decir otros ejemplos de tiempos perfectos. (x) Um, (xi) "habría ido", (xii) "habrás ido", (xiii) "has ido". [STATEMENT] (xiv) ¿Sabes cuál verbo es cada uno de esos o no? [QUESTION]
7	S:	(i) No [ANSWER]
8	E:	(i) Es "haber", (ii) de ahí viene- [STATEMENT]
9	S:	(i) Haber- [ACKNOWLEDGMENT]
10	E:	i) Entonces, (ii) yeah, (iii) have you. (iv) Entonces, (v) si yo te digo (vi) ¿tú has ido? (vii) Have you gone? [STATEMENT]
—	S:	[student nods]
11	E:	(i) ¿Okay? (ii) Entonces, (iii) ¿le llevó un haber de flores? (iv) ¿Viene de ese verbo o no? (v) Bueno, (vi) primero, (vii) es un verbo (laughter) (viii) entonces, (ix) ¿queda ahí la palabra? [QUESTION]
12	S:	(i) Le llevo un (.) [HESITATION]
13	E:	(i) Cualquier verbo que quieras poner, (ii) ¿va a describir eso? (iii) ¿O no? [QUESTION]
14	S:	(i) No [ANSWER]
15	E:	(i) Porque nec-, (ii) ¿qué es lo que necesitas (iii) si es algo de flores, (iv) ¿qué se- (v) qué se está usando? (vi) ¿Qué, (vii) uh, (viii) tipo de palabra? (ix) Adjetivo, (x) adverbio, (xi) verbo, (xii) sustantivo [QUESTION]
16	S:	(i) Adjetivo [ANSWER]

(Continued)

124 The Peer as the Expert

Turn	Speaker	Text
17	E:	(i) Perfecto, (ii) estás buscando un adjetivo (iii) o s- quizás sea un sustantivo por un tipo de flores [STATEMENT]
18	S:	(i) Mhmm [ACKNOWLEDGMENT]
19	E:	(i) ¿Vale? (.) (ii) Entonces, (iii) "has" viene del verbo. (iv) Si yo te digo hasta mañana (.) (v) ¿Qué es en inglés? [QUESTION] (vi) Tradúzcamelo [COMMAND]
20	S:	(i) Uhm, (ii) hasta mañana, (unint) (iii) until tomorrow? [QUESTION]
21	E:	(i) Bien [ACKNOWLEDGMENT]
22	S:	(i) So, (ii) until? [QUESTION]
23	E:	(i) Until. [ACKNOWLEDGMENT] (ii) ¿Funciona esa palabra ahí? [QUESTION]
24	S:	(i) No [ANSWER]
25	E:	(i) Okay (.) (ii) ¿qué es un asta? (iii) ¿Sabes qué es eso? [QUESTION]
26	S:	(i) ¿Asta? [HESITATION]
27	E:	(i) Asta sin h. [STATEMENT]
28	S:	(i) Asta (ii) como, como (.) [HESITATION]
29	E:	(i) Moose have them, (ii) reindeer have them [STATEMENT]
30	S:	(i) Ohhh [ACKNOWLEDGMENT]
31	E:	(i) Asta, (ii) entonces (iii) puede ser esto (iv) o también otra descripción para asta es como un shaft, (v) un tubo. [STATEMENT] (vi) ¿Queda eso? [QUESTION]
32	S:	(i) No [ANSWER]
33	E:	(i) Okay. (ii) Entonces (iii) el único que queda es haz, (iv) h-a-z. (v) Eso significa un bundle [STATEMENT]
34	S:	(i) Ahhh [ACKNOWLEDGMENT]
35	E:	(i) O un ramero [STATEMENT]
36	S:	(i) H-a-s [STATEMENT]
37	E:	(i) H-a-z [STATEMENT]
38	S:	(i) H-a-z [STATEMENT]
39	E:	(i) Bien [STATEMENT]
40	S:	(i) ah okay [STATEMENT]
41	E:	(ii) haz, (iii) entonces (iii) un haz de flores, (v) fue lo que se le dio [STATEMENT]
42	S:	(i) Haz [STATEMENT]
43	E:	(i) Bien. [ACKNOWLEDGMENT] (ii) ¿Número 6? [QUESTION]
44	S:	(i) un haz de- (ii) ah okay [ACKNOWLEDGMENT]

And, if the foregoing mood type analysis is quantified, the summary provided in Table 4.4 is true.

Esmeralda's approach in mediating this grammar exercise diverges significantly from that of Cristal's. Esmeralda is more assertive than Cristal in positioning herself as the expert; this is evidenced by the amount of full declarative clauses she uses in the exchange, including the fact that she does 76% of the talking, while the student only produces 17% of the exchanged clauses between the two of them. Esmeralda uses the greatest number of declarative clauses to

The Peer as the Expert 125

TABLE 4.4 Analysis of Lexico-Grammatical Resources in Esmeralda's Interaction

Mood (Clause Type)	Esmeralda	Student
Number of clauses and percentage in the interaction	90 (76%)	28 (17%)
Declarative full	35	6
Polar interrogative full	11	4
Tagged interrogative full	2	—
Wh-interrogative full	7	0
Imperative	1	—
Minor	25	11
Subject		
Most frequent subject choice	tú 11 palabra 10 you 2 verbo 5 nosotras 1 Various third-person singular 8	Various third-person singular 8
Language		
Percentage of language used in the interaction	Spanish (84 clauses, 93.3%) English (6 clauses, 6.7%)	Spanish (26 clauses, 92%) English (2 clauses, 8%)
Modalization	3	—
Modulation		
Obligation	—	—
Capability	—	

construct herself as taking an active, initiatory role in the interaction as she guides her student to the answer. Interestingly, she couples this strategy with a comparative use of English in three key moments: to illustrate the use of the auxiliary verb "haber" (one of the homophones in the exercise), when she asks the student (through the use of an imperative clause) to translate "hasta" so the student is able to eliminate it as a viable answer through a comparison in meaning, and as she continues to teach her student to rely on meanings in English. Thus, as noted in the thematic analysis of the same interaction, Esmeralda relies on her full repertoire to mediate the task with and for the student.

Similarly to Cristal, however, Esmeralda uses mostly Spanish in the interaction, likely given that both her and her students' metalinguistic repertoire comes from that learned in the formal curriculum of the program, which is carried out exclusively in Spanish. Even though Esmeralda creates less space for the student to take the floor, she consistently creates the need for her interlocutor to create a response as evidenced by the large use of polar interrogatives.

Towards the end of the interaction, when Esmeralda prompts her student to think about what kind of words she needs to produce (for example, recognizing that "it" isn't a verb, but a noun), she catches herself and abruptly switches from a declarative clause to a polar interrogative clause to prompt the student

126 The Peer as the Expert

TABLE 4.5 Summary of the Exchange Structure in Esmeralda's Interaction

Participants	Speech Function
Esmeralda	Acknowledgment (3)
	Statement (13)
	Question (10)
	Answer (2)
	Command (1)
Student	Acknowledgment (6)
	Statement (4)
	Question (3)
	Answer (5)
	Hesitation (3)

for a response (rather than provide it herself). Further, Esmeralda's modality also shows the way she combines assertiveness with space for participation, as she couples instances of [modulation; obligation] such as "hay que empezar aquí" (*we have to start here*) with instances of [modalization; probability] as in "cualquier verbo que quieras poner" (*any verb you want to use*) and "o quizás un sustantivo" (*or maybe a noun*), prompting her student to consider options as the comes up with the correct answer, instead of providing it herself. This is also illustrated by Esmeralda's most frequent subject use ("tú") versus the student's various third-person subjects related to the content of the grammar exercises.

Throughout this exchange, Esmeralda's tutee is visibly engaged as evidenced not just by her surprised reaction at the end of the excerpt, but especially indicated by the relatively large use of minor clauses, which again, encode follow-up reactions and position the speaker as compliant, as seen in Table 4.5.

The analysis of the exchange structure, in this case, explicitly shows Esmeralda's guiding student responses approach, one of the literacy practices discussed in Chapter 2. As noted, Esmeralda produces ten questions and the student three answers in addition to four statements (some of which are responses to Esmeralda's questions). Even though Esmeralda takes control of the session in terms of the quantity of speech, the student is still producing the greatest number of acknowledgments, thus illustrating the students' compliance with the task at hand. This is relevant too given the context of the task, as it is an explicitly grammar-oriented activity. Thus, initiating responses might be a more appropriate approach than one where there is less direct guidance from an expert (such as the one we see with Cristal).

In all, Cristal and Esmeralda mobilize very different approaches to constructing an academic persona as peer-to-peer tutors. Ultimately, however, they both mobilize expert identities in two distinct yet contextually situated ways. How they mobilize their expert identities responds to the task at hand, showing that their interpersonal resources are functionally motivated while mobilizing translanguaging practices.

Casual Talk Matters for Academic Literacy Development in Heritage Language Learning

As illustrated through an Appraisal analysis of the lexico-grammatical resources that tutors mobilize in the session, we see the varied strategies that tutors utilize to provide academic support to their students as they develop an academic persona, or as they position themselves as experts. Analysis of mood through modality within the speech event of tutor–tutee interactions shows that tutors mobilize specific types of clauses (of particular mood types) to create student-oriented interactions where tutees engage with rather than challenge the material being presented (including, for the most part, grammatical tasks such as the rules of accentuation and homophones in Spanish—both metalinguistic topics with which tutees struggle and on which tutors are experts). While the tutors analyzed in this section mobilize different lexico-grammatical resources, both interactions show the tutees' engagement with the task. Cristal mobilized a more student-centered approach where she allowed the student to use the highest number of minor and declarative clauses and produced "tú" (the informal, second-person singular pronoun) as the most commonly used subject. Further, her modulation facilitates a sense of capability in her student, and analysis of the exchange structure shows that both tutor and tutee use acknowledgments to a similar extent. Alternatively, Esmeralda mobilized a more teacher-oriented approach where she used the greatest number of declarative clauses, but where she also used polar interrogatives to allow space for the student to consider different answers to the task at hand. Further, Esmeralda's modality demonstrates how she combines assertiveness with space for participation, coupling obligation with probability to allow her student to consider various options, as opposed to Esmeralda providing the answer herself. Analysis of the exchange structure shows that, while Esmeralda is producing the greatest number of questions, it is her student who produces the greatest number of acknowledgments. The analysis shows that tutors create academic personas in distinct, contextually motivated ways that respond to the context and the task at hand, showing that their interpersonal resources, or "casual talk" is functionally motivated in this non-classroom, bilingually hybrid context.

Casual talk, therefore, and especially as it exists in academic spaces, is data that, while seldom studied, can illustrate the ways in which non-traditional academic repertoires are at play with the academic literacy development that students are expected to gain. Especially for heritage students, whose "casual" or "informal" repertoires have traditionally been invisible in the conception of new research epistemologies and traditional pedagogical methodologies, the careful, intentional, and critical study of heritage language practices can provide key information about how students are leveraging their linguistic repertoires in service of learning not just inside but especially outside the classroom. For a discussion of the pedagogical implications of the data findings, see Chapter 6.

128 The Peer as the Expert

In Chapter 5, I continue exploring the interpersonal and evaluative underpinnings of tutors' repertoires from an Appraisal Theory perspective. Yet, instead of illustrating tutors' contributions to their tutee's academic development, I share data that shows how—by mobilizing their own dynamic, hybrid repertoires—tutors actively design a student-led academic community that directly contributes to tutees' sense of belonging in literacy learning.

Note

1 Esmeralda likely meant "ramo", a commonly used word for "bouquet" in Spanish.

References

Achugar, M. (2009). Constructing a bilingual professional identity in a graduate classroom. *Language, Indentity, and Education, 8*(2–3), 65–97.

Achugar, M., & Oteíza, T. (2009). In whatever language people feel comfortable": Conflicting language ideologies in the U.S. Southwest border. *Text & Talk, 29*(4), 371–391.

Achugar, M., & Pessoa, S. (2009). Power and place: Language attitudes towards Spanish in a bilingual academic community in Southwest Texas. *Spanish in Context, 6*(2), 199–223.

Beaudrie, S. M., & Vergara, D. W. (2021). Reimagining the goals of HL pedagogy through critical language awareness. In S. Loza & S. Beaudrie (Eds.), *Heritage Language Teaching: Critical Language Awareness Perspectives for Research and Pedagogy* (pp. 63–79). London: Routledge.

Beaudrie, S. M., Ducar, C., & Potowski, K. (2014). *Heritage Language Teaching: Research and Practice.* New York: McGraw-Hill Education Create.

Eggins, S., & Slade, D. (1997). *Analyzing Casual Conversation.* London: Cassell.

Gutiérrez, K. D., Baquedano-López, P., & Tejeda, C. (1999). Rethinking diversity: Hybridity and hybrid language practices in the third space. *Mind, Culture, and Activity, 6*(4), 286–303.

Halliday, M. A. K. (1994). *An Introduction to Functional Grammar* (2nd ed.). London: Edward Arnold.

Hood, S. (2010). *Appraising Research: Evaluation in Academic Writing.* London: Palgrave Macmillan.

Hood, S., & Martin, J. R. (2007). Invoking attitude: The play of graduation in appraising discourse. In R. Hasan, C. M. I. M. Matthiessen, & J. Webster (Eds.), *Continuing Discourse on Language. A Functional Perspective* (Vol. 2, pp. 739–764). London: Equinox.

Loza, S., & Beaudrie, S. M. (Eds.). (2021). *Heritage Language Teaching: Critical Language Awareness Perspectives for Research and Pedagogy.* London: Routledge.

Macken- Horarik, M., & Isaac, A. (2014). Appraising appraisal. In G. Thompson & L. Alba- Juez (Eds.), *Evaluation in Context.* Amsterdam: John Benjamins Pu`blishing Company.

Martin, J. R., & White, P. R. R. (2005). *The Language of Evaluation: Appraisal in English.* New York: Palgrave.

Mori, M. S. (2014). *Negotiating Ownership when Incorporating Outside Sources: A Qualitative Study with Multilingual Undergraduate Students.* (Unpublished PhD Dissertation), University of California, Davis, CA.

Oteíza, T. (2009). Evaluative patterns in the official discourse of Human Rights in Chile: Giving value to the past and building historical memories in society. *Delta, 25*(Special Issue), 609–640.

Potowski, K., & Carreira, M. (2004). Teacher development and national standards for Spanish as a heritage language. *Foreign Language Annals, 37*(3), 427–437.

Showstack, R. E. (2012). Symbolic power in the heritage language classroom: How Spanish heritage speakers sustain and resist hegemonic discourses on language and cultural diversity. *Spanish in Context, 9*(1), 1–26.

Valdés, G., Fishman, J. A., Chávez, R., & Pérez, W. (2006). *Developing Minority Language Resources: The Case of Spanish in California.* Buffalo: Multilingual Matters.

Valdés, G. (1995). The teaching of minority languages as academic subjects: Pedagogical and theoretical challenges. *Modern Language Journal, 79*(3), 299–328.

Vergara, D. W., & Ibarra, C. E. (2015). Understanding the inheritors: The perception of beginning-level students toward their Spanish as a Heritage Language program. *Euro American Journal of Applied Linguistics and Languages, 2*(2), 85–101.

White, P. R. R. (2015). Appraisal theory. In K. Tracy, C. Illie, & T. Sandel (Eds.), *The International Encyclopedia of Language and Social Interaction.* Hoboken: John Wiley & Sons.

White, P. R. R. (2020). *The Appraisal Homepage. Appraisal: An Overview.* Retrieved from: https://www.grammatics.com/appraisal/appraisalguide/framed/frame.htm

5

THE PEER AS ALLY

Tutors Creating Community in an Academic Space

Creating an Academic Community: Mediating Collaborative Learning

Through the Use of Evaluative Language

As I conceived the framing of this last data chapter, I reflected on my own experience as an undergraduate student in the US. I attended college as an international student. I was (and still am) Latina. Spanish is my first language. Importantly, I had immigrated to the United States, leaving my family behind while navigating a system entirely foreign to me.

To secure my own academic success, I needed community. Certainly, this could apply to any student group with previous experiences and particular trajectories as they begin college—athletes, first-generation students, students moving away from home, etc. Regardless of what student group is in question, they all need institutions of higher education to intentionally create spaces within their campuses where students find like-minded peers to whom they can relate. This chapter illustrates the underpinnings of what those spaces can look like for students in a Spanish for heritage speakers program.

In a seminal 2016 article, Spanish as a Heritage Language scholar Glenn Martínez highlights the relevance of heritage language instruction as an optimal site for the development and improvement of heritage language communities. As such, he highlights that heritage language instruction, by intentionally assessing students' *capabilities* (and not simply their *competencies*), has not only the potential to develop the student but, importantly, to also advance the community. Martínez's view is that "community-based learning and teaching is not a tangential or supplementary activity to HL education but rather [...] a foundational

DOI: 10.4324/9781003191179-6

The Peer as Ally **131**

activity that is essential to the achievement of its educational goals" (2016, p. 48). When heritage students are afforded opportunities to participate actively and directly in language maintenance and language revitalization in their own peer communities, educators should align the relevance of formal instruction with the centrality of students' identity, potential, and active participation in communities in and out of school. This "embeddedness of community" is, as framed by Martínez, a powerful and imperative component of heritage education.

In the context of this book, "the community" is illustrated through the peer-tutoring room, including all tutoring sessions completed as part of this study. Both tutors (themselves heritage speakers) and tutees co-create an academic community that exudes a strong sense of belonging. As I have shown throughout the book, academic contexts of instruction such as the program described here can afford heritage speaker communities considerable influence. In this book, I subscribe to pedagogical models such as this tutoring program (see Chapter 3 for a full description of the peer-to-peer program) that provide students with the opportunity to mobilize expert identities, not only in consideration of what students can do (i.e., their proficiency) but also their roles (i.e., language speaker, community member, language partner, tutor, mentor, ally, etc.) and their impact in the community (Martínez, 2016). Additionally, I conceptualize the exploration of academic literacy in the heritage language as a process that is not just localized beyond the individual learner but also, and very critically, mobilized across communities of practice.

This chapter presents an additional discourse analysis of tutoring sessions using Appraisal Theory. In contrast to the analysis in Chapter 4, however, it focuses not on the lexico-grammatical resources mobilized by tutors but on the evaluative stances embedded in their discourse—that is, the ways they use language to express, negotiate, and naturalize inter-subject ideological positions (White, 2015). Evaluative stances, as per Appraisal Theory, allow speakers to mobilize judgments about what is being said and to whom it is being said. Analyzing speakers' evaluative stances per Appraisal Theory complements the discourse analysis of Chapter 4 by contextualizing how tutors, beyond constructing academic personas in unique ways, use language to construct an academic community that is welcoming, encouraging, and supportive and that, most critically, responds to the context and the task at hand, demonstrating that tutors' interpersonal resources are functionally motivated in this non-classroom context and are thus conducive to a collective sense of belonging, all while mobilizing hybrid linguistic repertoires.

In order to frame this evaluative language analysis, I identified and highlighted the discursive resources that, during tutoring sessions, signaled, inscribed, or evoked positive or negative evaluations of people, places, things, or events. As such, for this analysis, I focus on two semantic domains of Appraisal Theory: *affect*, which focuses on the emotional response of the speaker, and is expressed through the emotional dyads of *happiness* and/or *unhappiness*, *satisfaction* and/or *dissatisfaction*, and *security* and/or *insecurity*; and *appreciation*, which highlights how

132 The Peer as Ally

speakers evaluate the message—judgments about its *composition*, its *valuation*, and other systems of social value. Additionally, I note how speakers were raising or lowering these judgments through *graduation*, which illustrated how speakers can intensify a particular evaluation through *force* or *focus*.

This chapter extends the analysis of the evaluative language inscribed in the interactions between peer tutor and tutee, including illustrations of the varied ways in which tutors actively and intentionally create community as they work with their students and while they employ a variety of language resources (including "informal" and translingual resources) that evoke feelings of "community belonging"—the second set of themes discussed in Chapter 3. As mentioned, this analysis of attitudinal positionings was completed by identifying the discursive resources that signaled evaluation—positionings which are largely constructed through lexical selections. In all, analysis of tutors' evaluative language illustrates tutors' shaping their language (or their interpersonal resources) to adapt to the socially situated context of the tutoring room, thus depicting another way in which they shape their (and their tutees') belonging in an academic space.

Academic Empathy: Leveraging Tutees' Experiences for Learning

In Chapter 4, as I illustrate how Cristal positions herself as an expert and mobilizes a unique academic persona, we see an interaction between her and her tutee which includes the pair working through the rules of diacritic accentuation in Spanish. As we learn, the student begins the session anxious about their upcoming final exam that features a section on written accents in Spanish, and Cristal helps her internalize those rules. At the end of the interaction, we see the student finally realize how to appropriately apply the grammar rule that explains whether certain words are written with a diacritic or not, included here again for reference:

Student: Chávez (.)

Cristal: ¿Pero dices ChaVEZ?

But do you say ChaVEZ?

Student: ChaVEZ, no

Cristal: CHAvez, **right**?

Student: Ajá. Entonces digo ChAvez –

Uh huh. So I say ChAvez

Cristal: ((Mhm)) –

Student: Cesar Chávez. ¿En la e? ¿Sí, no?–

The Peer as Ally **133**

Cesar Chávez. On the e? Yes, no?

Cristal: No, ChavEz. ¿Cuál se-? [unint]

No. ChavEz. Which one do you- ?

Student: ChAvez. Cha. (...)

Cristal: <nods>

Student: Entonces si termina en dic- en la última (sílaba) no lo sigue (la regla) entonces va en Cha, en la a

So, if it ends in it- on the last one (syllable) it does not follow it (the rule) so it goes on Cha, on the a

Cristal: Mhm (.)

Student: Chávez

Cristal: Mhm

Student: (.) ChavEz, pero no digo Cesar ChavEZ. Entonces por eso no va en la- va en la a –

ChavEz, but I don't say Cesar ChavEz. So that's why it does go on the- it goes on the a

Cristal: Mhm –

Student: porque no lo sigue. –

Because it doesn't follow it

Cristal: Yeah –

Student: Cesar ChaVEZ. Con palabras más así como de dos sílabas es más fácil para mí como con palabras más largas porque me confundo. Okay, entonces fácil. Fa-cil

Cesar ChaVEZ. With words like that like with two syllables is easier for me like with words that are longer because I get confused. Okay, so "easy". Ea-sy.

<Cristal and Student begin working through specific words. Approximately four minutes go by>

Cristal: ¿**So** ya miraste? –

So you see?

Student: Okay yeah –

Cristal: Pero sub- subrayas el- el xxx-

But underline the- the-

134 The Peer as Ally

Student: Okay

Cristal: -de acuerdo con la regla es lo que dice

Following the rule, what does it say

Student: Ok y luego sílaba-

Ok and then the syllable-

Cristal: Ajá –

Student: Termina en: (.) en um vocal y la regla dice que las que terminan en vocal deben de llevarlo en la penúltima

It ends in- um a vowel and the rule says that those that end on a vowel should have the accent on the second to last

Cristal: Mhm

Student: Entonces aquí, síla- y digo silaBA. No digo silaBA. –

So here, "sila-" and I say "silaBA". I don't say "silaBA"

Cristal: No, dices siLAba –

No, you say "silaba"

Student: Aha –

Cristal: so dices SIlaba.

So you say "SIlaba"

Student: -laba

Cristal: So entonces –

So then

Student: Sílaba (.) entonces lo rompe y lleva en la i. En la i

"Sílaba" so it breaks it and has it on the i. On the i

Cristal: Mhm. Pero ya mirastes que el golpe lo debería-

Mhm. But you see that the emphasis should be-

Student: debería ir allí –

Should go there

Cristal: de caer allí, pero no cae ahí –

Should go there, but it doesn't go there

Student: ¡Oh! –

Cristal: Eso es lo que- (.) @@

    That's what-

Student: @@ Después de mil años ya entendí

    After a thousand years I got it

Cristal: Después de mil años ya entendí

    After a thousand years I got it

Student: Ya, ya entendí –

    Yes, I got it now

Cristal: Ayy –

Student: Eso es más fácil

    That's easier

Cristal: So yeah

Student: Uh!

Cristal: xxx

Student: Ah, me siento realizada

    Ah, I feel fulfilled

As noted, this detailed interaction shows instances of "tutor as expert" or, per the thematic analysis described in Chapter 3, any instance of tutors taking the role of the instructor or passing on information about the design of the course or any particular topic of content as a fact (grammar, content, writing, etc.). In Table 5.1, we see the Appraisal summary following the student's attitudinal positions during the session, which are guided by Cristal as the two work together. I note what lexical items are appraised as well as how they are appraised (*appreciation* or *affect*) and during what turn the appraised item happens. Additionally, I note any instances of graduation.

The Appraisal analysis presented in the table shows Cristal's overt contribution to her student feeling less insecure and more secure as the tutee navigates how to appropriately recognize words that take diacritic accentuation in Spanish. Evident in the analysis, the only evaluative stances of *Appreciation*—as mentioned, an attitudinal meaning speakers enact to index evaluation of a text or process—is that of valuation (e.g., evaluation of the message content being put across by the text or process.) The student mostly mobilizes valuation stances toward accentuation in Spanish, valuing it as "más fácil" or much easier at the end of the session. Thus, we know the student demonstrates that she can certainly access a sense of confidence when she conceives of herself as being able to appropriately place written accents. Importantly, at the beginning and throughout most of the

136 The Peer as Ally

TABLE 5.1 Appraisal Analysis in Cristal's Interaction with Student

Total Appraised Items	10	
in Interaction	135	
Total Clauses		
Attitudinal Positionings	Lexical Item → Appraised	Turn
Appreciation	⊘	
Reaction	⊘	
Composition	▶ (palabras de dos sílabas → más fácil)	▶ 13
Valuation	▶ (acentuación → más fácil)	▶ 107
	▶ (acentuación → fácil)	▶ 137
	▶ (acentuación → fácil)	▶ 141
	▶ (acentuación → más fácil)	▶ 167
Affect	⊘	
Un/happiness	▶ (yo → confusión) [insecurity]	▶ 13
In/security	▶ (palabras nuevas → confusión) [insecurity]	▶ 137
Dis/satisfaction	▶ (yo → sentirse realizada) [security]	▶ 169
	⊘	
Graduation	▶ (después de mil años [entendí]) (++)	▶ 163 and
Force	⊘	again in
Focus		181

session, the student's evaluative stances of *affect*—a second attitudinal meaning speakers utilize to encode the evaluation of emotional states—encode insecurity. The student is clear about how incapable she feels in terms of knowing where to write diacritic accentuation correctly in Spanish. What is relevant is that as the session proceeds, and with Cristal's guidance, her *affect* stance transforms into one of security by the very end of the session. In fact, this is the only stance that the student amplifies through force when she says, at the very end, when she uses a *graduation* resource to say "después de mil años, ya entendí" (*after a thousand years, I understood*). We then see how Cristal guides the student toward a more positive evaluative stance regarding accentuation in Spanish.

Cristal's effective strategies are evident as she creates an agentive learning process where students can feel free to make mistakes, take risks, and develop more positive evaluative stances vis-a-vis Spanish literacy. In an interview I conducted with Cristal, it is clear she has intentional awareness of the importance of aligning with where students are in relation to their learning:

Cristal: Pero es que me encanta como mi trabajo como tutora. **Like,** I mean, me encanta como aprender de mis estudiantes y sé que tengo que mejorar y aprender a adaptarme como enseñar como el currículo y todo el material, **so** entonces yo siempre trato como de adaptarme a las necesidades de mis estudiantes. **So** no puedo decir que no me gusta como nada de mi trabajo.

The Peer as Ally **137**

It's just that I love my job as a tutor. Like, I mean, I love like to learn from my students and I know I have to improve and learn to adapt to like teach the curriculum and the material, so I always try to like adapt to the needs of my students. So I can't say I don't like anything about my job.

Building Community for and with Tutees

At the evaluative level, tutors consistently engage with their tutees as they informally discuss several topics beyond the task at hand, including specific shared endeavors and experiences as undergraduate, first-generation, Latinx young people. Thus, as Eggins and Slade (1997) suggest, attitudinal positionings are essential devices to illustrate how individuals construct and signal degrees of solidarity in relationships and interactions. In this section, I present a handful of moments included in the "community building" theme from Chapter 3 per tutor and analyze the several instances of evaluative language—contextualizing the interaction for each and highlighting each interaction's contribution to a sense of belonging in this community of practice.

Concepción

As presented in Chapter 3, during the day before Thanksgiving break, Concepción and her student exchange conversation about the struggles of balancing school and being away from family. The student expresses feeling overwhelmed by the amount of work she must complete and not having enough money to visit family:

Concepción: Vas a estar bien ya mero terminamos

> *You'll be fine. We are almost done*

Student: I know (.) y todos modos la otra semana ni es una complete

> *I know. And then anyways next week isn't even a whole week*

Concepción: Va a ser el día de acción de gracias (.) ¿Vas a ir a casa o te

> quedas?

> *It's going to be Thanksgiving. Are you going home or are you staying?*

Student: No si– sé iba a quedar, pero mi amiga me dijo me dijo okay um mi

> papá va a venir quieres venir con nosotros, okay pues yo no quería

> pagar un avión porque muchos un ticket de avión pues todos quieren

> hacer eso, pero yo no tengo dinero para eso yo me quedo aquí no los

> miro hasta–

138 The Peer as Ally

> *I don't know- I was going to stay, but my friend told me okay um, my dad is going to come do you want to come with us, okay well I didn't want to pay for a plane ticket because a lot- many want to do that, but I don't have money for that so I am staying, I won't see them until-*

Concepción: The struggle

Student: Hasta el <laughs>

> *Until*

Concepción: Yeah it's hard bueno pues que te diviertas y comes mucho

> *Yeah it's hard well I hope you have a lot of fun and that you eat a lot*

In this brief interaction, Concepción mobilizes two appraisal instances, one of *affect* and the second one of *appreciation*, as seen in Figures 5.1 and 5.2.

Both instances of Concepción's evaluative language signal a direct acknowledgment of the types of struggles that her student is communicating to her, as well as Concepción's own recognition that she relates to the "struggle" (i.e., "the struggle is real"). First, Concepción assures her student, through an emotional instance of security, that the tutee will be fine as she continues to navigate the remainder of the academic quarter ("vas a estar bien" or *you will be okay*). Then, Concepción directly acknowledges the financial struggle the student is enduring, likely similar to her own struggle regarding access to plane tickets for family vacations. To highlight this last sense of shared experience around financial difficulties, Concepción appraises an instance of valuation, agreeing with her student and demonstrating that she too knows what it's like to struggle financially. Concepción's relatedness to her students' personal experiences mobilizes a sense of community belonging, considering a possible distinctive financial struggle.

Vanessa

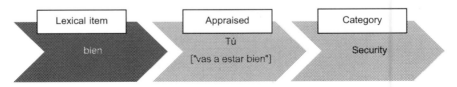

FIGURE 5.1 Affect Appraisal in Concepción's Interaction.

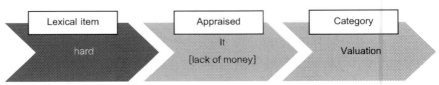

FIGURE 5.2 Appreciation Appraisal in Concepción's Interaction.

The Peer as Ally **139**

As Vanessa and her student are preparing to start the day's session, they chat about several events going on across campus. They exchange a few words about SPEAK's (Scholars Promoting Education Awareness and Knowledge) annual dinner ceremony organized by the student-run organization which focuses on supporting and empowering undocumented students at the university. Later, as they close the session, the same student shares with Vanessa that she has been sick for the last several days, and Vanessa engages:

Student: Fui a una cena acá, el- en el **Student Community Center**

I went to a dinner here, at the Student Community Center

Vanessa: Fuiste a es, ¿la de SPEAK?

You went to that one, the one for SPEAK?

Student: Ahuh, ((sí))–

Ahuh, yes

Vanessa: Ahh, muy bien, ¡qué bonito! ¿Cómo estuvo?

Oh, great, how nice! How was it?

Student: Bien, estuvo bien, había mucha gente

Good, it was good, there was a lot of people

Vanessa: ¿Verdad que sí?

Weren't there?

Student: Sí (.) <coughs> y fui pues, caminé, regresamos tarde y no tenía **sweater**

Yes and I went, well, I walked there, we came back late and I didn't have a sweater

Vanessa: Sí–

Yes

Student: Y el día siguiente estaba como que ¡AY mi garganta!

And the next day I was like OUCH my throat!

Vanessa: Sí, sí

Yes, yes

Student: Yeah, sí, um, el domingo me puse mal- peor y luego ayer estaba peor, [unint] estaba toda fónica

Yeah, yes, Sunday it was bad, worse, and then yesterday it was really bad, I was losing my voice

Vanessa: Sí, ay. ¿Pero te sientes mejor ahora?

Yeah, ouch. But you feel better now?

Student: Ehh

Vanessa: ¿Más o menos?

More or less?

Student: Sí, ahora sí mejor, bueno, más o menos

Yeah, now yes, well, more or less

In this short excerpt, there are two relevant interactions that carry evaluative language. In both instances, the student responds with the same category of appraisal to Vanessa, as seen in Figures 5.3 and 5.4.

As we see during the session, Vanessa gives priority to issues outside of the task at hand, engaging with her tutee about topics such as specific events on campus in support of undocumented students, as well as illness. She first appraises the SPEAK event, mobilizing a particularly empathic stance toward the event, and communicating her awareness and support for undocumented students (such as many heritage speakers at this institution). Later in the interaction, Vanessa tries to encourage her student by appraising the student's state of mind as hopefully "better". Then, the student, once again, uptakes the same instance of valuation by repeating she feels "better" or at least "more or less". She thus intentionally mobilizes valuation, illustrating how Vanessa ventures "beyond academics" to instill a sense of community belonging in the student. What is important here is the student's response, which matches the same instance of valuation and satisfaction as the pair relate. As Vanessa's student uptakes the same evaluative language in relation to the same appraised lexical items (the event as "bonito" or *nice* as well as "bien" or *good* and the students' state of being as "mejor" or *better*), we can safely assume that the tutee willingly and gladly receives this solidarity. During this short exchange, the two, guided by Vanessa, build a unique interpersonal interaction that, once again, builds on a sense of belonging.

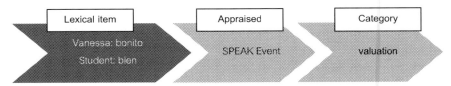

FIGURE 5.3 Appreciation Appraisal in Vanessa's Interaction.

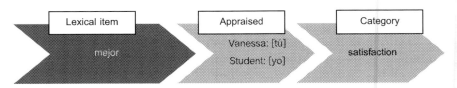

FIGURE 5.4 Affect Appraisal in Vanessa's Interaction.

FIGURE 5.5 Appreciation Appraisal in Esmeralda's Interaction.

Esmeralda and Maité

Esmeralda also uses evaluative language to establish solidarity with her students in relation to issues outside of the task at hand; this primarily features concerns stemming from life as an undergraduate and especially as a first-generation Latina. In this short excerpt, we see how Esmeralda uses *appreciation* to express the same feeling of dread experienced by her student when the pair discuss how much work is due in the upcoming week (see Figure 5.5). Appreciation is also expressed in addressing the relief that Veteran's Day is coming so that they both can take a break from schoolwork:

Esmeralda: Sí, va a ser muy pesada esta semana, pero el viernes es **Veteran's Day, yay. Thank you for all the veterans of our nation**

Yes, this week is going to be tough, but Friday is Veteran's Day, yay. Thank you for all the veterans of our nation

Student: I know right?

Esmeralda: Allowing us to not go to school <giggles>

In a different interaction and as they settle into the day's session, Maité talks to her student about having had limited time to eat anything throughout the day due to being so busy. Her student reacts to Maité's comments and engages in conversation about how difficult it is to juggle responsibilities at school as well as at work. As they vent together, Maité asks the student about her job outside of school:

Student: Estoy tratando de empezar todo a la misma vez

I'm trying to start everything at the same time

Maité: ¿Dónde trabajas?

Where do you work?

Student: En la Forever 21

At Forever 21

Maité: Oh how FUN

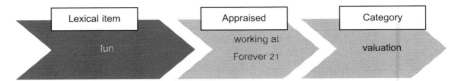

FIGURE 5.6 Appreciation Appraisal in Maité's Interaction.

After this short interaction and Maité's appraisal of *Appreciation* (see Figure 5.6), the student continues sharing with Maité the ins and outs of her job, the aspects of it she likes and dislikes, and the challenges that working while being a full-time student pose. Maité and her student continue building solidarity (that is, building community) throughout the first part of the session.

In all, excerpts in this section illustrate analyses of the evaluative language mobilized in the sessions that index a sense of community belonging. Specifically, the analysis shows the varied ways in which tutors actively and intentionally create community as they work with their students and as they use language that evokes academic empathy as a component of community belonging. I showed earlier, for example, that the attitudinal positioning of Cristal's tutee shows how she re-frames her *Affect* of diacritic accents from an insecure stance to a secure one as the tutor guides the session, thereby contributing to the tutee's sense of empowerment around a challenging metalinguistic task. Thus, beyond mobilizing a particular academic persona as well as a defined expert identity as we see in Chapter 4, tutors in this case use strategies to create a learning process where students can feel free to make mistakes, take risks, and develop more positive evaluative stances vis-à-vis Spanish literacy. This analysis of evaluative language often refers to unique shared endeavors and experiences that tutors and tutees share as undergraduate, first-generation Latinx young people. We see how the interpersonal stances—indexed through evaluative language and shared by tutors and tutees in the interaction—construct solidarity as tutors signal direct acknowledgment of tutees' struggles in and out of school activities, among other related topics.

Lastly, it is relevant to note that no instances of *Judgment* were coded, which evidences the prevalence of community belonging even in tutor–tutee interactions where tutors mobilized expert identities. The lack of *Judgment* as an appraised value is likely given that instances of judgment often encode opposition and interpersonal distance from the interlocutors. Thus, the tutors' and tutees' attitudinal positionings of *Affect* and *Appreciation* are consistently aligned, constructing students' experience of the tutoring session as a place where their affective involvement is widely engaged to positive evaluative meanings that, in turn, build an academic community to which both tutors and tutees are invested. Indeed, tutors consistently use specific attitudinal meanings of words in conversation with their tutors in order to mutually construct a community where students' experiences as related to their academics are shared, welcomed, and

The Peer as Ally **143**

TABLE 5.2 All Instances of Affect and Appreciation with Coding

Speaker	Lexical Item	Appraised	Affect or Appreciation Subcategory
Concepción	bien (*good*)	student	Security
	hard	lack of money	Valuation
Vanessa	bonito (*nice*)	SPEAK event	Valuation
	mejor (*better*)	student	Satisfaction
Esmeralda	pesada (*tough*)	esta semana	Composition
Maité	fun	working at Forever 21	Valuation

valid. Tutors consistently construct a community of shared feelings and values by sharing similar emotions and experiences with their students (Martin & White, 2005) and thus creating belonging through peer interactions.

Table 5.2 summarizes all instances of *affect* and *appreciation* described in all foregoing interactions.

The Appraisal Theory analysis built throughout Chapters 4 and 5 shows the different ways in which interpersonal meanings are inscribed in communication and how these meanings can construct specific realities. How tutors mobilize both lexico-grammatical resources inscribed in the mood structure of their interactions with their tutees as well as the interpersonal resources inscribed in their evaluative language demonstrate the intentional and functionally motivated linguistic practices they mobilize in the session. These linguistic practices build effective academic personas to the benefit of their tutees as tutors construct academic empathy and community building, making the tutoring session an accessible, positive component of students' academic experiences. This analysis is relevant for assessing student learning as it shows how interpersonal meanings are inscribed in communication and how these meanings construct the experience for students, showing a more precise illustration of the socially situated reality of, in this case, the heritage language peer-to-peer tutoring room.

Though it is beyond the scope of this analysis, it is important to consider the extent to which students are directly benefiting from tutors' interpersonal strategies. That is, what are the measurable effects that these particular attitudinal positions have on students' academic development? And how do these strategies affect students' experience in the program at large? Some of these questions are partially answered in a related study of the same tutoring program (Reznicek-Parrado, Patiño-Vega, & Colombi, 2018) where the authors complete analyses of evaluative language which show that tutees express an internalized lack of confidence regarding their linguistic skills through powerful emotions of insecurity when describing their feelings about their Spanish skills before joining the peer tutoring program.

However, the authors also demonstrate that students' emotional responses of insecurity regarding their own abilities in Spanish literacy contrast strikingly with the feelings of security and satisfaction they express when describing posterior emotions after just 11 weeks of working with a peer tutor. Additionally,

144 The Peer as Ally

instances of *appreciation*, both in the subcategories of valuation, reaction, and satisfaction, index students' positive evaluations of the course and the peer-to-peer program, which ultimately echoes renewed interest in, motivation for, and value of their Spanish-related repertoires. Overall, the data in that related study shows participants indexing a marked positive evaluative experience of the peer-to-peer interaction, the program, and, ultimately, their perceived emotional experience of their bilingual identity. Notably, after just 11 weeks of peer-to-peer collaboration as curricular support to this heritage program, participants' affective involvement is widely engaged or aligned to positive evaluative meanings of the bilingual identity. This combats previous negative evaluations of students' Spanish academic repertoires, suggesting that tutors' literacy and interpersonal strategies are highly effective and have positive consequences for students' academic experience not just related to the Spanish course but also to their experiences of belonging in Spanish learning and academic life.

Translating Peer Community Engagement and Heritage Literacy Practices into the Classroom

This book as a whole, and specifically the data analyses presented in Chapters 2 through 5, demonstrates that social approaches to literacy can give us insights into the ways in which Spanish heritage speakers mobilize particular translingual literacy repertoires to adapt to a socially situated academic context. In this case, we see how peer tutors mediate academic-related tasks with and for their students by using a range of literacy practices that reflect their sociodemographic and educational profile as first-generation, Latinx heritage speakers. Many of these literacy practices, as I demonstrate, are similar to and productive for the literacy and language practices expected in school. Thus, this represents one illustration of how literacy is actually mobilized by our students—a literacy shaped by practices patterned by their social and cultural values, power relations, historical patterns, and socially situated circumstances.

After establishing the socially meaningful and rich interactional power of heritage language practices throughout the data chapters, the next and final chapter of this book considers why such analysis presented in this book matters for heritage language instruction. It suggests the re-conceptualization of Spanish Heritage Language pedagogy to leverage students' translingual practices as crucial for teaching and learning. With the intention of transforming practitioners' critical lens in the field, I discuss a possible pedagogy that engages with the tension brought on by institutional standardization of most educational contexts where heritage pedagogies exist. I share a collection of pedagogical moves, activities, reflective prompts, and other ideas that highlight the deep importance and relevance of heritage speakers' sociocultural context, especially as it related to its realization in the heritage language classroom. I discuss how such a pedagogy can benefit both student and educator and how it can enrich the exploration of relevant content by recognizing and valuing the literacy practices of heritage students while developing advanced literacy skills in the heritage language. Additionally, I share a collection of relevant considerations for promoting peer-to-peer tutoring programs as a relevant and accessible pedagogical initiative to other Spanish for heritage student programs. Finally, as I illustrate a potential pedagogy, I also reflect on my last five years as Director of the Spanish for Bilingual/Heritage Speakers Program at my current institution, the University of Denver, considering how I have drawn on this research for the conception, design, and development of Spanish heritage courses. I illustrate the implications of this pedagogy by weaving in student voices through brief interviews with current and former students of our program.

References

Eggins, S., & Slade, D. (1997). *Analyzing Casual Conversation*. London: Cassell.

Martin, J. R., & White, P. R. R. (2005). *The Language of Evaluation: Appraisal in English*. New York: Palgrave.

Martínez, G. (2016). Goals and beyond in heritage language education. In M. Fairclough & S. Beaudrie (Eds.), *Innovative Strategies for Heritage Language Teaching: A Practical Guide for the Classroom* (pp. 39–55). Washington, DC: Georgetown University Press.

Reznicek-Parrado, L. M., Patiño-Vega, M. & Colombi, M.C. (2018). Academic peer-tutors and academic biliteracy development in students of Spanish as a heritage language. In S. Pastor Cesteros & A. F. Cabrera (eds.) L2 Spanish Academic Discourse: New Contexts, New Methodologies / El discurso académico en español como L2: nuevos contextos, nuevas metodologías. *Journal of Spanish Language Teaching, Special Issue, 5*(2), 152–167.

White, P. R. R. (2015). Appraisal theory. In K. Tracy, C. Illie, & T. Sandel (Eds.), *The International Encyclopedia of Language and Social Interaction*. Hoboken: John Wiley & Sons.

6

STUDENTS' HYBRID LANGUAGE PRACTICES AT THE CORE OF SHL PEDAGOGY

How to Foster Equitable Pedagogies in SHL

Heritage Language Learning for Institutional Belonging

Not long ago, a former student of the University of Denver's Spanish Program for Heritage/Bilingual Speakers shared with me:

> [Esta clase] me ayudó a clasificar específicamente qué hablante de español soy yo, así que yo soy una hablante de herencia, y es algo que yo no sabía qué significaba, um, cuál era la definición, así que definitivamente me ayudó con esa parte de mi identidad, um, y creo que también me hizo sentir mucho más (.) orgullosa de poder hablar español, y estar en un salón en donde soy considerada un hablante de herencia del español, um. Creo que es algo que en otros cursos (.) no se hace porque eres la minoría en veces, si estás en una clase de español para personas que están hablando español como segundo idioma, um, en veces es raro que [haya] (.) um, hispanohablantes pero este curso definitivamente aseguró esa parte de mi identidad, y me ayudó a clasificarla mejor.

> *This class helped me recognize specifically what type of Spanish speaker I am. So I am a heritage speaker, and that is something I did not know what it mean, um, what the definition was, so it definitely helped me with that part of my identity, um, and I think it also helped me feel prouder to be able to speak Spanish, and be in a classroom where I am considered a Spanish heritage speaker. I think it is something that in other courses you don't do because you are the minority sometimes. If you are in a Spanish class for people who are speaking Spanish as a second language, um, sometimes it is weird that there are [Latinx] Spanish speakers, but this course definitely established that part of my identity, and it helped me classify it better.*

DOI: 10.4324/9781003191179-7

This student's realization of their identity as a Spanish heritage speaker and the resulting positive impact that self-identifying as such presented for their learning is evidence that spaces of belonging are crucial in heritage students' overall academic trajectories, not just in their academic literacy learning. Thus, as I prepared to outline an accessible, useful, and effective way to illustrate the pedagogical relevance of the data presented in this book, I conceived why and how I consistently make an effort to foment heritage language practices as an integral part of my pedagogy in the way that peer tutors do following the analysis in Chapters 2 through 5. As such, I kept needing to revisit the many stories of belonging that my heritage students have shared with me throughout the last five years and as I have been directing the Spanish Program for Heritage/Bilingual Speakers at the University of Denver which I founded in 2018. Here, I begin by remembering that while teaching Spanish to heritage students has traditionally been broadly about the development of their academic literacy in Spanish, my pedagogical mission and vision are fundamentally guided by the many ways I have seen my students find themselves as Spanish speakers in my classroom. The constant, consistent, and intentional validation of the heritage language practices that students weave throughout their repertoires has, time and time again, awakened their sense of individual and collective belonging. It is imperative to remind the reader that the work of heritage language pedagogy is, firstly, about nurturing the sense of belonging that has so often been stripped from students during their early years of education, and that academic literacy development in Spanish, while essential, must come only after that. It is my view that if our pedagogical framework in Spanish Heritage Language Pedagogy prioritizes and adheres to that order, our pedagogical design will not just teach students how to write academic texts, but it will also—quite literally—change their lives.

In the Fall of 2018, I was hired by the University of Denver (DU), a midsized, private university in the heart of urban Colorado, to design and implement a Spanish program for heritage students. At the time and still today, our institution was and has continued to be invested in the recruitment and retention of first-generation students, many of which are Spanish-speaking Latinxs. While Latinxs only comprise approximately 13% percent of DU's student population as of 2021 (DU Institutional Research Analysis, 2022), it was evident that, at the time of my hiring, the university's leadership was aware of the powerful, unfolding sociodemographic national and statewide changes that evidence the rapid expansion of Latinx young students entering higher education. As illustrated by the US Census Data, Latinxs in Colorado account for about 21.8% of the population in the last census data available (2021), a jump from 17% just ten years prior (US Census Bureau, 2021). Additionally, the Latino Leadership Foundation (LLF), a local leadership partner invested in increasing Latinx leadership, forecasts growth in Colorado's current share of this population (21.8%) to 33% in just 20 years, estimating that one in four Coloradans will identify as Latinx by the end of the decade (Latino Leadership Institute, 2022). The LLF

148 Student's Language Practices for Teaching

also documents the significantly younger median age of Latinxs in the state, with those in Colorado being an average of 27 years old compared to 42 years old for non-Hispanic whites. While at 13%, Latinx students remain a small share of the student population at DU, their enrollment has increased since Fall 2016, when enrollment of Hispanic/Latinx students was 10%.

As I established the Spanish Program for Heritage/Bilingual Speakers, now five years old, I realized early on that the optimal way to conceive a long-term vision was to ground my efforts not just as pedagogy, but most importantly, as a recruitment and retainment endeavor, knowing all too well that an opportunity to connect with each other would result in a sense of "being seen" for this underrepresented student population. Certainly, my interests still laid in recruiting students so we have enough young people to teach, but importantly, my goal was especially fostering belonging as the primary source for student retention and as a core aspect of students' academic trajectory in our program and at our institution. It was crucial, therefore, to establish connections with other academic and professional support services across campus that identify the interests and well-being of Spanish-speaking Latinx students as part of their mission. For that reason, I spent many hours connecting with support staff in Admissions, across Student Support Services and student groups, as well as with other faculty who work tirelessly to support this underrepresented, on-campus student community.

Since 2019, we have enrolled 110 Spanish heritage students. Of those students, 87% were first-generation college students, and 39 of them continued to pursue a minor or major in Spanish after taking our Spanish heritage courses (DU Banner Data, 2022). Our goals are to continue growing course sections, hire more peer-to-peer tutors, and become a hub of belonging in the institution through the pedagogical model explained here. To illustrate, a former student explains what this sense of belonging looked like for them:

> Creo que, um, definitivamente las clases son un espacio donde todas las diferentes formas de español sean aceptables, ya sea (.) el Spanglish, que es un concepto que discutimos en esta última clase, um y la importancia de reconocer que hay diferentes variedades del español y que no es sólo una forma correcta de hablar el español, um (.) creo que me siento más: cómoda hablando en una clase donde sé que no me voy a ver diferente si uso una palabra en inglés, no me van a juzgar si es que uso, um, el Spanglish en la clase, um, y no importa qué diferente español yo hable a comparación con mis compañeros. Creo que su estilo de enseñar [de la profesora] transmite que ese lugar sea, um, definitiva muy- muy inclusivo a todos los diferentes dialectos del español y variedades del español. [...] Así que creo que no es tan estr- estricta con like sólo académico, sólo (.) académico en la escuela, creo que ella hace (.) una experiencia muy buena en este concepto.

> *I think that um, definitely the classes are are a safe space where all the different types of Spanish are acceptable, be it Spanglish, which is a concept that we discussed in the last class, ym and the importance of recognizing that there are different varieties of*

Spanish and not just one that is the correct way of speaking Spanish. Um, I think I feel more comfortable speaking in a class where I know I am not going to be different if I use a word in English, nobody is going to judge me for that, for using Spanglish in class, um, and it doesn't matter what Spanish I use in relation to my peers. I think her style of teaching [the professor's] communicates that that place is, certainly very inclusive to all different dialects of Spanish and varieties of Spanish. So I think she is not so strick like with just academic academic [language] in school. I think she creates a great experience in relation to that concept.

In the next sections, I illustrate the program's four key motions from which the program's pedagogical design is based. I use the term "motion" to highlight the strategic moves that a pedagogy such as the one described here takes on—echoing what García et al. group as "translanguaging stance, design and shift" (2017), which stem from a specific, ideological system acknowledging that heritage students mobilize many different language practices together and not separately. The end-result of such pedagogy is seeing such language repertoires as resource, and never as deficit. This pedagogical design intentionally integrates home, school, and community language practices, designs assessment that includes the voice of others, and gives students "opportunities to perform tasks with assistance from other people and resources" (García et al., 2017, p. xiii). For each motion, I will share concrete examples of what this pedagogy might look in the classroom as I illustrate how consistently mobilizing a framework that intentionally incorporates heritage language practices for learning is crucial for belonging in heritage language teaching and learning. Finally, as I illustrate each motion in our pedagogy, I will include several voices of students who have completed the program at DU and who explain, from a personal point of view, how these pedagogies have made a difference in their Spanish learning trajectories. These voices will remain anonymous.

The Spanish Program for Heritage/Bilingual Speakers at the University of Denver

The University of Denver's decision to create and grow a Spanish program for heritage students was not based entirely on demand; that is, we, at the time, were not, and still today are not, a majority-Latinx institution, nor did we enroll high numbers of Latinx students in our Spanish program at the time of my hiring. Rather, the institutional decision to bring resources and energy to this mission was based on an intentional commitment of providing relevant pedagogy for this group, echoing recent scholarship in Spanish heritage pedagogy that advocates curricular design in language learning with the unique profiles of bilingual/heritage students at the forefront (Torres, Pascual, & Beusterein, 2017; Beaudrie et al, 2014; Samaniego & Warner, 2016; Beaudrie & Fairclough, 2012). This program was thus born to break the cycle for heritage students in the institution—the cycle that deemphasizes heritage language practices to frame heritage

150 Student's Language Practices for Teaching

students as "not a good fit" for beginner courses where second language learners do not yet have the sociolinguistic knowledge to integrate with heritage speakers and as "not good enough" for advanced courses, wherein heritage speakers do not yet have the academic literacy skills to produce the academic texts deemed obligatory in those spaces.

Key Theoretical Notions Guiding the Pedagogical Work

Before illustrating the key motions in our program, it is important to explore theoretical notions that represent the backbone of this pedagogical approach. Importantly, these notions have guided my understanding of best practices in the Spanish heritage language classroom. The first of these is knowing that heritage students mobilize bilingualism dynamically, and that this set of repertoires uniquely shapes their linguistic practices (Palmer & Martínez, 2013). This dynamic bilingualism presents a need for pedagogical design that leverages and supports heritage students' fluid, flexible, and complex process of linguistic integration across multiple repertoires in the classroom and critically, beyond the classroom. I share Palmer and Martínez's observation, for example, that while pedagogical efforts exist to more "appropriately" teach Spanish to heritage speakers, pedagogical literature in the field tends to focus on the particular "needs" of students, seeking to provide instructors with methods and strategies necessary to "help mitigate" such needs. However, in these (traditional) methods of Spanish heritage instruction, learning is often equated with "learning academic Spanish", and heritage language practices—often rich, hybrid language practices that include translanguaging practices—are rarely acknowledged, nor are they considered as tools to facilitate learning. Researchers and educators need tools to help instructors unpack the dynamics of heritage language practices as essential to the teaching and learning process. Otherwise, heritage students will continue to be othered, and hybrid language practices will continue to be invisible in spaces of teaching and learning. Thus, the notion of dynamic bilingualism seeks to normalize being bilingual as "doing bilingualism" (Palmer & Martínez, 2013) or mobilizing all language practices, including those that incur a low social status in academic spaces.

What we understand as dynamic heritage language practices (referenced earlier) is illustrated through the notion of translanguaging practice, or the ability to make meaning across linguistic boundaries in any socially situated context (Canagarajah, 2013). As such, when individuals mobilize—in this case, heritage (trans)languag(ing) practices, they are using all the language varieties they possess to varying degrees of proficiency and legitimacy. This notion, then, expands how we comprehend and assess what the legitimate linguistic resources are of any individual that crosses any social boundary, essentially counteracting the traditional notion that bilingualism represents an already-achieved competence in exactly two languages. Certainly, the notion of translanguaging practice complements what García and Wei (2014) define as translanguaging, or "the multiple discursive practices in which bilinguals engage to make sense of their bilingual worlds'" (p. 22), which is a useful notion in shaping pedagogies that frame learning as a dynamic exchange of linguistically hybrid practices that make meaning. Within the contexts of learning about academic literacy, wherein heritage students are exposed to a register intended to grant them access to public spaces of the privileged mainstream, Molle (2015) highlights the need to develop more productive and inclusive notions of academic literacy—notions with the potential to reflect an academic reality encompassing all student literacies, and not just those of the so-called "standard". It is such a framework that guides the pedagogical design explained in the following. (For an overview of the implications of translanguaging for heritage language pedagogy and heritage language literacy, see the Introduction as well as Chapter 1.)

The Four Motions for Equitable Pedagogies in Spanish Heritage Learning

Collaboration

A sense of belonging relates to the ability to see oneself reflected in the teaching and learning space of a particular course. For this former student, belonging was directly a part of the content of the courses' discussion. As they illustrate:

> Yo creo que la: tema que, um, se me hizo más interesante fue: cuando ((estábamos)) aprendiendo- no aprendiendo porque ((estábamos)) leyendo textos que: eran de- no Spanglish- sí eran de Spanglish, y: había una historia de un señor que estaba hablando de su experiencia de ser un hispanohablante, de ser alguien de:- latino aquí en América, y: habló de cómo se sentía que no tenía país: y eso como, sentí como que todos teníamos una conexión, y todos hablábamos como- especialmente, pues conecta a nuestra experiencia aquí en DU, que DU um, es como: (.) es un **predominantly white institution**, y: a veces como que no tenemos nuestra comunidad, y cuando estábamos en esta clase, nos tenemos un lugar donde- como nos podemos desahogar, y pudimos estar en un cuarto y sentimos como que estamos representados, y que pudimos hablar español sin que: haya como esa tensión de que: hay como personas mirando, pero, sentí como que esa tema en: específico como que todos (.) tenían algo que decir.

> *I think that the topic that was most interesting to me was when we were learning, well, not learning but we were reading texts that were not about Spanglish. Well, yes actually they were about Spanglish, and there was a story of this man that was talking about his experience of being a Spanish-speaker, of being someone who was Latino here in America. And he talked about how he felt he did not have a country, and that, like, I felt that we all had a connection with that, and we were all talking about how especially, it connects to our experience here at DU, because DU is a*

predominantly white institution and sometimes we don't have our community, and when we were in class, we have a place where we can like vent. And we could be in a room and feel like we were represented, and that we could speak Spanish without there being that tension of like, there are people watching. But I felt that that topic specifically like we all had something to say.

One of the most foundational aspects of heritage language programs, and the general ability to have a pedagogical design exclusively for heritage speakers, is the option of relying on students themselves for collaboration. That is, when heritage students come together in a class, and soon realize they share a unique, non-traditional literacy experience, *collaboration*, which is key for community development, is one of the most effective resources available to those of us who design and teach said courses. In other words, a course designed for heritage speakers makes most sense for students when they understand that relying on each other for learning—rather than primarily on the instructor—is the most fulfilling way to learn.

Given the pivotal role of students in their own learning process, it is imperative that educators rely on student linguistic resources for the design of both course activities and course assessment. For example, taking into consideration that students rely on the knowledge that is relevant to the class already, educators can leverage this knowledge as their frame of reference for discussion questions, topics of analysis, types of texts to be written, and especially, student learning objectives. In other words, the realization that student background knowledge can completely guide an educator's pedagogical design, should, in my view, be prioritized in heritage pedagogy design.

Our program prioritizes a peer-to-peer tutoring component in the course design given the crucial place that collaboration holds in Spanish for heritage speaker programs and as illustrated by my previous research (Reznicek-Parrado, 2018a, 2018b, 2020, 2022). For that reason, the initial stages of the program and course design involve the direct incorporation of weekly, one-hour, mandated peer tutor sessions held outside of the course's class sessions. As students develop ideas, learn to write argumentatively, review grammar topics, and learn to collect evidence, a peer tutor—a more advanced heritage speaker who has completed the program—will provide one-on-one support. This unique collaboration not only good for any student, but in the case of heritage students, the collaboration is highlighted through providing multiple academic spaces where heritage language literacy repertoires are prioritized, modeled, and importantly, relevant for learning. Thus, my annual searches for potential peer tutors are directly conducted among the group of students that take my courses. As such, I provide attractive pay and consistent professional development support and frame the experience as an opportunity to develop collaboration as a career-relevant skill. At the end of this chapter, I will offer additional details on how our peer-to-peer program is designed and ideas on how to mobilize peer tutoring as a pedagogical initiative.

Recently, one of our tutors described how joining the team has impacted their own learning trajectory:

> The most meaningful aspect of being a tutor was being able to connect with others at such an intimate level when it comes to language and identity. **Como hablantes de herencia, nuestra lengua no sólo es una destreza sino también un gran aspecto de nuestra identidad cultural. Para las/os estudiantes que no recibieron escolarización formal con el español, el no poder expresarse sí misma/o con fluidez resulta en vergüenza.** After going through the program and developing so much myself, it was an impactful experience to be able to look across the table and say, "**no te preocupes**". [...] Knowing that our classroom was full of other students who had similar ambitions around the language. Everyone had their own reasons for pushing to be in that class, and it was inspiring to see that drive translate to progress. As I was helping them foment their linguistic foundations, they were helping me sharpen my rhetoric. This strong sense of community is what really stood out to me.

> *The most meaningful aspect of being a tutor was being able to connect with others at such an intimate level when it comes to language and identity. As heritage speakers, our language is not just a skill but also an important aspect of our cultural identity. For students who did not receive formal schooling in Spanish, not being able to express themselves with fluency results in shame. After going through the program and developing so much myself, it was an impactful experience to be able to look across the room and say, "Don't worry". Knowing that our classroom was full of other students who had similar ambitions around the language, everyone had their own reasons for pushing to be in that class, and it was inspiring to see that drive translate to progress. As I was helping them foment their linguistic foundations, they were helping me sharpen my rhetoric. This strong sense of community is what really stood out to me.*

Beyond the peer-to-peer component of our program, in-class discussions also leverage heritage language practices for collaborative teaching and learning. It is easy, in my view, to highlight the interconnectedness between students' lived experiences vis-à-vis students' practices with literacy through using any opportunity to highlight students' voices as part of the teaching and learning process. As such, for the first day of class, while we explore the important reasons for being together, I ask students to reflect upon their lived experiences while defining what they see as their personal relationship with the Spanish language. After this initial reflective exercise, I ask them to collectively explore why we are together while considering varying ways to describe their positionality toward Spanish as a language, and Spanish as their language (see Figure 6.1).

In this exercise, students take a moment to jot down a "definition" of their personal relationship with Spanish. As I explain in the activity prompt:

154 Student's Language Practices for Teaching

En el espacio a continuación, escribe algo en particular que *define tu relación con el español.*

Esta "definición" puede referirse a cualquier aspecto de tu historia con el español. esto puede ser una anécdota o historia personal, un viaje que hiciste, algún aspecto sobre la variedad que hablas, algo que te encanta o que detestas del español, alguna experiencia específica que hayas tenido, un temor o ilusión que te inspira el español, algo que te intriga del español, lo que te inspira hablar español, lo importante (o no) que es el español para ti, etc., etc.,etc.

FIGURE 6.1 Reflection Prompt: "Defining Your Relationship with the Spanish Language".

This definition can refer to any aspect of your story with Spanish. It can be an anecdote or a personal story, a trip you have taken, some aspect of the variety you speak, something you love or hate about Spanish, some specific experience you have had, a fear or illusion that inspires you about Spanish, something you are curious about the language, what inspires you to speak Spanish, that which is important (or not important) to you about Spanish, etc., etc., etc.

Afterward, students receive a large piece of paper where they jot down their thoughts. They are asked not to include their names and to simply free-write as they see fit.

As I have completed this activity throughout the years, I have observed that student answers often involve personal stories of inadequacy about their Spanish skills—anecdotes of interactions with family members or former teachers where they are told, and have thus internalized, that their Spanish is limited, or "mocho" (*broken*). I often hear students' struggles to adapt to standard conventions of the language (accents, orthography, etc.), while expressing a sense of incompleteness especially in relation to their otherwise advanced academic skills in English. However, student answers also very often involve powerful stories of Spanish as being a defining factor in their identity, as it is frequently used to support individuals who don't speak English or help community members participate in events or access public spaces. Interestingly, students generally experience a strong sense of feeling "complete" when speaking Spanish or using it to facilitate experiences. They also identify a great sense of desire to maintain the language and pass it on to future generations. Time and time again, opposing senses of incompleteness versus completeness, of true love at the same time as true insecurity, come together in this simple activity (see Figure 6.2):

Top Note: Something I like about Spanish is that it has given me the opportunity to travel to countries where being a native (speaker) has benefitted me.

Middle Note: I feel like I speak Spanish a little broken and I want to improve that aspect.

Student's Language Practices for Teaching 155

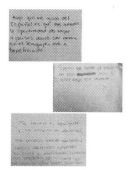

FIGURE 6.2 Students' Responses to Reflection Prompt "Define Your Relationship with the Spanish Language".

Bottom Note: I love Spanglish and the mix of language; I love it when native speakers learn English and pronounce words that start with "s" like "-es". For example, "Estarbucks", "especial".

When students are finished writing, I collect the pieces of paper and shuffle them. I then ask students to form a circle in the classroom, with me seated outside of it. I begin to read the stories found in the pieces of paper that students wrote and ask them to take a step into the circle if they "relate to what is being spoken". Time after time, I read a story out loud, and most students move in and out of the circle in unison. The movement across the circle is dynamic, and while subtle, there is consistent dance in and out for as long as stories are shared.

After we discuss the collective reality that these lived experiences are, quite surprisingly for some students, shared experiences, I ask the students to complete a second reflection (see Figure 6.3).

This time, students reflect for a moment and write down just two words. Framing the general question of "Why study Spanish as a heritage language?", I ask students identify two adjectives that, for them, describe Spanish. First, I ask them to think of a word that describes the Spanish as a "universal/global

---

¿Por qué estudiar el español como lengua de herencia?

Quiero que exploremos esta pregunta juntas/os.

Primero, quiero que pienses en dos adjetivos que, para ti, describen el español; el primer adjetivo, debe ser un adjetivo que describa el español en general, mientras que el segundo, debe ser un adjetivo que describa TU español.

Luego, vamos a explorar algunas situaciones personales a las que algunas personas, quienes hablan español, se han enfrentado. ¿Te conectas con estas experiencias en particular? ¿Por qué sí o por qué no? Conversemos.

FIGURE 6.3 Reflection Prompt: "Why Study Spanish as a Heritage Language?".

language"—that is, a language spoken by people *in the world*. Secondly, I ask them to think of a word that more intimately describes their own Spanish—that is, Spanish as spoken by and through them, or Spanish *in their world*.

After students have time to reflect, I use an anonymous poll service (e.g., PollEv.com) to collect students' answers and illustrate them in a word cloud (see Figures 6.4 and 6.5).

Just as the sticky notes from the foregoing activity often illustrate a contrasting reality (i.e., speaking Spanish as shameful but also as liberating), the word clouds show a similar juxtaposition. It is visually clear that, as a collective, students regard Spanish highly; they describe the Spanish language as "poetic", "beautiful", "a source of pride", "complex", as representing a "heritage", and, beautifully, as "necessary". However, when asked to describe the language at a more intimate level, students tended to collectively produce adjectives illustrating their struggle of feeling like the language does not truly belong to them. Among others, the most recurring adjectives were "different", "Spanglish", "basic", "shameful", and, strikingly, "strange". While the contrasting illustration perhaps does not come as a surprise, the collective contrasting experience is particularly salient.

FIGURE 6.4 Students' Word Cloud for "Adjectives That Describe Spanish as a 'Universal' Language" Collected in the Fall Course, 2019.

FIGURE 6.5 Students' Word Cloud for "Adjective That Describes 'my Spanish'" Collected in the Fall Course, 2019.

Student's Language Practices for Teaching **157**

I call this first motion "collaboration" to highlight the cooperative aspect that learning holds in a Spanish for heritage speakers course, and especially to illustrate how educators can design activities that highlight and expand the shared lived experiences of students as their basis for learning together. It is necessary, in my view, to establish an intentional, collaborative pedagogical lens within the course design's base as we make space for heritage language practices that are crucial for student learning in our pedagogical design.

Exploration

An additional layer of collaboration utilizes intentional *exploration* of content that reflects the literacy lives of heritage students. Not only is the collective awareness I describe earlier necessary to establish a collaborative learning space where students have a sense of belonging among the group and where the instructor can begin to extrapolate salient themes, but it is also crucial for students to generate and tap into the same sense of belonging across communities and/or individuals outside of the classroom, and especially *outside of the academic context*. Specifically, the motion of exploration refers to the study of content that reflects the lived experiences of individuals that speak and validate stories of uprooting, immigration, biculturalism, belonging, etc. as an additional opportunity for heritage students to realize that they are part of a much larger group of communities who face similar life and literacy stories of strife and success. Indeed, if students can engage with texts that not only reflect a similar story to theirs but that also mobilize similar literacy practices in relation to their own, the exploration of both content and text can strengthen a sense of belonging for heritage students, both at the personal and collective levels.

To achieve the type of exploration of content I describe, I give students opportunities to both engage with multimodal texts as readers as well as take on new identities through writing in light of those same texts. I primarily rely on two social media platforms, Twitter and Facebook, to find texts that speak to social movements that illustrate the realities of Spanish-speaking communities across the world before introducing other more traditional formal genres. Similar to the multimodal activity that Foulis and Alex (2019) describe in their Spanish for Heritage Speakers open access textbook, through a basic search for any trending hashtag related to a social movement, students explore a variety of Spanish-language texts, written by individuals who mobilize a variety of literacy practices beyond those found in the traditional language textbook. Throughout our weeks together, each student chooses the hashtag they want to explore and curates Spanish-language posts as comments. They interact with the text by replying directly to the original post or replying indirectly on the course's learning management system (LMS). Students also have the freedom to mobilize whatever literacy practices they see fit as they explore participation in the virtual conversation about a relevant topic. Importantly, this activity can be replicated with other mediums of social media such as TikTok or Instagram.

158 Student's Language Practices for Teaching

The multimodal features of platforms such as Twitter and Facebook allow students to access a variety text types and formats, ranging from newspaper articles that mobilize standard literacy practices to individuals' personal reflections, arguments, and expressed feelings about the content. This also includes visual images and video content, among other types of modes. As such, it is the optimal space where heritage students can connect with relevant content through a realistic, holistic literacy (see Figure 6.6).

Al Punto con Jorge Ramos ✓
@AlPunto

El actor @antoniobanderas responde si se considera una "persona de color", esto luego de que varias publicaciones lo catalogaran como tal tras recibir la nominación como mejor actor a los #Oscars. La entrevista completa este domingo en #AlPunto con @jorgeramosnews 10AM/9C/1P.

FIGURE 6.6 Twitter Entry Following the Hashtag #LatinoPride.

Student's reply (see Figure 6.7):

> @juanita123 Enseñale de lo que eres! Diles de donde eres! #Latinopride

Felicitas Bonavitta
@FelicitasBV

Duele. Hoy nos despertamos con esta noticia. Camila fue asesinada a balazos frente a sus hijes y parece que esto no se termina más. Basta de matarnos. Basta de violencia machista. #NiUnaMenos ✊

FIGURE 6.7 Twitter Entry Following the Hashtag #NiUnaMenos.

Student's reply:

> @JuanaXY Una tía mía fue asesinada afuera de una tienda en Mexico. Su marido la asesinó. Han sido 15 años desde que se murió. Yo no la conocí mucho pero mi papá, quiern era el hermano de mi tía, habla de ella. Ojalá algún día todo esto termine. #NiUnaMenos

Through exploration of real-life, multimodal texts that present a variety of literacy practices around social movements related to the Spanish-speaking world, students also complete a diary writing activity; they must take on the identity of a fictional or real individual who is or was directly participating in social movement they choose to explore. Ideally, their selected hashtag social movement connects directly with the diary character, allowing students to explore relevant content from different angles. Through this activity, students must write entries that reflect their character's experiences, thoughts, feelings, and emotions. Often, students choose a real character of political, artistic, or other prominence (Mexican journalist Jorge Ramos and activist Puerto Rican singer René Pérez "Residente" are two popular choices). They can also create fictional characters that are immersed in the daily struggle of a particular sociopolitical context (for example, a "Central American immigrant who is separated from their child at the border" or "a Venezuelan refugee seeking asylum in Perú" are other possibilities). Students submit weekly diary entries that directly reflect any current event relevant to the life of their character. Week after week, students write entries that mobilize a variety of literacy practices, while they intertwine their own identities as Spanish speakers with their imagined characters' identities. At the end of the experience, students share with the class the sociopolitical context related to their character, a series of events that happened to the character in relation to the context in which they are, and a diary entry from their quarter-long assignment (see Figure 6.8).

Providing heritage students consistent opportunities to take on new identities through hybrid literacies broadens and expands the literacy practices they

La imagen de arriba enseña a mi persona llamada Grisel Rodriguez. Aunque mi persona no es alguien cuya identidad ya existía, pude crear un personaje de la información que coleccione a través del internet.

Como mencioné, mi personaje es Grisel Rodriguez y es una mujer en Venezuela que está sufriendo las consecuencias de la pandemia, COVID-19. Grisel es una mamá viviendo en pobreza en Venezuela. Al no tener suficientes recursos para llevar a su esposo al hospital o para comprarle sus medicinas- por la crisis económica y la pandemia- su esposo, Jose Luis, falleció. Ahora, Grisel es mamá soltera que tiene que cuidar a su familia durante estos tiempos difíciles. En desesperación, Grisel está contemplando irse a Colombia en busca de una vida mejor o quedarse en Venezuela con la esperanza de sobrevivir las condiciones devastadoras.

Lo siguiente es un poco de mi diario. " En realidad, todo cambio cuando se nos fue mi esposo José Luis. La oposición de Maduro catalizo una crisis económica. Ya andábamos en malos pasos, pero la pandemia del COVID-19 empeoró nuestra situación. José Luis se puso mal. Sus huesos lentamente le fallaban y su fiebre seguía subiendo. Sin gasolina en el carro y nada de dinero, no había manera de llevarlo al hospital. Aunque trate con todo mi esfuerzo a cargar su cuerpo en mis hombros, no podía ayudarlo."

FIGURE 6.8 Student's Final Reflection Presentation on Diary Assignment.

160 Student's Language Practices for Teaching

are exposed to and are encouraged to employ inside of the classroom. The stories students create frequently relate—albeit indirectly—to their own stories of immigration, uprooting, and the like. However, because these contexts spring from a variety of countries and communities, many times outside of their own, students can feel connected to Spanish-speaking communities across the world, and not just tied solely to their lived experiences. Additionally, students' internalization of literacy as a process of belonging, to me, is the first step toward academic literacy development. It is not until I know my students are comfortable writing in their own ways (and their own stories) that I then introduce the exploration of traditional academic literacy, such as argumentation, academic registers, and other grammatical tools to explore the creation of an academic text, as additional options—just as valid as non-academic tools—to create text.

Finally, the exploration of academic texts can also happen through student connection to content related to the lived experiences of heritage students. Following the diary exercise, students complete a research project in the program's second course. For this project, students continue researching the context of their selected social movement, but they then access academic texts such as newspaper articles, government archives, and other artifacts that consistently present standard academic literacy practices. By this level, students have already had the opportunity to explore a variety of texts and are ready to delve into how academic texts approach the same topic of research. Students collect texts each week, summarize them, outline their main arguments, and submit a minimum of three new vocabulary words from the text before preparing a final presentation that showcases their research. A former student states:

> A mí me gustó mucho la: investigación, porque pue- podíamos tomar en cualquier (.) manera que quisiéramos, y a mí se me- o sea, yo soy muy interesada como a la manera que: las políticas sirven, por todo el mundo, y pues eso- o sea yo nunca tenía esa oportunidad de mirar cómo, o sea cómo están las políticas en México, en xxx a la:- al movimiento de (justicia reproductiva), y: me hizo muy interesante como aprender cómo personas se andan organizando, y andan por- protestando, y andan como, escribiendo legislaciones para, o sea, dar más como: (.) um, cómo se dice.. (.) um, oportunidades para las mujeres, y:- y sí, se me hizo muy fascinante como (.) aprender, y también como: (.) o sea yo nunca: ando leyendo cosas en español, y fue (una de las veces) que estaba mirando como artículos en español, y: estaba explorando como sitios de webs que, o sea yo ni sabía que existían , o sea, sí- y um, ¡pues sí! Se me- me hizo muy bien, um, esa parte en- uh en particular, y también se me hizo muy interesante oír las otras presentaciones, y aprender, o sea lo que está pasando, um, por todo el mundo.

> *I really liked the research project because we could do it any way we wanted to. Like, I am really interested in the ways that legislation works, around the world, and so I*

Student's Language Practices for Teaching 161

had never had the opportunity to see how these policies work in Mexico, in terms of reproductive justice, and it was interesting like to learn how people are organizing, and they are striking, and they are, like, writing policy to, like—how do you say—give women more opportunities. And I just thought it was fascinating also to learn like, I had never read things in Spanish, and I was looking at articles in Spanish, and I was exploring websites that I didn't even know existed, like, and yes. It was great, that part in particular, and also it was interesting to hear other presentations, and learn, like what is happening around the world.

At the culmination of the course, students provide academic oral presentations on their research topic, featuring how it relates to the pertinent social movement they have been analyzing since the beginning of the program. In preparation for this presentation, which is completed through exclusively mobilizing standard academic literacy practices, we complete a variety of modules on academic language, including argumentation, text cohesion, and standard orthography (see Figure 6.9).

Creating and performing their final presentation and submitting their accompanying research report present students with the challenge of producing texts that are solely academic. This experience provides the much-needed space to establish a sense of belonging in literacy so students can then feel safer as they explore and adapt to a literacy that traditionally existed outside of their comfort zone. Thus, the primary and intentional analysis of relevant, multimodal texts

FIGURE 6.9 Student's Final Presentation on Researching Femicides and Women's Rights Movements in Mexico.

162 Student's Language Practices for Teaching

that mobilize both hybrid literacies and the subsequent exploration of traditional academic literacies is key for heritage language writing instruction, as it provides an opportunity to equate both literacies as valid, and not simply the latter. As eloquently illustrated by a former student:

> Hmm, creo que en general la presentación, um, y la investigación periodística, um, fue algo que me gustó mucho porque fue un tema que me interesaba a mí, que yo escogí, que yo quería investigar en español, algo que no, no había hecho antes, así que creo que ese- esa actividad fue muy divertida y muy, um, buena para (.) que- seguir, um, usando el español en diferentes contextos, contextos de que en este contexto, usé el español para leer diferentes artículos en español, algo que no había hecho antes, um y creo que por eso hizo la experiencia más memorable, porque sentía que estaba usando (.) el español en diferentes maneras (.) a comparación como antes.

> *Hmm, I think in general the presentation, um, and the newspaper research project, um, was something that I liked a lot because it was a topic that interested me, that I chose, that I wanted to research in Spanish—something that I hadn't done before, so I think that is—that activity was fun and very, um, good to continue using Spanish to read in different articles in Spanish, something I had not done before. And I think that's why it made it a more memorable experience, because I felt I was using Spanish in different ways in comparison to before.*

Production

While the intentional and consistent inclusion of heritage language practices through text analysis is crucial for academic literacy instruction in Spanish heritage pedagogy, student production of a variety of texts beyond heritage-centered texts is also paramount. The previous motion of exploration highlights the importance of intentionally incorporating texts that build on students' experiences and stories (both personal and literacy stories); here, the motion of *production* elaborates on the process through which students are guided to access the conventions of academic language in order to produce a variety of texts, including those traditionally framed as academic in content and composition.

As I discussed in the Introduction, it is imperative to weave in the relevance and space that academic literacy practices hold within heritage language pedagogies, while leveraging and intentionally validating heritage language practices in the ways described earlier. As I clarified, appropriateness models of writing pedagogies that equate formal and "standard" language as exclusively "appropriate" for participation in academic spaces are detrimental to heritage students' development of academic literacy. Instead, I envision doing away with the notion of appropriateness altogether in order to more effectively leverage heritage language practices as inherent tools for academic literacy development. As such, the intentional incorporation of what has traditionally been understood as "academic

Student's Language Practices for Teaching   **163**

language"—standard ways of meaning often used in academic spaces—needs to be nestled within tenets of Critical Language Awareness. The motion of production describes how I weave the norms of academic writing into the process of text exploration and belonging in my classroom so that heritage literacy practices continue to be incorporated even as students explore a new type of literacy.

As such, and given the unique social context of heritage students participating in courses where they develop additional literacies in the language of their heritage, it is crucial to provide enough opportunities for students to interact with a variety of multimodal texts—both texts that mobilize heritage literacy practices (such as hybrid language, informal registers, and the like) and texts that abide by the traditional academic norms of literacy. As illustrated by a former student when asked about the relationship between the establishment of heritage literacy practices as part of her academic writing journey, the student's response demonstrates that this dual process can make academic literacy less intimidating for heritage speakers:

Interviewer: ¿Sentís que: esa libertad en expresarte, ehm, bueno de, de la forma en que siempre hablabas, ¿no? O sea tu <air quotes> español. ¿Sentís que: um, estar más cómoda con eso y tener esa libertad contribuyó en alguna forma a, a desarrollar tu escritura, o tu español: más?

Do you feel that, that freedom of expression, um, of the way you had always talked, no? Like your "Spanish". Do you feel that being more comfortable with that and having that freedom contributed in some way to developing your writing, or your Spanish?

Student: Sí, creo que definitivamente no me enfocaba tanto en si mi español estaba correcto, si mi español estaba- um, si era académico, **if it was like, good enough, um,** creo que más me enfoqué en desarrollar mis ideas y presentar mi reporte con más fluidez y más naturaleza al contrario que estar preocupada si iba a ser, um, mirado diferente tal vez no era, um, tal vez sonaba diferente. Pero creo que eso definitivamente me ayudó.

Yes, I think definitely I was not focusing so much on whether my Spanish was correct, if my Spanish was, um, if it was academic, if it was, like good enough. Um, I think the more I focused on developing my ideas and presenting my report with more fluency and more naturally and not worried that it was going to be seen differently if it sounded different. But I think that it definitely helped.

Additionally, when exposing students to texts that solely use academic language features, one must consider the significant potential for student learning in analyzing and interacting with a variety of texts, and not just the traditional argumentative essay so often expected in writing courses.

As such, while completing the collaboration and exploration of content through the two first motions explained earlier and establishing a shared sense of belonging in the learning experience, I weave in lessons on argumentation

164 Student's Language Practices for Teaching

through explicit instruction on basic tenets of academic literacy such as argument development, the structure of argumentative texts, and cohesion tools such as lexical chains, connectors, and relative pronouns. As in a traditional writing course, students complete in-class writing workshops where they are expected to apply academic features of writing to exercises. While this process may come across as de-contextualized, or perhaps too mechanical, I deem it necessary to support the process of belonging through literacy to which heritage students have the right.

It is my experience that, by the time I incorporate the production of academic literacy practices, students welcome the process, knowing that it is safe since they have learned that heritage language practices can still be mobilized as part of the learning trajectory. Additionally, key to the acquisition of academic literacy for heritage students is the opportunity to mobilize these newly acquired skills in a variety of academic texts tied to a specific social context—not just via the argumentative essay. In the sequential course offered in our program I expose heritage students to a variety of academic texts which require critical consideration of the socially situated context in which the text exists. These texts are intrinsically connected to class discussion topics, so students can contextualize where to use them. Thus, while these writing assignments emphasize academic literacy practices and not heritage literacy practices, the social relevance of the context in which they exist, in my view, serves as a bridge across this—often intimidating—literacy jump.

To emphasize the social context of every academic text that students create in class, I designed each text to serve as an opportunity to critically examine a particular issue before practicing the creation of strong, evidence-based, written arguments. For example, while completing a unit on global technology inequity and access (or lack thereof) to technology in education, students must create a formal e-mail written to their professor who has established a new policy in class that forbids students to use technology. To counter the argument that "students use technology mostly to get distracted and use social media platforms", students prepare their arguments to cohesively follow academic literacy practices as they convince their professor that their new policy is detrimental to their learning. In doing so, they incorporate evidence from course materials, course discussions, and, of course, their own research. Following introduction of the context for the text and the common agreement that the text must follow academic literacy practices, students begin a three-week process of text creation, editing, and applying peer tutor feedback. They revise different versions of their text with a peer tutor, then receive feedback from the professor, before being graded on the assignment.

Adapted from Potowski (2010), Table 6.1 gives an explanation of the types of socially situated academic texts students create as relevant to the discussion topic.

The process of academic text production reflects a variety of literacy practices, including, certainly, heritage literacy practices, as students work through outlines, drafts, and peer conversations around argumentation, evidence, citing, and

Student's Language Practices for Teaching **165**

TABLE 6.1 Relationships Between Topics of Discussion and Analysis Taking Place in the Classroom and Subsequent Academic Texts Assigned

Topic of Discussion and Analysis[a]	Academic Text to Produce
Global technology inequity and access/technology use in education	Formal e-mail to professor with arguments against newly established anti-technology policies for the classroom
Gender (in)equality in modern society	Product review supporting or rejecting the purchase of a children's toy
LGBTQ rights	Blog entry that critically frames the act of "coming out" in LGBTQ communities
Literature written in Spanish in the US context	Brief literary analysis of a passage in a literary text written in Spanish by a US author

[a]Topics of discussion are mostly from the thematic chapters in the Spanish for Heritage Speakers textbook *Conversaciones escritas* (Potowski, 2010).

the like. The key is to open up channels for the mobilizing of all literacy practices as students adapt and expand their linguistic repertoires. In this way, students already know they belong in literacy learning, before opening up to a literacy that, while intimidating, in the end also belongs to heritage students. Through this process, then, students know that they, too, can belong in academic literacy.

Self-Reflection

A last foundational pedagogical motion, one that is likely already an essential layer of teaching and learning in a variety of contexts and especially when furthering critical pedagogies, is the motion of *self-reflection* regarding the learning process. Any language course, but especially a heritage course, should include intentional self-reflection as inherent in its design. Unique about the heritage language context, however, is the need to specifically and intentionally instill reflection that addresses the recognition, validation, and relevance of heritage literacy practices for learning. As illustrated by a former student:

> Yeah, um, creo que (.) [esta clase] me da mucho la oportunidad de hacer, (.) **like,** reflexión en la clase, um porque obviamente, **like, no** (.) no sólo hablo español, también hablo inglés, y no sólo hablo inglés, también hablo español, entonces es esa experiencia como **like,** así única, que **um, like** @@ que me ha gustado mucho porque siento que aquí en la clase cuando puedo hablar español y tomar ese tiempo para hablar español con, um, mis, **like, classmates** y todo, pero también**, like,** no me siento mal si no sé una palabra, lo que sea, lo puedo decir en inglés, en español, um, es **like** el único espacio, más o menos, aquí, um, que puedo hacer eso y que la profesora me entiende la gente en la clase me entiende, y creo que, como ella nos, nos deja, **like,** decir nuestras experiencias y me ayuda, a **like–** a reflejar en, en lo que estamos aprendiendo, y es algo que, **like,** mis otros profesores incorporan un poco pero no tanto, y

166 Student's Language Practices for Teaching

creo que es muy beneficioso, hacer esa reflexión, y poder hablar en español y inglés en clase.

Yeah, um, I think this class gives me the opportunity of doing reflection in class, um, because obviously like, I don't just speak Spanish. I also speak English, and I don't just speak English, I also speak Spanish. So that experience, like, is so unique, that um, that I have liked a lot because I feel that here in class when I can speak Spanish and take time to speak Spanish with um, my classmates and all, but also like, I don't feel bad if I don't know a word, whatever, I can say it in English, in Spanish, it is like the only space, more or less, here at DU, where I can do that and have the professor understand me and people in class understand me. And I think like, she lets us say our own experiences and that helps me reflect on, on what we are learning, and it is something that my other professors do but not as much. And I think it is helpful, doing that reflection, and being able to speak in Spanish and English in class.

Self-reflection regarding the use of hybrid literacy practices for language learning is inscribed, for example, in discussions and activities that foment *collaboration* (see earlier). Additionally, self-reflection is inscribed in the production of academic texts described in the motion of *production*, especially as students continue to grapple with literacy insecurities while navigating academic literacy, sometimes for the first time. Additionally, peer-to-peer sessions are crucial spaces for self-reflection. Students and student peers discuss the validity of students' heritage literacy practices in earlier drafts, the relevance of academic registers, and the relationship between the academic standard for argumentation and participation in the social world. A consistent layer of self-reflection is necessary for a student's successful transition from belonging through heritage literacy practices into belonging in academic literacy practices.

Self-reflection is the foundation of dialogical discourse that must happen intentionally as an individual and within student-to-peer and student-to-instructor relationships. As the Freirian perspective sustains, critical reflection through structured dialogue must be a crucial goal in learning, "with language development as a by-product of authentic purposeful social interaction" (Faltis, 1990). If literacy learning in heritage pedagogy is devoid of self-reflection, it becomes de-contextualized, losing its social meaning. Thus, academic literacy continues to be an impersonal, meaningless, and—importantly—intimidating process for heritage students who may never find belonging in texts that exist outside of their purview.

I hope the foregoing description of the four motions of heritage language pedagogy is as useful as it has been to me in developing spaces for belonging and sustaining equitable pedagogies that respond to heritage students' linguistic hybridity and its potential for language teaching and learning.

Before concluding the book, I return to the relevance of the data analysis presented throughout Chapters 3–5, highlighting the peer-to-peer instructional model as an initiative with much potential for programs that support heritage language pedagogy.

The Peer-Effect: Heritage Student Tutors Mirroring Equitable Pedagogies in Spanish Heritage Language Instruction

Throughout this book, I have described the many ways heritage peer tutors have taught me that heritage literacy practices have a critical place in heritage pedagogical design. As an illustration of how tutors talked about the relevance of their repertoires for the larger student community and as a way to recall my admiration for tutors' consistent commitment to the heritage student community, the words of Esmeralda, a former heritage tutor, come to mind. Several years ago, while I was at UC Davis, she eloquently explained to me what she saw as the meaning of being a tutor as well as aspects of her role that she most appreciated, showing her deep commitment to her peers:

> Aprecio ofrecer como un sistema de apoyo. Si estás pidiendo esto deberías ir a tal oficina o si estás teniendo tal problema en casa quizás esto es una cosa que puedes intentar como remedio. Y ayudar que tengan un ambiente muy positivo hacia el español. Porque muchas veces y muchos estudiantes que llegan siempre dicen, no pues mis padres dicen que pa' qué voy a tomar esto si hablo español. Les digo, no, pero es mucho más que eso. Yo quiero ser una asociación positiva con el programa. Lo que yo estoy allí para ser es su mentor, aparte soy su tutor, pero **I'm**- les digo yo, **I'm your mentor before anything else.** Estoy aquí para ayudarte.

> *I appreciate, like, being able to offer a support system. If you are asking for this you should go to that office or if you are having that problem at home maybe this is something you can try to help. And helping so that they have a positive environment towards Spanish. Because many times and many students that come [to the program] always say, well my parents say why take these classes if I already speak Spanish. I tell them, no, but this is so much more than that. I want to create a positive association with the program. What I am there for is to be their mentor, yes I am their tutor, but I'm- I tell them, I'm your mentor before anything else.*

In illustrating her commitment as a "sistema de apoyo" or support system to her students, Esmeralda implies that to do her job, she must hold and exhibit direct regard for students' overall experience, not just as students who are taking Spanish courses, but also as students navigating a complex, challenging, and difficult new context—much as she did herself during her early undergraduate years. As she sees it, her role is not only to generate a direct impact on students' Spanish literacy development but to also develop a positive outlook on what it means to study Spanish as a heritage speaker. She states, "es mucho más que eso" (*it is so much more than that*) in referencing some students' perceptions that taking Spanish might be useless since they already speak the language. Further, Esmeralda has a deep sense of her potential impact as a mentor, and that she has the tools, through her own language and literacy, to help students navigate not

168 Student's Language Practices for Teaching

just Spanish academic literacy development, but just as importantly, campus life through community building.

The type of commitment to her students that Esmeralda expresses is shared by other tutors such as Joaquín and Maité:

Joaquín: So, si tuviera que describir mi rol es como de ayudar aquellos que me necesitan y a quien yo pueda ayudar

So, if I had to describe my role it is like helping those that need me and those I can help

Maité: Entonces eso es un aspecto que me gusta mucho y obviamente ayudar a los estudiantes porque en esa manera me estoy ayudando a mí misma a mejor mi propia lengua.

And so it's an aspect I like a lot and obviously helping students because in that way I am helping myself to improve my own language.

Tutors have a clear vision of achieving much more than fostering the literacy development of (and with) the students they mentor. As shown through the analyses in Chapters 2 through 5, tutors consistently mobilize literacy practices and interpersonal resources that reflect their cultural and linguistic shared experiences, both among tutors as well as with tutees. Further, tutors consistently discuss that by being involved in the program, they make an impact that goes "beyond academics" by supporting peers not just academically but also personally.

Thus, as tutors work with students one-on-one in this non-classroom academic context, they deploy literacy and linguistic practices that echo the interrelatedness between literacy development and community building. My analysis illustrates the powerful impact that promoting the development of standardized language skills—while intentionally leveraging heritage students' linguistic practices—has in terms of creating powerful student-led academic communities of belonging. Additionally, the pedagogical approach described in this chapter illustrates how educators can intentionally facilitate the mobilizing of such interrelatedness in the classroom. This additive approach, which seeks not to replace students' heritage language practices but incorporate them in literacy development, attempts to show how reframing "the problem of language diversity by emphasizing respect for the [heritage] linguistic practices of minoritized students while acknowledging the importance of developing standardized language skills" (Flores & Rosa, 2015, p. 149) key to the development of equitable pedagogies in Spanish Heritage Pedagogy.

Peer-to-Peer Tutoring for Spanish Heritage Language Instruction: Considerations

It is my view that anyone can implement a peer-to-peer tutoring program as a core component of a Spanish for heritage speakers program. If there are students enrolling in courses for heritage speakers and since these students are the ones who later become tutors, the human resources necessary to implement a

Student's Language Practices for Teaching **169**

peer-to-peer tutoring program as a program initiative are already there. I now share several considerations in the process of establishing the student-led, nontraditional pedagogy initiative described throughout the book.

Firstly, and based on the relevance of community building as part of the learning experience of students in this type of tutoring program, efforts to include cross-contextual opportunities for literacy learning should be student-led. One of the most powerful aspects of this tutoring community, as shown in the analysis, is the extent to which peer tutors have a deep commitment to their students' academic experience, including their overall well-being as undergraduate Latinxs who in a lot of cases are the first ones in their families to attend college. Thus, the literacy resources that students have themselves are the ones impacting the success of the program, powerfully demonstrating to tutees that their own linguistic practices can make a similar difference. Additionally, furthering opportunities for students to mobilize expert identities demonstrates the positive impact that a student community can have on itself. While the tasks guiding the tutoring session are structured to support the formal curriculum, the autonomy with which tutors mediate these tasks models to all students the opportunity to mobilize their entire linguistic repertoire, opening space up for the types of alignments shown in this analysis.

Given the importance of community building and student-led learning in this academic space outside of the classroom, it also seems imperative to give value to students' contributions as related to literacy learning. This means that becoming a peer tutor must be seen as a desirable role for prospective students who may want to apply for the position. While there are many ways to achieve this, I have found that an application must include basic requirements such as the completion of basic program courses. While the application should demonstrate students' awareness of particular writing conventions and academic genres (one way of achieving this is by requiring an essay as part of the application), their experiences as students in the program will be crucial in order to get to know the curriculum to which tutees will also be exposed. Further, if requiring an essay as part of the application, it is important to focus the topic around questions that will allow candidates to express their motivations to become peer tutors as well as what they consider are their contributions to students and to the program at large. While advanced written proficiency is not a crucial requirement, candidates must be able to demonstrate basic academic literacy such as the ones tutees will be developing during their time in the program. To see a sample interview questionnaire, see Appendix C.

Candidates' ability for community building can be assessed through a short personal interview, where the Program Director, course instructors, and former peer tutors participate and assess a candidate's ability to converse and connect to the program's larger mission of providing positive academic experiences for the heritage speaker community. Beyond gathering a sample of a candidate's academic oral skill, candidates must be able to listen, respond, and reflect as they connect their own educational and personal experiences to the larger objectives

170 Student's Language Practices for Teaching

of the program. Lastly, tutors must be compensated well—an hourly salary of a typical student-worker would be appropriate as remuneration for their work, but certainly not less than that.

Also, when recruiting for tutors, I have consistently found it crucial to frame the peer-to-peer program as an opportunity for professional development and to offer potential candidates the chance to develop and polish teaching, coaching, and professional skills. For example, a workshop component could be incorporated into the peer-to-peer tutoring experience, such that tutors receive training in student mental health issues and resources, writing across the curriculum, and community-building skills, among other potential topics. In the end, it is crucial to frame the experience of being a peer tutor as a collection of professional activities that students can use in their CVs as they continue on with their careers after college. This way, students are not only contributing to the student community with which they work, but they are also actively developing their own academic and professional trajectories.

In terms of the weekly structure of tutoring sessions, it is necessary to consider the resources and context of each program. Both peer-to-peer programs at UC Davis and DU require a consistent, weekly meeting with a tutor, ranging from 30 minutes to one hour. Additionally, varying the goals of each session is useful in framing the writing process as just that—a process—that involves attention to a variety of linguistic and functional aspects that should be discussed. For example, a single session should be devoted to dialogue around the topic at hand, ideas, arguments, evidence, and the like. It should involve some note-taking and perhaps mutual brainstorming. Another session for a particular writing assignment should be devoted to discussing the text structure, following functional features of academic writing studies in class. And a third session, for example, could be devoted to polishing grammar, accentuation, and orthography. Any and all of the objectives for the session should be discussed mobilizing students' and tutors' *full* linguistic repertoires. It is important, however, to establish that if tutees bring up other topics of discussion, such as personal problems they are having with a professor, or a particular challenge related to their academic life, tutors should feel free to engage with students in that way as well. For more information on tutoring session design, two iterations of the tutoring session format and goals that I have used at DU are described at length in Reznicek-Parrado and Gonzales (2022) and in Appendix D.

Academic Literacy in Spanish as a Heritage Language

Though this book does not specifically examine academic writing development, nor does it investigate the direct impact of the tutoring sessions, or the pedagogical approaches described in this last chapter on students' academic literacy gains, it does carry implications for the overall conception of "academic literacy" in the Spanish heritage context. It is imperative that the field begins to not only consider the specific features of academic literacy that students are socialized into in schools, but also how students themselves already mobilize language to navigate the demands of academic literacy. In other words, work in academic literacy in Spanish as a heritage language must consider the existence of the many literacies that students consistently mobilize. This includes but is not limited to those described by multiple modes of representation, lexico-grammatical resources, and interpersonal stances that are inscribed beyond the text such as the ones analyzed throughout Chapters 3–5. Critically, the incorporation of social approaches to academic literacy in Spanish as a heritage language allows for a crucial distinction between practices that have the potential to "give students the skills and knowledge they need to achieve their aspirations" (Cazden et al. 1996, p. 63) and practices that simply take place in school settings (Molle, 2015).

While the academic practices of school have an impact on students' academic success, simply socializing students into those practices without regard for their full linguistic repertoires represents a missed opportunity. Indeed, an exclusive focus on academic and professional registers may erode heritage speakers' local use of their own vernacular and the particular sociocultural heritage identities that they index (Samaniego & Warner, 2016). As early as 2016, linguists Samaniego and Warner cautioned that the field of Spanish Heritage Pedagogy currently lacks a literacy framework that prompts understanding of advanced literacy development as the expansion of learners' resources for meaning-making, that is, "a framework that embraces the multiplicity and polysemy of language use" (p. 193). Such a narrow yet unfortunately common approach may altogether erode heritage students' sense of identity and belonging in academic contexts of higher education. As Flores (2015) pointedly exclaims, the traditional notion of "academic language" may be irrelevant for diverse contexts of teaching and learning:

> How is it possible for the dominant representation of the language practices of Latino students to clash so starkly with the unofficial interactions that we have observed in our research? This is possible because the concept of academic language is fundamentally flawed. It begins from the premise that language can be dichotomized into "academic" and "non-academic" forms and presupposes that Latino children inevitably come to school without a strong foundation in the academic forms. The deficit perspective produced by this narrative has become so ingrained that regardless of what Latino children do with language they will always be positioned as lacking a strong foundation in academic language.

This book evidences that Spanish heritage students are anything but devoid of meaningful, relevant literacy. As the relevance of multiple literacy repertoires in the field gains interest, especially as a social justice framework in education, researchers are paving the way to better understand how heritage speakers' repertoires are crucial for the development of a pedagogy that can better reflect

172 Student's Language Practices for Teaching

students' literacy reality, therefore enhancing their sense of belonging as they see themselves more directly reflected in the literacy practices of the classroom. It is this last area of emphasis, the exploration of Spanish heritage student language and literacy practices for belonging in the teaching and learning of a heritage language, to which this book contributes. I explore the conviction that heritage learners "do not merely acquire the genres that are out there in the world, but that they redesign them through individual instantiations of meaning-making" (Samaniego & Warner, 2016, p. 198). This book illustrates how and why such a redesign is the optimal way for educators and researchers to envision a heritage language pedagogy rooted in social justice that considers difference as a *resource*, and never as an obstacle.

It is time for the field to recognize and leverage the wide range of linguistic and cultural resources that heritage students bring into the classroom and to the lives of those with whom they share academic spaces.

Belonging in Both Heritage and Academic Literacies

This book demonstrates that social approaches to literacy can give us insights into the ways in which Spanish heritage speakers mobilize particular translingual literacy repertoires to adapt to a socially situated academic context while experiencing a sense of belonging in their learning trajectories. It also provides ideas of how educators can leverage heritage language repertoires in the classroom. In the context of this study, we see how peer tutors mediate academic-related tasks with and for their students by using a range of translingual literacy practices which reflect their sociodemographic and educational profile as first-generation, Latinx heritage speakers—many of which are similar to the practices expected in school. This analysis represents one illustration of how literacy is practiced by heritage students; that is, a literacy shaped by practices patterned from social and cultural values, power relations, historical patterns, and socially situated circumstances all of whom are expressed through hybrid, dynamic, and translingual literacy practices. By recognizing and valuing these situated, everyday practices of Spanish heritage speakers for both research and pedagogy, this book holds that educators and researchers alike must continue to better understand "the relationship among instructional schemes in the skills of reading and writing and the ways that those skills are taken up and transformed by students in their lived-in cultures" (Purcell-Gates, 2005, p. x). If we can achieve such an endeavor, I am convinced we can transform the Spanish learning experience into one in which heritage speakers can truly, and finally, *belong*.

References

Beaudrie, S. M., & Fairclough, M. A. (2012). Spanish as a heritage language in the United States: *The State of the Field* (p. 203). Washington, DC: Georgetown University Press.

Beaudrie, S. M., Ducar, C., & Potowski, K. (2014). *Heritage Language Teaching: Research and Practice*. New York: McGraw-Hill Education Create.

Canagarajah, A. S. (2013). *Translingual Practice: Global Englishes and Cosmopolitan Relations.* Abingdon, Oxon: Routledge.

Cazden, C., Hope, B., Fairclough, N., Gee, J. (1996). A pedagogy of multiliteracies. Designing social futures. *Harvard Educational Review.* Spring 66(1), 60–92.

DU Banner Data. (2022). Internal faculty enrollment information. Retrieved through: www.MyDU.edu

DU Institutional Research Analysis (2022). *Data Insights and Enrollment Reports.* Retrieved from: https://datainsights.du.edu:9443/theia/#/gameboard/WDI

Faltis, C. (1990). Spanish for native speakers: Freirian and Vygotskian perspectives. *Foreign Language Annals,* 23, 117–126.

Flores, N. (2015). Is it time for a moratorium on academic language? https://educationallinguist.wordpress.com/2015/10/01/is-it-time-for-a-moratorium-on-academic-language/

Flores, N., & Rosa, J. (2015). Undoing appropriateness: Raciolinguistic ideologies and language diversity in education. *Harvard Educational Review,* 85(2), 149–171.

Foulis, E., & Alex, S. (2019). *Mi idioma, mi comunidad: Español para bilingües.* Open Source. https://ohiostate.pressbooks.pub/idiomacomunidad/

García, O., & Wei, L. (2014). *Translanguaging: Language, Bilingualism and Education.* New York and London: Palgrave MacMillan.

García, O., Johnson, S. I., Seltzer, K., & Valdés, G. (2017). *The Translanguaging Classroom: Leveraging Student Bilingualism for Learning.* Philadelphia: Caslon.

Latino Leadership Institute. (2022). Latinos and Colorado: Colorado's demographic destiny. Retrieved from: https://latinoslead.org/latinos-colorado/#:~:text=Over%20the%20next%2020%20years,the%20end%20of%20this%20decade

Molle, D. (2015). Academic language and academic literacies: Mapping a relationship. In D. Molle, E. Sato, T. Boals, & C. A. Hedgspeth (Eds.), *Multilingual Learners and Academic Literacies* (pp. 13–32). New York: Routledge.

Palmer, D., & Martínez, R. A. (2013). Teacher agency in bilingual spaces: A fresh look at preparing teachers to educate Latina/o bilingual children. *Review of Research in Education,* 37(1), 269–297.

Potowski, K. (2010). *Conversaciones escritas: Lectura y redacción en contexto.* Hoboken: Wiley & Sons.

Purcell-Gates (2005). Foreword. In J. Anderson & M. Kendrick (Eds.), *Portraits of literacy across families, communities, and schools.* Mahwah, NJ: Lawrence Erlbaum Associates.

Reznicek-Parrado, L. M. (2018). *Peer-to-Peer Tutoring in Spanish as a Heritage Language Development: A Qualitative Study of Student Literacy Practices* (Unpublished Doctoral Dissertaion), University of Califoria, Davis.

Reznicek-Parrado, L. M. (2020). Peer-to-peer translanguaging academic spaces for belonging: The case of Spanish as a heritage language. *International Journal of Bilingual Education & Bilingualism.* https://doi.org/10.1080/13670050.2020.1799320

Reznicek-Parrado, L.M, & Gonzales, A. (2022). Curricular integration of academic support services: Supporting heritage writing. *Spanish Heritage Language Journal,* 2(2), 250–267.

Samaniego, M., & Warner, C. (2016). Designing meaning in inheritage languages: A multiliteracies approach to HL instruction. In M. Fairclough & S. M. Beaudrie (Eds.), *Innovative Strategies for Heritage Language Teaching* (pp. 191–213). Georgetown University Press.

Torres, J., Pascual y Cabo, D., & Beusterien, J. (2017). What's next? Heritage language learners shape new paths in Spanish teaching. *Hispania,* 100(5), 271–278.

U.S. Census Bureau. (2021). Retrieved from: https://data.census.gov/cedsci/table?q=Race%20Colorado&tid=DECENNIALPL2020.P2

APPENDIX A

FIGURE A.1 Tutor Recruitment Flyer.

APPENDIX B

Interview Protocol: Tutors

Preguntas sobre tu rol como tutor/a

¿Qué es lo que más aprecias sobre tu rol como tutor/a académica/o en el Programa para hablantes nativos? (¿Ejemplo?)

¿Qué es lo que más te desafía en tu rol como tutor/a académica/o en el Programa para hablantes nativos? (¿Ejemplo?)

¿Qué es lo que menos te gusta sobre tu rol como tutor/a académica/o en el Programa para hablantes nativos? (¿Ejemplo?)

Preguntas sobre las estrategias de tutoría

¿Qué haces (en general) para establecer una buena relación interpersonal que funcione bien con tus estudiantes? (¿Ejemplo?)

¿Utilizas el inglés en general durante las sesiones? ¿Por qué sí o por qué no? (¿Ejemplo?)

¿Qué haces en general cuando un estudiante parece atascarse, ya sea mientras trabajan ejercicios de gramática o cuando no logra escribir, o generar ideas para un escrito, o durante la sesión en general? (¿Ejemplo?)

OPCIONAL: ¿Utiliza humor durante las sesiones? Si sí, ¿crees que el humor juega un rol importante para desarrollar una buena relación entre el/la tutor/a y el/la estudiante? ¿Puedes pensar en una situación en particular en la que el humor jugó un papel importante durante alguna sesión?

¿De qué manera prefieres comunicarte con tus estudiantes fuera de la sesión de tutoría? ¿Por qué?

Escritos

¿Animas a tus estudiantes a que completen un poco de escritura previa a la sesión? Si sí, ¿qué tipo de escritura (versión borrador, notas, ideas, etc.)?

¿Hablas con tus estudiantes sobre los cambios a alguna versión del escrito? Es decir, ¿comparas versiones, estudias los comentarios de la/del instructor/a, etc.?

¿Utilizas algún tipo de recurso externo durante las sesiones? Por ejemplo, un diccionario, el libro de texto del curso, el internet, otra/o tutor/a, un/a instructor/a, etc. Si sí, ¿qué tan seguido piensas que lo haces? (Muy seguido, de seguido, más o menos seguido, para nada seguido)

¿Puedes pensar en un ejemplo específico de alguna vez en la que utilizaste algún recurso externo durante alguna sesión de tutoría? ¿Fue útil o no fue útil¿ ¿Cómo?

Creando comunidad

Fuera de escribir escritos o completar las actividades de gramática para la clase, ¿hay algún otro tema que discutas con tus estudiantes durante las sesiones? Por ejemplo, hobbies por fuera de la clase, intereses en general, tradicionales familiares, escuela, etc.? ¿Qué tan seguido dirías que discutes temas que no están relacionados con la clase durante las sesiones? (Muy seguido, de seguido, más o menos seguido, para nada seguido)

APPENDIX C

Interview Questions: Interview to Become a Peer Tutor in Spanish for Heritage/Bilingual Students

Preguntas entrevista
Tutores, Programa de español para hipanohablantes
University of Denver

- Cuéntanos sobre tu proceso con el español aquí en DU. ¿Cómo llegaste al programa? ¿Por qué decidiste tomar los cursos de español para hispanohablantes?
- En tu opinión, ¿cuál es el rol del español como lengua a nivel personal, académico y por fuera de la institución? En otras palabras, ¿cuál es la relevancia del español en estos tres niveles?
- Comenta sobre tu habilidad para trabajar en equipo, y en especial para ser tutor—alguien que apoya y ayuda a otros estudiantes a nivel individual.
- ¿Cuáles te parecen que son algunas habilidades que quisieras desarrollar a través de esta oportunidad?
- ¿Cuál es tu posición ante tu propio desarrollo de habilidades para la escritura académica en español? ¿Piensas que estás en la capacidad de apoyar a estudiantes de herencia con su propio proceso de desarrollo? ¿Qué recursos utilizarías para apoyar a estudiantes en su desarrollo de la lectoescritura en español?
- ¿Qué sugerencias, cambios, etc., recomendarías para mejorar el programa, basado en tu experiencia?
- ¿Alguna pregunta para nosotros?

APPENDIX D

Sample Tutoring Session Format and Objectives

The Heritage Spanish Writing Center
Consultation Series for the Spanish Heritage Program

Consultation #1 (to Happen During Weeks 3 and 6)

Students will meet with consultant for 30 minutes, individually.

This first consultation is referred to as an "*intervención y sesión de planeación*" where "*el o la estudiante y el asesor discutirán ideas para el proyecto de escritura, desglosando las instrucciones y generando ideas y estrategias para poder escribir*".

Objectives

At the end of this session, students will:

- Have a sound idea of what their argument will be.
- List their argument (also referred to as thesis or proposal), their audience, and at least three elaborations or evidence to support their argument.
- List the source of information students will include in their essays.

In order to achieve the objectives above, students should be able to fill out the following statement before leaving the session:

180 Appendix D

> "En este ensayo, voy a proponer _____ (argumento/ propuesta) a _____ (grupo/audiencia). Los tres detalles de mi propuesta son:
>
> 1. _____
> 2. _____
> 3. _____
>
> Además, la información que voy a citar incluye:
> c Experiencias personales o de familiares. ¿Cuáles?
> c Datos de páginas web, libros, etc. ¿Cuáles?
> c Entrevistas. ¿A quiénes?
> c ¿Otro?

Consultation #2 (to Happen During Weeks 4 and 7)

Students will meet with the same tutor but will have to bring a digital copy of their essays. This consultation is referred to as *"revisión estructural"* since the main objective is to work on essay structure—mainly, checking that the main arguments/thesis are sound, that each paragraph contains a main argument relating to the (larger) argument, and that there is enough evidence/details to support it.

Objectives

At the end of this session, students will:

- Be able to explain how their thesis is debatable and provide enough evidence and details.
- Recognize their main arguments in each paragraph as well as the evidence and examples that support their arguments (which, in turn, support their thesis).
- Recognize the specific structure of each of their paragraphs.

In order to achieve the objectives above, students will submit the following information after the session:

> 1) Escribe tu tesis aquí. Luego, responde: ¿es tu tesis a) clara (¿la entiendes?), b) específica, y c) debatible?
> 2) Luego parafrasea (es decir, escribe en otras palabras, de manera concisa) los dos argumentos principales de tu ensayo:
>   - El primer argumento de mi propuesta es...
>   - El segundo argumento de mi propuesta...

Después, responde:

¿Cómo son estos argumentos? ¿Son claros? ¿Tienen una conexión obvia con la tesis?

¿Se relacionan los dos argumentos entre sí? ¿Se complementan bien?

3) Ahora, discutamos la evidencia y o los ejemplos de tu ensayo. Explica lo siguiente:

- La evidencia o ejemplo que utilizo para mi primer argumento es...
- La evidencia o ejemplo que utilizo para mi segundo argumento es...

¿De qué manera se relaciona la evidencia con cada argumento? Explica.

4) Revisa la estructura del párrafo que vimos en clase durante la Semana 2. Escoge un párrafo y subraya cada sección con el color correspondiente:

Argumento central. Elaboración. Ejemplo de apoyo. Elaboración. Conclusión.

Recuerda que debes seguir esta estructura.

The consultant will facilitate this interaction by visiting the breakout rooms and providing feedback as needed.

Consultation #3 (to Happen During Weeks 5 and 8)

Students will meet with the same tutor and will bring the most updated digital copy of their work. This consultation is referred to as *"revisión de gramática y estilo"* since the main objective is to work on accentuation and orthography; mainly, checking that there are no errors with accent use, spelling, and other stylistic features.

Objectives

At the end of this session, students will:

- Have a nearly complete draft of their work, after recognizing any errors in accentuation and grammar.
- Students should be able to explain why any word should or should not take a written accent after working with the tutor.
- Students should be able to provide an example of a grammatical error improved for the last draft.

ACKNOWLEDGMENTS

Gracias por tanto

- To the study's participants: Concepción, Maité, Joaquín, Esmeralda, Cristal, and Vanessa—you know who you are. This book would have never been possible without your inspiration, commitment, and selfless participation.
- To all heritage students of Spanish whom I have had the pleasure of knowing and teaching and from whom I have learned so much throughout the last ten years at UC Davis and DU; these young people deeply inspire the contributions to which I aspire in my work. Their resiliency, sense of community, and potential will never cease to impress me.
- To the University of California Institute for Mexico and the United States (UC Mexus) which supported early iterations of this work through a dissertation grant.
- To my former students, Josué Vidrio Virula and Evan Hess, who helped me collect heritage student voices at the University of Denver to generate a more personal recount of what we do in community.
- To Dr. Julia Menard-Warwick, for believing in the project since 2016 and convincing me more recently that a book proposal on this work was worthy. Her initial feedback and reactions to the project were crucial in its development.
- To Dr. Damián Vergara Wilson, for his genuine, constructive, and honest reactions to early drafts of the book manuscript.
- To my editor Leslie Poston from A Draft Supreme and support by the DU Latinx Center, especially by Dr. Deb Ortega.
- To my colleagues Dr. Kathleen Guerra, Dr. Tracy Quan, Dr. Marinka Swift, Dr. Adrienne Gonzalez, and Dr. Cecilia Colombi, for their selfless *acompañamiento* and encouragement to continue engaging with work that matters—their presence fuels me more than they will ever know.

Acknowledgments **183**

- To colleagues at the University of Denver, for committing to making intentional spaces of belonging for heritage language learners in our Spanish program.
- To those outside the academic doors who pushed me to continue writing and engaging with this work even as I was ready to give up, especially my neighbor Reese and my mother-in-law Dianne.
- To my husband, Jeff, who did what he had to do and lovingly gave me space and support to cross the finish line.

Y a Lucía y Manuel, dos hablantes de herencia del español en Estados Unidos, por darme las ganas de seguir siempre.

INDEX

Page numbers in **bold reference tables.
**Page numbers in *italics* reference figures.
**Page numbers with n reference notes.

academic advising 61–63
academic communities, creating 130–132
academic discourse: as practice 28; as situated 27–28
academic empathy 50, **51**, 92–93; evaluative language 132–137
academic language 10, 25–26, 75, 162–163, 171; *see also* academic literacy
academic learning space 101–107
academic literacies model 27, 84
academic literacy 23, 75–76, 170–172; as social 24–29; *see also* academic language
academic literacy development: academic empathy 92–93; academic support 84–88; belonging to community 94–96; casual talk 127; community building 92; tutors as experts 88–92
academic persona, analysis of lexico-grammatical resources *see* lexico-grammatical resources
academic support **51**, 84–88; providing academic support 109–120
academic writing 163–164; defining norms of 67–72
accents 65
Achugar, M. 102
Affect 105–106, 131, 135–136, 138, 142, **143**
Affect appraisal *140*

American Association of Teachers of Spanish and Portuguese (AATSP) 7
Appraisal *141–142*
Appraisal analysis 102, 135–136
Appraisal Resources *103*
Appraisal Theory 102, 107, 131, 143
Appreciation 104–105, 135, 138, *141–142*, **143**, 144
appropriateness 162
appropriateness model 21
asking metalinguistic questions 57–61
attitudes, graduation 106
attitudinal positionings 137
autonomous model of literacy 22–23
axial coding 50

Basic Interpersonal Communicative Skills (BICS) 25
Beaudrie, S. M. 101
belonging 2, 131, 151–152, 172; to communities **51**, 94–96; institutional belonging 146–149; in language learning 42–45; non-classroom, pedagogical spaces 30
BICS *see* Basic Interpersonal Communicative Skills
bilingual 5
bilingual education 5–8
bilingualism 90, 150
building community 137–144

Index 185

CAL *see* Center for Applied Linguistics
California, bilingual education 7
CALP *see* Cognitive Academic Language Proficiency
Canada, Heritage Language Programs of Ontario 4
capabilities 130
casual conversation 100
casual talk 99–100; academic literacy development 127
Center for Applied Linguistics (CAL) 8
CLA *see* critical language awareness
class activities: reflection prompts 153–156; research project on social movement 157–162
clausal mood types 103; lexico-grammatical resources 109–120
cognition, literacy and 52
Cognitive Academic Language Proficiency (CALP) 25
collaboration, equitable pedagogies in Spanish heritage learning 151–157
commands 108
community building 90–94, 169; collaboration 151–152; for/with tutees 137–144
community languages 4
composition 104, 132
consulting an expert 57–61
context-embedded communication 25
context-reduced communication 25
critical language awareness (CLA) 101, 163
Critical Language Awareness (CLA) frameworks 9
cultural pluralism 1
culture of power 28
culture of school 28
Cummins, J. 25

data analyses performed per data chapters **52**
data collection, for peer-to-peer tutoring program 39–42
demographic growth of Latinxs 31–32
dialectal variation 82
dual-language education 5–6
dynamic bilingualism 150
dynamic heritage language practices 150

Eggins, S. 100, 102, 108, 137
embeddedness of the community 13, 131
English for the Children movement 7
English-Only movement 7

equitable pedagogies in Spanish heritage learning; collaboration 151–157; exploration 157–162; production 162–165; self-reflection 165–166
ethnographic methodology 49
evaluative language 130–132; academic empathy 132–137; community building 137–144
exchange structure 103
exploration, equitable pedagogies in Spanish heritage learning 157–162

field notes, from tutoring sessions 39–41
First Heritage Languages in America 8
First Nations languages 4
focus 106, 132
force 106, 132

García, O. 77
Genishi, C. 49
goals of Spanish heritage language research 9
graduation 106, 132, 136
grammatical analysis of mood 117–120
guiding student responses 67–72; metalinguistic knowledge 120–126

heritage language 3–5
heritage language instruction 130
heritage language learners 3–5
heritage language learning for institutional belonging 146–149
heritage language practices 21
Heritage Language Programs of Ontario (Canada) 4
heritage language repertoires 29–30
heritage language speakers 30
heritage language writing 24–29
Hernandez-Chavez, Eduardo 1
heterogeneity 9
Hispanic Serving Institution 32
home language 4
HSI *see* Hispanic Serving Institution
hybridity, linguistic hybridity 76–83

identity 159; as Spanish heritage speaker 146–147
ideological model of literacy 22–23
immigrant languages 4
immigrant minority language 4
informal talk *see* casual talk
initiating student responses 67–72
Insecurity 136
interview protocol, tutors 176–177

186 Index

interview questions for tutors 178
invisible academic practices 57, 61

Judgment 106, 142

@LaCasaBlanca 7
language learning, belonging 42–45
Latino Leadership Foundation (LLF) 147
Latinxs 6; demographic growth of 31–32
Lau v Nichols 6
Lea, M. R. 27, 84
Leeman, Jennifer 10
LEP *see* Limited English Proficient
LES *see* Limited English Speakers
lexico-grammatical resources 107–
    109; analysis of interactions **125**;
    metalinguistic knowledge 120–126;
    providing academic support 109–120
Limited English Proficient (LEP) 6
Limited English Speakers (LES) 6
linguistic biography 64–65
linguistic hybridity 22, 76–77, 83
linguistic repertoires 77
literacy 1; cognition and 52; as practice
    27; *see also* academic literacy
literacy instruction, old and new basics
    in **23**
literacy practices 21, 53–54, 83–84;
    asking metalinguistic questions 57–61;
    guiding student responses 67–72;
    personal storytelling 63–67; searching
    the Internet for academic information
    61–63; talking about social media
    54–57
literacy repertoires 77
literacy standards, Spanish as a Heritage
    Language Pedagogy 100–101
LLF *see* Latino Leadership Foundation
Loza, S. 101

mannequin challenge 54–55
Martínez, Glenn 26–27, 130
matrix queries 50
metalinguistic knowledge 120–126
metalinguistic questions, asking 57–61
mirroring equitable pedagogies 167–168
modality 108, 118, 126
modalization 103, 108, 119
modulation 103, 108
Molle, D. 26–27, 75
mood 108; grammatical analysis of
    117–120
mood clauses, with illustrations **107**
multi-level analysis 49
multilingual students 74–75

multiliteracies 10
multimodal texts 157–159
multiple literacies perspective 28

National Foreign Language Center
    (NFLC) 8
National Symposium on Spanish as a
    Heritage Language (NSSHL) 8
native language 1
Native Speakers of Spanish 7
New Literacy Studies (NLS) 21
NFLC *see* National Foreign Language
    Center
NLS *see* New Literacy Studies
non-academic language 12
non-classroom, pedagogical spaces:
    academic learning space 101–107;
    belonging 30; tutoring rooms
    100–101
NSSHL *see* National Symposium on
    Spanish as a Heritage Language

open coding 50
origin language 4

Pascual y Cabo, Diego 8
peer education 13
peer tutors 30–31; *see also* tutors
peer-to-peer academic advising 61–63
peer-to-peer collaborative academic
    language learning 83
peer-to-peer collaborative academic
    learning space 101–107
peer-to-peer tutor programming 12
peer-to-peer tutoring: considerations for
    168–170; data collection 39–42; by and
    for heritage students of Spanish 33–34;
    hours of video recording **40–41**;
    participant selection and background
    34–39; sample tutoring session format
    and objectives 179–181
peer-tutoring room 131
personal storytelling 63–67
positionality 42–45
production, equitable pedagogies in
    Spanish heritage learning 162–165
Proposition 227 8, 15n3
providing academic support, lexico-
    grammatical resources 109–120

Reaction 104
reflection prompts, class activities
    153–156
research project on social movement
    157–162

Index **187**

sample tutoring session format and objectives 179–181
Satisfaction 140
Scholars Promoting Education Awareness and Knowledge (SPEAK) 139
searching the Internet for academic information 61–63
second language acquisition 25
Security 138
self-reflection, equitable pedagogies in Spanish heritage learning 165–166
service-learning experiences 12
SFL *see* System Functional Linguistics
Slade, D. 100, 102, 108, 137
social acts, academic literacy as 24–29
social approaches to literacy 22–23
social esteem 106
social literacy theory 21–22
social media: exploration 157; talking about social media as literacy practice 54–57
social sanction 106
sociolinguistic ethnography 49–51
Spanish as a Heritage Language Pedagogy, literacy standards 100–101
Spanish for Native Speakers Program 32–33
Spanish heritage education 5–8
Spanish heritage language research, goals of 9–10
Spanish Program for Heritage/Bilingual Speakers (University of Denver) 147–150
SPEAK *see* Scholars Promoting Education Awareness and Knowledge
Street, B. V. 22, 27, 84
student enrollment, for program for native speakers (2012-2017) **33**
student-led learning 92, 169
System Functional Linguistics (SFL) 48, 102

talking about social media, literacy practices 54–57
Teaching of Spanish to Native Speakers (SNS) 7
themes, definition of **51**
transcription conventions **53**
translanguaging 11, 54–57, 75, 96, 150–151; in context 51–53; linguistic hybridity 76–83
tutor as expert 50, **51**, 88–92, 135
tutor interviews 41–42
tutor participants, demographic and educational profile **36**
tutoring 12–13
tutoring rooms 100–101
tutors: as experts 88–92; interview protocol 176–177; interview questions for 178; language and literacy practices 51–53; linguistic hybridity 76–83; literacy practices for academic development and community building 83–96; mirroring equitable pedagogies 167–168; translanguaging 77–83, 96
Twitter, exploration 157–159

University of Denver, Spanish Program for Heritage/Bilingual Speakers (University of Denver) 147–150

Valdés, Guadalupe 5, 7
Valuation 132, 140
Vergara, D. W. 101
video recordings, of tutoring sessions 39–41
Villa, D. 26–27, 82
viral phenomena, as literacy practice 55

Wh- interrogatives 108
White, P. R. R. 102
writing development 26–27; academic writing 163–164; defining norms of academic writing 67–72

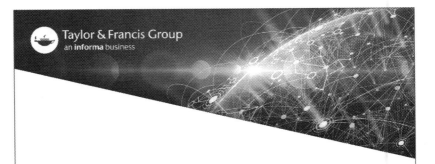

Taylor & Francis eBooks

www.taylorfrancis.com

A single destination for eBooks from Taylor & Francis with increased functionality and an improved user experience to meet the needs of our customers.

90,000+ eBooks of award-winning academic content in Humanities, Social Science, Science, Technology, Engineering, and Medical written by a global network of editors and authors.

TAYLOR & FRANCIS EBOOKS OFFERS:

- A streamlined experience for our library customers
- A single point of discovery for all of our eBook content
- Improved search and discovery of content at both book and chapter level

REQUEST A FREE TRIAL
support@taylorfrancis.com

Printed in the United States
by Baker & Taylor Publisher Services